W9-CAV-707

Cisco Secure Virtual Private Networks

Andrew G. Mason, CCIE #7144

Cisco Press
201 W 103rd Street
Indianapolis, IN 46290 USA

Cisco Secure Virtual Private Networks

Andrew G. Mason

Copyright© 2002 Cisco Systems, Inc.

Published by:
Cisco Press
201 West 103rd Street
Indianapolis, IN 46290 USA

Printed in the United States of America 3 4 5 6 7 8 9 0

Library of Congress Cataloging-in-Publication Number: 2001086624

ISBN: 1-58705-033-1

Third Printing May 2002

Warning and Disclaimer

This book is designed to provide information about Cisco virtual private networks. Every effort has been made to make this book as complete and as accurate as possible, but no warranty or fitness is implied.

The information is provided on an "as is" basis. The author, Cisco Press, and Cisco Systems, Inc. shall have neither liability nor responsibility to any person or entity with respect to any loss or damages arising from the information contained in this book or from the use of the discs or programs that may accompany it.

The opinions expressed in this book belong to the author and are not necessarily those of Cisco Systems, Inc.

Trademark Acknowledgments

All terms mentioned in this book that are known to be trademarks or service marks have been appropriately capitalized. Cisco Press or Cisco Systems, Inc. cannot attest to the accuracy of this information. Use of a term in this book should not be regarded as affecting the validity of any trademark or service mark.

Feedback Information

At Cisco Press, our goal is to create in-depth technical books of the highest quality and value. Each book is crafted with care and precision, undergoing rigorous development that involves the unique expertise of members from the professional technical community.

Readers' feedback is a natural continuation of this process. If you have any comments regarding how we could improve the quality of this book, or otherwise alter it to better suit your needs, you can contact us through e-mail at feedback@ciscopress.com. Please make sure to include the book title and ISBN in your message.

Publisher	John Wait
Editor-in-Chief	John Kane
Executive Editor	Brett Bartow
Cisco Systems Management	Michael Hakkert
	Tom Geitner
	William Warren
Managing Editor	Patrick Kanouse
Development Editor	Andrew Cupp
Project Editor	Marc Fowler
Copy Editor	Ginny Kaczmarek
Course Developers	Bob Eckhoff
	Steven D. Hanna
	Leon Katcharian
	Mike Westrom
Technical Editors	Kelly McGrew
	Mark J. Newcomb
Team Coordinator	Tammi Ross
Book Designer	Gina Rexrode
Cover Designer	Louisa Klucznik
Production Team	Argosy Publishing
Indexer	Larry Sweazy

CISCO SYSTEMS

Corporate Headquarters
Cisco Systems, Inc.
170 West Tasman Drive
San Jose, CA 95134-1706
USA
http://www.cisco.com
Tel: 408 526-4000
    800 553-NETS (6387)
Fax: 408 526-4100

European Headquarters
Cisco Systems Europe
11 Rue Camille Desmoulins
92782 Issy-les-Moulineaux
Cedex 9
France
http://www-europe.cisco.com
Tel: 33 1 58 04 60 00
Fax: 33 1 58 04 61 00

Americas Headquarters
Cisco Systems, Inc.
170 West Tasman Drive
San Jose, CA 95134-1706
USA
http://www.cisco.com
Tel: 408 526-7660
Fax: 408 527-0883

Asia Pacific Headquarters
Cisco Systems Australia, Pty.,
Ltd
Level 17, 99 Walker Street
North Sydney
NSW 2059 Australia
http://www.cisco.com
Tel: +61 2 8448 7100
Fax: +61 2 9957 4350

Cisco Systems has more than 200 offices in the following countries. Addresses, phone numbers, and fax numbers are listed on the Cisco Web site at www.cisco.com/go/offices

Argentina • Australia • Austria • Belgium • Brazil • Bulgaria • Canada • Chile • China • Colombia • Costa Rica • Croatia • Czech Republic • Denmark • Dubai, UAE • Finland • France • Germany • Greece • Hong Kong • Hungary • India • Indonesia • Ireland • Israel • Italy • Japan • Korea • Luxembourg • Malaysia • Mexico • The Netherlands • New Zealand • Norway • Peru • Philippines • Poland • Portugal • Puerto Rico • Romania • Russia • Saudi Arabia • Scotland • Singapore • Slovakia • Slovenia • South Africa • Spain • Sweden • Switzerland • Taiwan • Thailand • Turkey • Ukraine • United Kingdom • United States • Venezuela • Vietnam • Zimbabwe

About the Author

Andrew G. Mason, CCIE #7144, CSS-1, CCNP: Security, and CCDP, is the CEO of three UK-based companies: Mason Technologies, CCStudy.com, and Boxing Orange. He specializes in Cisco consulting for numerous companies. Andrew has 11 years experience in the networking industry and is currently consulting for the largest ISP in the UK. He is involved daily in the design and implementation of complex secure hosted solutions utilizing products from the Cisco Secure Product range.

About the Technical Reviewers

Kelly McGrew is a Cisco Certified Systems Instructor (CCSI) and vice-president of mcgrew.net inc., a network training and course development firm. He has worked as a trainer throughout the world. Kelly holds the CCNP-Voice Access Specialist and CCDA certifications. He has more than 15 years of experience in the networking industry, including experience with a variety of LAN and WAN protocols seldom seen in today's IP-centric world. Kelly has held a variety of positions for leaders in the networking industry. These include positions as a network systems engineer for CompuServe Network Services and MCI/WorldCom, an instructor/consultant for Chesapeake Computer Consultants, Inc., a program manager for Microsoft Corporation, and an instructor/consultant under a leased-employee relationship for Cisco Systems, Inc. He is a graduate of The Evergreen State College (B.A.) and obtained an M.B.A. from City University. Kelly is an associate member of the IEEE and member of the ASTD. Kelly currently focuses on teaching and course development in the Voice over Layer 2/IP arena. He currently resides in Olympia, Washington, with his wife, Tammy (also a CCSI and the president of mcgrew.net inc.), their son, Duncan, and the world's best doggie, Lady Buttons.

Mark J. Newcomb, CCNP Security and CCDP, is a senior consulting network engineer for Aurora Consulting Group (www.auroracg.com), a Cisco Premier Partner located in Spokane, Washington. Mark provides network design, security, and implementation services for clients throughout the Pacific Northwest.

Mark has over 20 years experience in the microcomputer industry. His current projects include designing secure communication systems for wireless devices and providing comprehensive security services to the banking industry.

Dedication

I would like to dedicate this book to my recently born son, Jack and my 2-year-old daughter, Rosie. Words cannot describe the love I feel for my children or the happiness they bring. I would also like to thank my wife, Helen, for being such a wonderful and supportive mother and wife. I am sure my children will grow to be a testament to the time and love invested by Helen.

Acknowledgments

In writing this book I had the opportunity to work with a very professional team of colleagues. I would like to thank Brett Bartow of Cisco Press for pulling all of this together and always emanating a joyful and helpful attitude. I would like to thank Drew Cupp, also from Cisco Press, for his superb attention to detail and his vast knowledge of the finer grammatical points of the English language. Appreciation is also due to the rest of the Cisco Press team as well as the original course developers, Bob Eckhoff, Steven D. Hanna, Leon Katcharian, and Mike Westrom, in bringing this book to print.

Thanks go out to the technical reviewers, Kelly McGrew and also my good friend Mark J. Newcomb for their technical insight and supportive comments along the way.

Contents at a Glance

Contents

Foreword

In January 2001 Cisco Systems, Inc. announced a new family of professional certifications called Cisco Qualified Specialist. The first CQS released was the Cisco Security Specialist 1. CSS1 is designed to certify your skills and knowledge in general network security, concentrating on intrusion detection systems, firewalls, and virtual private networks. The demand for qualified network security professionals has never been greater. Each day organizations find themselves engaged in a never-ending battle to keep their networks secure from those intent on damaging systems or gaining unauthorized access. Proper employment of virtual private networks is a critical skill for the network security professional.

Cisco Secure Virtual Private Networks uses book format to present the knowledge contained in the lab-intensive, instructor-led courses and the e-learning courses of the same title. While releasing the information in book format cannot compete with the hands-on experience gained by attending Cisco-authorized training delivered by a Cisco Learning partner, it is a valuable component in meeting the worldwide demand for Cisco training. This book will allow you to describe, configure, verify, and manage IPSec features in the Cisco VPN 3000 product family, PIX Firewalls, and Cisco routers. You will learn how to configure and manage VPNs for remote access and site-to-site applications. Both the CSVPN course and the Cisco Press book are dedicated to the highest standards of quality and knowledge transfer. Whether you are preparing to complete the CSS1 certification or are interested in installing, configuring, and operating Cisco VPNs, this book will enhance your understanding of virtual private networks.

This is another in a series of Cisco Press books dedicated to the transfer of knowledge and skills critical to the success of the network security professional. Additional Cisco Press books developed to support the CSS1 certification include *Managing Cisco Network Security, Cisco PIX Firewall*, and *Cisco Intrusion Detection Systems*.

Rick Stiffler

Manager, VPN and Security Training

Cisco Systems, Inc.

September 2001

Introduction

Cisco Secure Virtual Private Networks is a comprehensive, results-oriented book, designed to give readers a basic knowledge to plan, administer, and maintain a virtual private network (VPN). With *Cisco Secure Virtual Private Networks,* the reader will be able to accomplish specific tasks, including:

- Identifying the features, functions, and benefits of Cisco Secure VPN products

- Identifying the component technologies which are implemented in Cisco Secure VPN products

- Identifying the procedure, steps, and commands required to configure and test IPSec in Cisco IOS software

- Identifying the procedure, steps, and commands required to configure and test IPSec in the Cisco Secure PIX Firewall

- Installing and configure the Cisco VPN Client to create a secure tunnel to a Cisco VPN Concentrator and PIX Firewall

- Configuring and verify IPSec in the Cisco VPN Concentrator, Cisco router, and the Cisco Secure PIX Firewall

- Configuring the Cisco VPN Concentrator, Cisco router, and the Cisco Secure PIX Firewall for interoperability

Overall, the readers will not only understand the theory behind VPNs (and their obvious benefit) but will also learn actual configurations through detailed steps. This will allow for immediate functionality within their environments.

Cisco Secure Virtual Private Networks is structured into distinct chapters, each chapter gives the reader established learning objectives. Whether theory or implementation, the reader will be able to achieve the knowledge provided in each chapter in a clear and concise manner most effective in adult learning. This book will also provide the reader with graphic representations, providing visual accompaniment to the text.

Audience

Cisco Secure Virtual Private Networks is aimed at intermediate readers, with first hand knowledge of system administration. Care is also taken to include beginners who understand the need for secure VPNs within their infrastructure and are reading with the objective of achieving a greater understanding of interconnection. The most common reader in the audience will be system administrators who intend to implement a VPN solution using equipment already in place or soon to be purchased. It is also likely that students will be reading this book in an effort to broaden their understanding—on the road to certification. The book covers the required objectives for the Cisco-provided exam: 9EO-570 CSVPN.

Audience Prerequisites

The content in this book assumes that the reader is familiar with general networking concepts and terminology. This includes a thorough understanding of the network protocol TCP/IP, and a familiarity of the topics covered in the Cisco Press books *Internetworking Technologies Handbook* and *IP Routing Fundamentals*.

What Is Covered

This book is organized into 12 chapters:

- **Chapter 1, "VPNs and VPN Technologies"**—This chapter provides an overview of VPNs and a detailed look at IPSec.

- **Chapter 2, "Cisco VPN Family of Products"**—This chapter covers the available products in the Cisco product line for establishing virtual private networks.

- **Chapter 3, "Configuring Cisco IOS Routers for Preshared Keys Site-to-Site"**—This chapter looks at configuring IPSec site-to-site VPNs using Preshared keys on Cisco IOS Routers.

- **Chapter 4, "Configuring Cisco IOS Routers for CA Site-to-Site"**—This chapter looks at configuring IPSec site-to-site VPNs using digital certificates on Cisco IOS Routers.

- **Chapter 5, "Troubleshooting Cisco IOS VPNs"**—This chapter covers the troubleshooting tools and techniques that are available for troubleshooting Cisco IOS VPNs.

- **Chapter 6, "Configuring the Cisco PIX Firewall for Preshared Keys Site-to-Site"**—This chapter looks at configuring IPSec site-to-site VPNs using Preshared keys on Cisco Secure PIX Firewalls.

- **Chapter 7, "Configuring the Cisco PIX Firewall for CA Site-to-Site"**—This chapter looks at configuring IPSec site-to-site VPNs using digital certificates on Cisco Secure PIX Firewalls.

- **Chapter 8, "Troubleshooting Cisco PIX Firewall VPNs"**—This chapter covers the troubleshooting tools and techniques that are available for troubleshooting Cisco Secure PIX Firewall VPNs.

- **Chapter 9, "Configuring the Cisco VPN 3000 for Remote Access Using Preshared Keys"**—This chapter covers the configuration of Remote Access VPNs on the Cisco VPN 3000 Concentrator using Preshared keys.

- **Chapter 10, "Configuring the Cisco VPN 3000 for Remote Access Using Digital Certificates"**—This chapter covers the configuration of Remote Access VPNs on the Cisco VPN 3000 Concentrator using digital certificates.

- **Chapter 11, "Monitoring and Administration of Cisco VPN3000 Remote Access Networks"**—This chapter covers the monitoring and administration of Cisco VPN 3000 Remote Access Networks.
- **Chapter 12, "Scaling Cisco IPSec Virtual Private Networks"**—This chapter builds on the previous chapters looking at the scalability solutions available within IPSec VPNs.

Appendix A contains the answers to each chapter's Review Questions.

Command Syntax Conventions

Command syntax in this book conforms to the following conventions:

- Commands, keywords, and actual values for arguments are **bold**
- Arguments (which need to be supplied with an actual value) are *italic*
- Optional keywords and arguments are in brackets []
- A choice of mandatory keywords and arguments is in braces { }

Note that these conventions are for syntax only.

PART I

Virtual Private Network Fundamentals

Chapter 1   VPNs and VPN Technologies

VPNs and VPN Technologies

This chapter defines virtual private networks (VPNs) and explores fundamental Internet Protocol Security (IPSec) technologies. This chapter covers the following topics:

- Overview of VPNs and VPN technologies
- Internet Protocol Security (IPSec)
- IPSec crypto components
- IKE overview
- How IPSec works
- IPSec security associations
- CA support overview

Overview of VPNs and VPN Technologies

Cisco products support the latest in VPN technology. A VPN is a service that offers secure, reliable connectivity over a shared public network infrastructure such as the Internet.

Figure 1-1 shows various VPNs between a main site and branch offices and small office, home office (SOHO) workers.

VPNs maintain the same security and management policies as a private network. They are the most cost effective method of establishing a virtual point-to-point connection between remote users and an enterprise customer's network. There are three main types of VPNs.

- **Access VPNs**—Provide remote access to an enterprise customer's intranet or extranet over a shared infrastructure. Access VPNs use analog, dial, ISDN, digital subscriber line (DSL), mobile IP, and cable technologies to securely connect mobile users, telecommuters, and branch offices.

- **Intranet VPNs**—Link enterprise customer headquarters, remote offices, and branch offices to an internal network over a shared infrastructure using dedicated connections. Intranet VPNs differ from extranet VPNs in that they allow access only to the enterprise customer's employees.

- **Extranet VPNs**—Link outside customers, suppliers, partners, or communities of interest to an enterprise customer's network over a shared infrastructure using dedicated connections. Extranet VPNs differ from intranet VPNs in that they allow access to users outside the enterprise.

Figure 1-1   *Examples of VPNs*

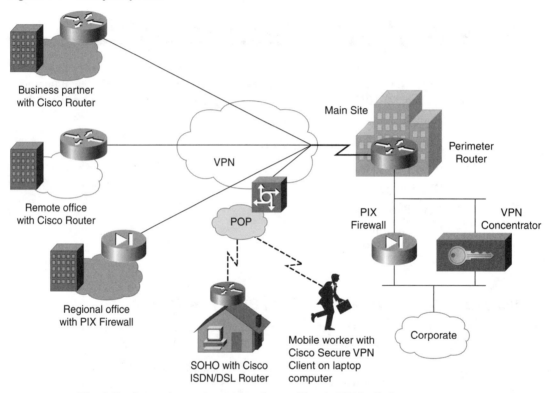

The following main components make up Cisco's VPN offerings:

- **Cisco VPN routers**—Use Cisco IOS software IPSec support to enable a secure VPN. VPN-optimized routers leverage existing Cisco investment, perfect for the hybrid WAN.

- **Cisco Secure PIX Firewall**—Offers a VPN gateway alternative when the security group "owns" the VPN.

- **Cisco VPN Concentrator series**—Offers powerful remote access and site-to-site VPN capability, easy-to-use management interface, and a VPN client.

- **Cisco Secure VPN Client**—Enables secure remote access to Cisco router and PIX Firewalls and runs on the Windows operating system.

- **Cisco Secure Intrusion Detection System (CSIDS) and Cisco Secure Scanner—** Can be used to monitor and audit the security of the VPN.
- **Cisco Secure Policy Manager and Cisco Works 2000—**Provide VPN-wide system management.

These components can all be seen in Figure 1-2.

Figure 1-2   *Cisco Secure VPN Components*

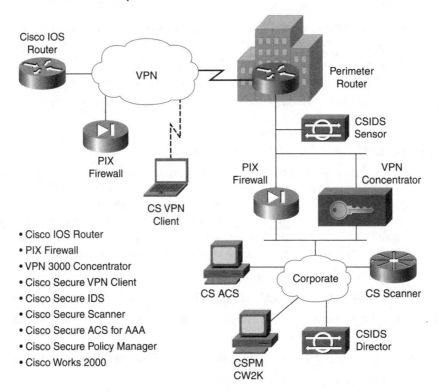

- Cisco IOS Router
- PIX Firewall
- VPN 3000 Concentrator
- Cisco Secure VPN Client
- Cisco Secure IDS
- Cisco Secure Scanner
- Cisco Secure ACS for AAA
- Cisco Secure Policy Manager
- Cisco Works 2000

The main Cisco VPN product offerings are discussed in more detail in Chapter 2, "Cisco VPN Family of Products."

Internet Protocol Security (IPSec)

Cisco IOS uses the industry-standard IPSec protocol suite to enable advanced VPN features. The PIX IPSec implementation is based on the Cisco IOS IPSec that runs in Cisco routers.

IPSec acts at the network layer, protecting and authenticating IP packets between a PIX Firewall and other participating IPSec devices (peers), such as other PIX Firewalls, Cisco routers, the Cisco Secure VPN Client, the VPN 3000 Concentrator series, and other IPSec-compliant products.

IPSec enables the following Cisco IOS VPN features:

- **Data confidentiality**—The IPSec sender can encrypt packets before transmitting them across a network.

- **Data integrity**—The IPSec receiver can authenticate packets sent by the IPSec sender to ensure that the data has not been altered during transmission.

- **Data origin authentication**—The IPSec receiver can authenticate the source of the IPSec packets sent. This service is dependent upon the data integrity service.

- **Antireplay**—The IPSec receiver can detect and reject replayed packets.

IPSec Overview

IPSec is a framework of open standards that provides data confidentiality, data integrity, and data authentication between participating peers at the IP layer. IPSec can be used to protect one or more data flows between IPSec peers. IPSec is documented in a series of Internet RFCs, all available at http://www.ietf.org/html.charters/ipsec-charter.html. The overall IPSec implementation is guided by "Security Architecture for the Internet Protocol," RFC 2401. IPSec consists of the following two main protocols:

- Authentication Header (AH)
- Encapsulating Security Payload (ESP)

IPSec also uses other existing encryption standards to make up a protocol suite, which are explained in the next sections.

IPSec has several standards that are supported by Cisco IOS and the PIX Firewall.

- IP Security Protocol
    - Authentication Header (AH)
    - Encapsulating Security Payload (ESP)
- Data Encryption Standard (DES)
- Triple DES (3DES)
- Diffie-Hellman (D-H)
- Message Digest 5 (MD5)
- Secure Hash Algorithm-1 (SHA-1)

- Rivest, Shamir, and Adelman (RSA) Signatures
- Internet Key Exchange (IKE)
- Certificate Authorities (CAs)

IP Security Protocol—Authentication Header (AH)

Authentication Header (AH) provides authentication and integrity to the datagrams passed between two systems.

It achieves this by applying a keyed one-way hash function to the datagram to create a message digest. If any part of the datagram is changed during transit, it will be detected by the receiver when it performs the same one-way hash function on the datagram and compares the value of the message digest that the sender has supplied. The one-way hash also involves the use of a secret shared between the two systems, which means that authenticity can be guaranteed.

AH can also enforce antireplay protection by requiring that a receiving host sets the replay bit in the header to indicate that the packet has been seen. Without this protection, an attacker might be able to resend the same packet many times: for example, to send a packet that contains "withdraw $100 from account X." Figure 1-3 shows two routers and confirms that the data between them is sent in clear text.

Figure 1-3   *Authentication Header*

Router A   Router B

All data in clear text

- Ensures data integrity
- Provides origin authentication—ensures packets definitely came from peer router
- Uses keyed-hash mechanism
- Does NOT provide confidentiality (no encryption)
- Provides optional replay protection

The AH function is applied to the entire datagram except for any mutable IP header fields that change in transit: for example, Time to Live (TTL) fields that are modified by the routers along the transmission path. AH works as follows:

Step 1   The IP header and data payload is hashed.

Step 2   The hash is used to build a new AH header, which is appended to the original packet.

Step 3 The new packet is transmitted to the IPSec peer router.

Step 4 The peer router hashes the IP header and data payload, extracts the transmitted hash from the AH header, and compares the two hashes. The hashes must match exactly. Even if one bit is changed in the transmitted packet, the hash output on the received packet will change and the AH header will not match.

This process can be seen in Figure 1-4.

Figure 1-4 *AH Authentication and Integrity*

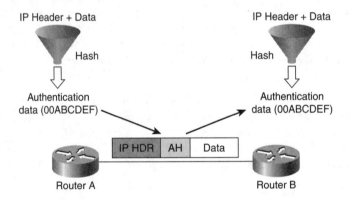

IP Security Protocol—Encapsulating Security Payload (ESP)

Encapsulating Security Payload (ESP) is a security protocol used to provide confidentiality (encryption), data origin authentication, integrity, optional antireplay service, and limited traffic flow confidentiality by defeating traffic flow analysis. Figure 1-5 shows that the data payload is encrypted with ESP.

ESP provides confidentiality by performing encryption at the IP packet layer. It supports a variety of symmetric encryption algorithms. The default algorithm for IPSec is 56-bit DES. This cipher must be implemented to guarantee interoperability among IPSec products. Cisco products also support use of 3DES for strong encryption. Confidentiality can be selected independent of all other services.

Figure 1-5   *Encapsulating Security Payload*

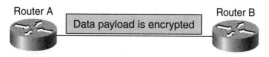

- Data confidentiality (encryption)
- Limited traffic flow confidentiality
- Data integrity
- Optional data origin authentication
- Anti-replay protection
- Does not protect IP header

NOTE   Deciding whether to use AH or ESP in a given situation might seem complex, but it can be simplified to a few rules, as follows. When you want to make sure that data from an authenticated source gets transferred with integrity and does not need confidentiality, use the AH protocol. If you need to keep data private (confidentiality), then you must use ESP. ESP will encrypt the upper-layer protocols in transport mode and the entire original IP datagram in tunnel mode so that neither are readable from the wire. However, ESP can now also provide authentication for the packets. This situation is covered later in this chapter in the "ESP Tunnel Versus Transport Mode" section.

DES Algorithm

DES uses a 56-bit key, ensuring high-performance encryption. DES is used to encrypt and decrypt packet data. DES turns clear text into ciphertext with an encryption algorithm. The decryption algorithm on the remote end restores clear text from ciphertext. Shared secret keys enable the encryption and decryption.

Triple DES Algorithm (3DES)

Triple DES (3DES) is also a supported encryption protocol for use in IPSec on Cisco products. The 3DES algorithm is a variant of the 56-bit DES. 3DES operates similarly to DES in that data is broken into 64-bit blocks. 3DES then processes each block three times, each time with an independent 56-bit key. 3DES effectively doubles encryption strength over 56-bit DES.

Diffie-Hellman (D-H)

Diffie-Hellman (D-H) is a public-key cryptography protocol. It allows two parties to establish a shared secret key used by encryption algorithms (DES or MD5, for example) over an insecure communications channel. D-H is used within IKE to establish session keys. 768-bit and 1024-bit D-H groups are supported in the Cisco routers and PIX Firewall. The 1024-bit group is more secure because of the larger key size.

Message Digest 5 (MD5)

Message Digest 5 (MD5) is a hash algorithm used to authenticate packet data. Cisco routers and the PIX Firewall use the MD5 hashed message authentication code (HMAC) variant that provides an additional level of hashing. A hash is a one-way encryption algorithm that takes an input message of arbitrary length and produces a fixed length output message. IKE, AH, and ESP use MD5 for authentication.

Secure Hash Algorithm-1 (SHA-1)

Secure Hash Algorithm-1 (SHA-1) is a hash algorithm used to authenticate packet data. Cisco routers and the PIX Firewall use the SHA-1 HMAC variant, which provides an additional level of hashing. IKE, AH, and ESP use SHA-1 for authentication.

Rivest, Shamir, and Adelman (RSA) Signatures

Rivest, Shamir, and Adelman (RSA) is a public-key cryptographic system used for authentication. IKE on the Cisco router or PIX Firewall uses a D-H exchange to determine secret keys on each IPSec peer used by encryption algorithms. The D-H exchange can be authenticated with RSA signatures or preshared keys.

Internet Key Exchange (IKE)

Internet Key Exchange (IKE) is a hybrid protocol that provides utility services for IPSec: authentication of the IPSec peers, negotiation of IKE and IPSec security associations, and establishment of keys for encryption algorithms used by IPSec.

NOTE   IKE is synonymous with Internet Security Association Key Management Protocol (ISAKMP) in Cisco router or PIX Firewall configurations.

Certificate Authorities (CAs)

The Certificate Authority (CA) offered by Cisco routers and the PIX Firewall allows the IPSec-protected network to scale by providing the equivalent of a digital identification card to each device. When two IPSec peers wish to communicate, they exchange digital certificates to prove their identities (thus removing the need to exchange public keys manually with each peer or to specify a shared key manually at each peer). The digital certificates are obtained from a CA. CA support on Cisco products uses RSA signatures to authenticate the CA exchange.

Tunnel and Transport Modes

IPSec can be run in either *tunnel* or *transport* modes. Each of these modes has its own particular uses, and care should be taken to ensure that the correct one is selected for the solution. Figure 1-6 shows that transport mode should be used for end-to-end sessions and tunnel mode should be used for everything else.

Figure 1-6 *Tunnel and Transport Mode IPSec*

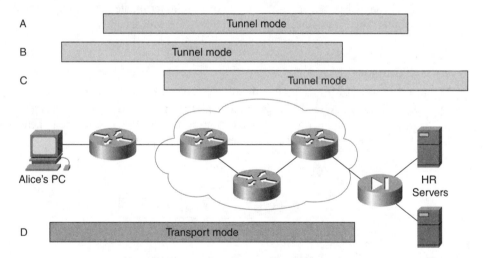

Figure 1-6 illustrates situations where a tunnel or a transport mode is used. Tunnel mode is most commonly used between gateways or from an end station to a gateway. The gateway acts as a proxy for the hosts behind it. Transport mode is used between end stations or between an end station and a gateway, if the gateway is being treated as a host; for example, in an encrypted Telnet session from a workstation to a router, the router is the actual destination.

Using Figure 1-6, consider some examples of when to use tunnel or transport mode.

- **Example A**—Tunnel mode is most commonly used to encrypt traffic between secure IPSec gateways, such as between the Cisco router and the PIX Firewall, as shown in Example A in Figure 1-6. The IPSec gateways proxy IPSec for the devices behind them, such as Alice's PC and the HR servers in the figure. In Example A, Alice connects to the HR servers securely through the IPSec tunnel set up between the gateways.

- **Example B**—Tunnel mode is also used to connect an end station running IPSec software, such as the Cisco Secure VPN Client, to an IPSec gateway, as shown in Example B.

- **Example C**—In Example C, tunnel mode is used to set up an IPSec tunnel between the Cisco router and a server running IPSec software. Note that Cisco IOS software and the PIX Firewall set tunnel mode as the default IPSec mode.

- **Example D**—Transport mode is used between end stations supporting IPSec or between an end station and a gateway if the gateway is being treated as a host. In Example D, transport mode is used to set up an encrypted Telnet session from Alice's PC running Cisco Secure VPN Client software to terminate at the PIX Firewall, enabling Alice to remotely configure the PIX Firewall securely.

AH Tunnel Versus Transport Mode

Figure 1-7 shows the differences that the IPSec mode makes to AH. In transport mode, AH services protect the external IP header along with the data payload. AH services protect all the fields in the header that do not change in transport. The AH goes after the IP header and before the ESP header, if present, and other higher-layer protocols.

Figure 1-7   *AH Tunnel Versus Transport Mode*

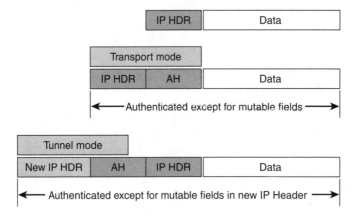

In tunnel mode, the entire original header is authenticated, a new IP header is built, and the new IP header is protected in the same way as the IP header in transport mode.

AH is incompatible with Network Address Translation (NAT) because NAT changes the source IP address, which will break the AH header and cause the packets to be rejected by the IPSec peer.

ESP Tunnel Versus Transport Mode

Figure 1-8 shows the differences that the IPSec mode makes to ESP. In transport mode, the IP payload is encrypted and the original headers are left intact. The ESP header is inserted after the IP header and before the upper-layer protocol header. The upper-layer protocols are encrypted and authenticated along with the ESP header. ESP does not authenticate the IP header itself. Please note that higher-layer information is not available because it is part of the encrypted payload.

Figure 1-8 *ESP Tunnel Versus Transport Mode*

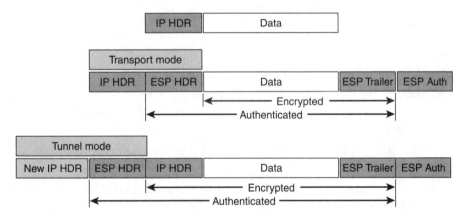

When ESP is used in tunnel mode, the original IP header is well protected because the entire original IP datagram is encrypted. With an ESP authentication mechanism, the original IP datagram and the ESP header are included; however, the new IP header is not included in the authentication.

When both authentication and encryption are selected, encryption is performed first, before authentication. One reason for this order of processing is that it facilitates rapid detection and rejection of replayed or bogus packets by the receiving node. Before decrypting the packet, the receiver can detect the problem and potentially reduce the impact of denial-of-service attacks.

ESP can also provide packet authentication with an optional field for authentication. Cisco IOS software and the PIX Firewall refer to this service as ESP HMAC. Authentication is calculated after the encryption is done. The current IPSec standard specifies SHA-1 and MD5 as the mandatory HMAC algorithms.

The main difference between the authentication provided by ESP and that provided by AH is the extent of the coverage. Specifically, ESP does not protect any IP header fields unless those fields are encapsulated by ESP (tunnel mode). Figure 1-9 illustrates the fields protected by ESP HMAC.

Figure 1-9 *ESP Encryption with a Keyed HMAC*

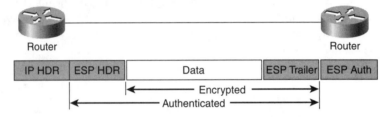

• Provides ESP confidentiality with encryption

• Provides integrity with a keyed HMAC

IPSec Transforms

An IPSec *transform* specifies a single IPSec security protocol (either AH or ESP) with its corresponding security algorithms and mode. Some example transforms include the following:

- The AH protocol with the HMAC with MD5 authentication algorithm in tunnel mode is used for authentication.

- The ESP protocol with the 3DES encryption algorithm in transport mode is used for confidentiality of data.

The ESP protocol with the 56-bit DES encryption algorithm and the HMAC with SHA authentication algorithm in tunnel mode is used for authentication and confidentiality.

Transform Sets

A *transform set* is a combination of individual IPSec transforms designed to enact a specific security policy for traffic. During the ISAKMP IPSec security association negotiation that occurs in IKE phase 2 quick mode, the peers agree to use a particular transform set for protecting a particular data flow. Transform sets combine the following IPSec factors:

- **Mechanism for payload authentication**—AH transform

- **Mechanism for payload encryption**—ESP transform

- **IPSec mode (transport versus tunnel)**

Transform sets equal a combination of an AH transform, an ESP transform, and the IPSec mode (either tunnel or transport mode).

IPSec Crypto Components

This section covers in detail the component technologies used in IPSec. This section covers the following:

- DES encryption
- Diffie-Hellman (D-H) key agreement
- HMAC

DES Encryption

The components of DES encryption are as follows:

- Encryption and decryption algorithms
- Matching shared secret keys on each peer
- Input clear text data to be encrypted

At the core of DES is the encryption algorithm. A shared secret key is input to the algorithm. Clear text data is fed into the algorithm in fixed-length blocks and is converted to ciphertext. The ciphertext is transmitted to the IPSec peer using ESP. The peer receives the ESP packet, extracts the ciphertext, runs it through the decryption algorithm, and outputs clear text identical to that input on the encrypting peer. The DES encryption algorithm can be seen in action in Figure 1-10. In Figure 1-10, a preshared key is in use.

Figure 1-10 *DES Encryption*

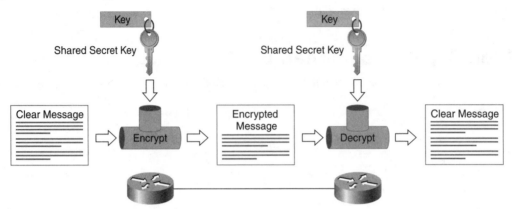

- Encryption turns clear text into ciphertext.
- Decryption restores clear text from ciphertext.
- Keys enable encryption and decryption.

Diffie-Hellman Key Agreement

The Diffie-Hellman (D-H) key agreement is a public key encryption method that provides a way for two IPSec peers to establish a shared secret key that only they know, although they are communicating over an insecure channel.

With D-H, each peer generates a public and private key pair. The private key generated by each peer is kept secret and never shared. The public key is calculated from the private key by each peer and is exchanged over the insecure channel. Each peer combines the other's public key with its own private key and computes the same shared secret number. The shared secret number is then converted into a shared secret key. The shared secret key is never exchanged over the insecure channel.

As you can see in Figure 1-11, Diffie-Hellman key exchange is a complicated process. This adds to the effectiveness of the encryption algorithm.

Figure 1-11 *Diffie-Hellman Key Agreement*

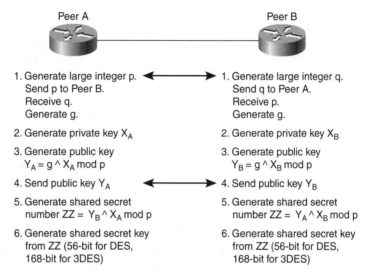

Peer A   Peer B

1. Generate large integer p.   1. Generate large integer q.
   Send p to Peer B.   Send q to Peer A.
   Receive q.   Receive p.
   Generate g.   Generate g.

2. Generate private key X_A 2. Generate private key X_B

3. Generate public key   3. Generate public key
   $Y_A = g \wedge X_A$ mod p $Y_B = g \wedge X_B$ mod p

4. Send public key Y_A 4. Send public key Y_B

5. Generate shared secret   5. Generate shared secret
   number ZZ = $Y_B \wedge X_A$ mod p   number ZZ = $Y_A \wedge X_B$ mod p

6. Generate shared secret key   6. Generate shared secret key
   from ZZ (56-bit for DES,   from ZZ (56-bit for DES,
   168-bit for 3DES)   168-bit for 3DES)

NOTE   Diffie-Hellman is very important because the shared secret key is used to encrypt data using the secret key encryption algorithms specified in the IPSec security associations, such as DES or MD5.

The Diffie-Hellman Process

The Diffie-Hellman process is as follows:

Step 1   The D-H process starts with each peer generating a large prime integer, p and q. Each peer sends the other its prime integer over the insecure channel. For example, Peer A sends p to Peer B. Each peer then uses the p and q values to generate g, a primitive root of p.

Step 2   Each peer generates a private D-H key (Peer A: Xa, Peer B: Xb).

Step 3   Each peer generates a public D-H key. The local private key is combined with the prime number p and the primitive root g in each peer to generate a public key: Ya for Peer A and Yb for Peer B. The formula for Peer A is Ya =g^Xa mod p. The formula for Peer B is Yb =g^Xb mod p. The exponentiation is computationally expensive. The ^ character denotes exponentiation (g^Xa is g to the Xa power); mod denotes modulus.

Step 4   The public keys Ya and Yb are exchanged in public.

Step 5   Each peer generates a shared secret number (ZZ) by combining the public key received from the opposite peer with its own private key. The formula for Peer A is ZZ=(YbXa) mod p. The formula for Peer B is ZZ=(YaXb) mod p. The ZZ values are identical in each peer. Anyone who knows p or g, or the D-H public keys, cannot guess or easily calculate the shared secret value largely because of the difficulty in factoring large prime numbers.

Step 6   Shared secret keys are derived from the shared secret number ZZ for use by DES or HMACs.

NOTE   Each IPSec peer has three keys:

- **A private key that is kept secret and is never shared**—It is used to sign messages.

- **A public key that is shared**—It is used by others to verify a signature.

- **A shared secret key that is used to encrypt data using an encryption algorithm (DES, MD5, and so on)**—The shared secret key is derived from Diffie-Hellman key generation.

HMAC

The fundamental hash algorithms used by IPSec are the cryptographically secure MD5 and SHA-1 hash functions. Hashing algorithms have evolved into HMACs, which combine the proven security of hashing algorithms with additional cryptographic functions. The hash produced is encrypted with the sender's private key, resulting in a keyed checksum as output.

In Figure 1-12, the hash function takes as input the variable-length clear text data that needs to be authenticated and a private key. The private key length is the same as that of the output of the hash. The HMAC algorithm is run, with a resultant fixed-length checksum as output. This checksum value is sent with the message as a signature. The receiving peer runs an HMAC on the same message data that was input at the sender, using the same private key, and the resultant hash is compared with the received hash, which should exactly match.

Figure 1-12 *Hashed Message Authentication Codes (HMAC)*

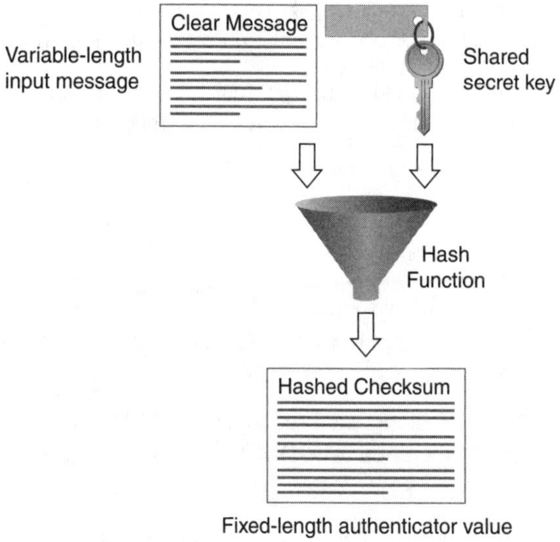

Fixed-length authenticator value

HMAC-MD5-96

The HMAC-MD5-96 (also known as HMAC-MD5) encryption technique is used by IPSec to ensure that a message has not been altered. HMAC-MD5 uses the MD5 hash developed by Ronald Rivest of the Massachusetts Institute of Technology and RSA Data Security Incorporated and is described in RFC 1321.

HMAC-MD5 uses a 128-bit secret key. It produces a 128-bit authenticator value. This 128-bit value is truncated to the first 96 bits. Upon sending, the truncated value is stored within the authenticator field of AH or ESP-HMAC. Upon receipt, the entire 128-bit value is computed, and the first 96 bits are compared to the value stored in the authenticator field.

MD5 alone has recently been shown to be vulnerable to collision search attacks. This attack and other currently known weaknesses of MD5 do not compromise the use of MD5 within HMAC, as no known attacks against HMAC-MD5 have been proven. HMAC-MD5 is recommended where the superior performance of MD5 over SHA-1 is important.

HMAC-SHA-1-96

The HMAC-SHA-1-96 (also known as HMAC-SHA-1) encryption technique is used by IPSec to ensure that a message has not been altered. HMAC-SHA-1 uses the SHA-1 specified in FIPS-190-1, combined with HMAC (as per RFC 2104), and is described in RFC 2404.

HMAC-SHA-1 uses a 160-bit secret key. It produces a 160-bit authenticator value. This 160-bit value is truncated to the first 96 bits. Upon sending, the truncated value is stored within the authenticator field of AH or ESP-HMAC. Upon receipt, the entire 160-bit value is computed and the first 96 bits are compared to the value stored in the authenticator field.

SHA-1 is considered cryptographically stronger that MD5, yet it takes more CPU cycles to compute. HMAC-SHA-1 is recommended where the slightly superior security of SHA-1 over MD5 is important.

IKE Overview

IKE negotiates the IPSec security associations (SAs). This process requires that the IPSec systems first authenticate themselves to each other and establish ISAKMP, or IKE, shared keys.

In phase one, IKE creates an authenticated secure channel between the two IKE peers that is called the IKE Security Association. The Diffie-Hellman key agreement is always performed in this phase.

In phase two, IKE negotiates the IPSec security associations and generates the required key material for IPSec. The sender offers one or more transform sets that are used to specify an allowed combination of transforms with their respective settings. The sender also indicates the data flow to which the transform set is to be applied. The sender must offer at least one transform set. The receiver then sends back a single transform set, which indicates the mutually agreed-on transforms and algorithms for this particular IPSec session. A new Diffie-Hellman agreement can be done in phase two, or the keys can be derived from the phase one shared secret.

Figure 1-13 shows the role that IKE takes in the IPSec VPN creation process.

NOTE   A security association (SA) is a relationship between two or more entities that describes how the entities will use security services to communicate securely. SAs are covered in detail later in this chapter in the "IPSec Security Associations" section.

Figure 1-13 *The Function of IKE*

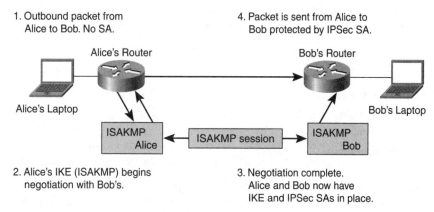

1. Outbound packet from
   Alice to Bob. No SA.

4. Packet is sent from Alice to
   Bob protected by IPSec SA.

2. Alice's IKE (ISAKMP) begins
   negotiation with Bob's.

3. Negotiation complete.
   Alice and Bob now have
   IKE and IPSec SAs in place.

* IKE sets up a secure channel to negotiate the IPSec security associations.

IKE authenticates the peer and the IKE messages between the peers during IKE phase one.
Phase one consists of main mode or aggressive mode. Potential peers in an IPSec session
must authenticate themselves to each other before IKE can proceed. Peer authentication
occurs during the main mode exchange during IKE phase one. The IKE protocol is very
flexible and supports multiple authentication methods as part of the phase one exchange.
The two entities must agree on a common authentication protocol through a negotiation
process. IKE phase one has three methods to authenticate IPSec peers in Cisco products,
which are as follows:

* **Preshared keys**—A key value entered into each peer manually (out of band) used to
  authenticate the peer

* **RSA signatures**—Use a digital certificate authenticated by an RSA signature

* **RSA encrypted nonces**—Use RSA encryption to encrypt a nonce value (a random
  number generated by the peer) and other values

A common value used by all authentication methods is the peer identity (ID), which helps
identify the peer. Some ID values used are as follows:

* IP address of the peer (four octets), such as 172.30.2.2

* Fully qualified domain name (FQDN), such as student@cisco.com

Preshared Keys

With preshared keys, the same preshared key is configured on each IPSec peer. IKE peers
authenticate each other by computing and sending a keyed hash of data that includes the
preshared key. If the receiving peer is able to create the same hash independently using its
preshared key, it knows that both peers must share the same secret, thus authenticating the

other peer. Preshared keys are easier to configure than manually configuring IPSec policy values on each IPSec peer. However, preshared keys do not scale well because each IPSec peer must be configured with the preshared key of every other peer with which it will establish a session.

RSA Signatures

The RSA signatures method uses a digital signature, where each device digitally signs a set of data and sends it to the other party. RSA signatures use a CA to generate a unique identity digital certificate that is assigned to each peer for authentication. The identity digital certificate is similar in function to the preshared key, but provides much stronger security.

RSA is a public-key cryptosystem used by IPSec for authentication in IKE phase 1. RSA was developed in 1977 by Ronald Rivest, Adi Shamir, and Leonard Adelman.

The initiator and the responder to an IKE session using RSA signatures send their own ID value (IDi, IDr), their identity digital certificate, and an RSA signature value consisting of a variety of IKE values, all encrypted by the negotiated IKE encryption method (DES or 3DES).

RSA Encryption

The RSA-encrypted nonces method uses the RSA encryption public key cryptography standard. The method requires that each party generates a pseudorandom number (a nonce) and encrypt it in the other party's RSA public key. Authentication occurs when each party decrypts the other party's nonce with a local private key (and other publicly and privately available information) and then uses the decrypted nonce to compute a keyed hash. This system provides for deniable transactions. That is, either side of the exchange can plausibly deny that it took part in the exchange. Cisco IOS software is the only Cisco product that uses RSA encrypted nonces for IKE authentication. RSA encrypted nonces use the RSA public key algorithm.

CAs and Digital Certificates

The distribution of keys in a public key scheme requires some trust. If the infrastructure is untrusted and control is questionable, such as on the Internet, distribution of keys is troublesome. RSA signatures are used by CAs, which are trusted third-party organizations. Verisign, Entrust, and Netscape are examples of companies that provide digital certificates. To get a digital certificate, a client registers with a CA. After a CA verifies the client's credentials, a certificate is issued. The digital certificate is a package that contains information such as a certificate bearer's identity: his or her name or IP address, the certificate's serial number, the certificate's expiration date, and a copy of the certificate bearer's public key. The standard digital certificate format is defined in the X.509

specification. X.509 version 3 defines the data structure for certificates and is the standard that Cisco supports. Figure 1-14 identifies some key points of CA operation.

Figure 1-14 *CAs and Digital Certificates*

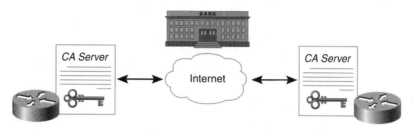

- Certificate Authority (CA) verifies identity.
- CA signs digital certificate containing device's public key.
- VeriSign OnSite, Entrust PKI, Baltimore CA, Microsoft CA.

How IPSec Works

IPSec involves many component technologies and encryption methods. Yet IPSec's operation can be broken down into five main steps. The five steps are summarized as follows:

Step 1 **Interesting traffic initiates the IPSec process**—Traffic is deemed interesting when the IPSec security policy configured in the IPSec peers starts the IKE process.

Step 2 **IKE phase one**—IKE authenticates IPSec peers and negotiates IKE SAs during this phase, setting up a secure channel for negotiating IPSec SAs in phase two.

Step 3 **IKE phase two**—IKE negotiates IPSec SA parameters and sets up matching IPSec SAs in the peers.

Step 4 **Data transfer**—Data is transferred between IPSec peers based on the IPSec parameters and keys stored in the SA database.

Step 5 **IPSec tunnel termination**—IPSec SAs terminate through deletion or by timing out.

This five-step process is shown in Figure 1-15.

Figure 1-15 *The Five Steps of IPSec*

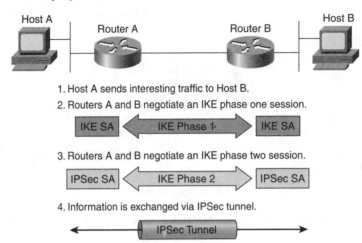

1. Host A sends interesting traffic to Host B.
2. Routers A and B negotiate an IKE phase one session.
3. Routers A and B negotiate an IKE phase two session.
4. Information is exchanged via IPSec tunnel.
5. IPSec tunnel is terminated.

Step 1: Defining Interesting Traffic

Determining what type of traffic is deemed interesting is part of formulating a security policy for use of a VPN. The policy is then implemented in the configuration interface for each particular IPSec peer. For example, in Cisco routers and PIX Firewalls, access lists are used to determine the traffic to encrypt. The access lists are assigned to a crypto policy such that permit statements indicate that the selected traffic must be encrypted, and deny statements can be used to indicate that the selected traffic must be sent unencrypted. With the Cisco Secure VPN Client, you use menu windows to select connections to be secured by IPSec. When interesting traffic is generated or transits the IPSec client, the client initiates the next step in the process, negotiating an IKE phase one exchange.

Step 1 is shown in Figure 1-16.

Figure 1-16 *Defining Interesting Traffic*

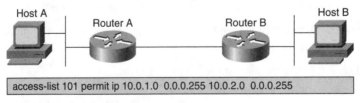

access-list 101 permit ip 10.0.1.0 0.0.0.255 10.0.2.0 0.0.0.255

Access lists determine traffic to encrypt.

• Permit—Traffic must be encrypted.
• Deny—Traffic sent unencrypted.

Step 2: IKE Phase One

The basic purpose of IKE phase one is to authenticate the IPSec peers and to set up a secure channel between the peers to enable IKE exchanges. IKE phase one performs the following functions:

- Authenticates and protects the identities of the IPSec peers
- Negotiates a matching IKE SA policy between peers to protect the IKE exchange
- Performs an authenticated Diffie-Hellman exchange with the end result of having matching shared secret keys
- Sets up a secure tunnel to negotiate IKE phase two parameters

IKE phase one occurs in two modes:

- Main mode
- Aggressive mode

Main Mode

Main mode has three two-way exchanges between the initiator and receiver.

- **First exchange**—The algorithms and hashes used to secure the IKE communications are agreed upon in matching IKE SAs in each peer.
- **Second exchange**—This exchange uses a Diffie-Hellman exchange to generate shared secret keying material used to generate shared secret keys and to pass nonces, which are random numbers sent to the other party, signed, and returned to prove their identity.
- **Third exchange**—This exchange verifies the other side's identity. The identity value is the IPSec peer's IP address in encrypted form. The main outcome of main mode is matching IKE SAs between peers to provide a protected pipe for subsequent protected ISAKMP exchanges between the IKE peers. The IKE SA specifies values for the IKE exchange: the authentication method used, the encryption and hash algorithms, the Diffie-Hellman group used, the lifetime of the IKE SA in seconds or kilobytes, and the shared secret key values for the encryption algorithms. The IKE SA in each peer is bidirectional.

Aggressive Mode

In the aggressive mode, fewer exchanges are done and with fewer packets. In the first exchange, almost everything is squeezed into the proposed IKE SA values, the Diffie-Hellman public key, a nonce that the other party signs, and an identity packet, which can be used to verify the initiator's identity through a third party. The receiver sends everything back that is needed to complete the exchange. The only thing left is for the initiator to confirm the exchange. The weakness of using the aggressive mode is that both sides have exchanged information before there is a secure channel. Therefore, it is possible to sniff the wire and discover who formed the new SA. However, aggressive mode is faster than main mode.

Step 2 is shown in Figure 1-17.

Figure 1-17 *IKE Phase One*

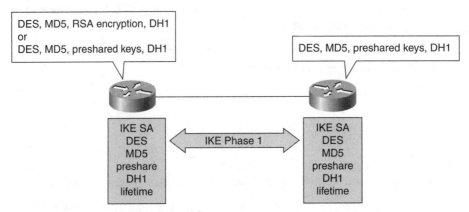

- Authenticates IPSec peers
- Negotiates matching policy to protect IKE exchange
- Exchanges keys via Diffie-Hellman
- Establishes IKE security association

Step 3: IKE Phase Two

The purpose of IKE phase two is to negotiate IPSec SAs to set up the IPSec tunnel. IKE phase two performs the following functions:

- Negotiates IPSec SA parameters protected by an existing IKE SA
- Establishes IPSec security associations
- Periodically renegotiates IPSec SAs to ensure security
- Optionally performs an additional Diffie-Hellman exchange

IKE phase 2 has one mode, called quick mode. Quick mode occurs after IKE has established the secure tunnel in phase one. It negotiates a shared IPSec policy, derives shared secret keying material used for the IPSec security algorithms, and establishes IPSec SAs. Quick mode exchanges nonces that provide replay protection. The nonces are used to generate new shared secret key material and prevent replay attacks from generating bogus SAs.

Quick mode is also used to renegotiate a new IPSec SA when the IPSec SA lifetime expires. Base quick mode is used to refresh the keying material used to create the shared secret key based on the keying material derived from the Diffie-Hellman exchange in phase one.

Perfect Forward Secrecy

If perfect forward secrecy (PFS) is specified in the IPSec policy, a new Diffie-Hellman exchange is performed with each quick mode, providing keying material that has greater entropy (key material life) and thereby greater resistance to cryptographic attacks. Each Diffie-Hellman exchange requires large exponentiations, thereby increasing CPU use and exacting a performance cost.

Step 4: IPSec Encrypted Tunnel

After IKE phase two is complete and quick mode has established IPSec SAs, information is exchanged by an IPSec tunnel. Packets are encrypted and decrypted using the encryption specified in the IPSec SA. This IPSec encrypted tunnel can be seen in Figure 1-18.

Figure 1-18 *IPSec Encrypted Tunnel*

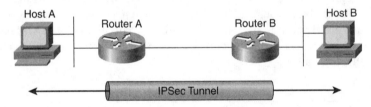

Step 5: Tunnel Termination

IPSec SAs terminate through deletion or by timing out. An SA can time out when a specified number of seconds have elapsed or when a specified number of bytes have passed through the tunnel. When the SAs terminate, the keys are also discarded. When subsequent IPSec SAs are needed for a flow, IKE performs a new phase two and, if necessary, a new phase one negotiation. A successful negotiation results in new SAs and new keys. New SAs can be established before the existing SAs expire so that a given flow can continue uninterrupted. This can be seen in Figure 1-19.

Figure 1-19 *Tunnel Termination*

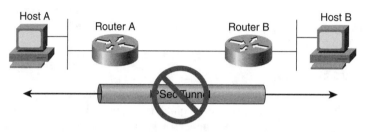

IPSec Security Associations (SAs)

The concept of a security association (SA) is fundamental to IPSec. An SA is a relationship between two or more entities that describes how the entities will use security services to communicate securely. IPSec provides many options for performing network encryption and authentication. Each IPSec connection can provide encryption, integrity, authenticity, or all three. When the security service is determined, the two IPSec peers must determine exactly which algorithms to use (for example, DES or 3DES for encryption, MD5 or SHA for integrity). After deciding on the algorithms, the two devices must share session keys. As you can see, there is quite a bit of information to manage. The security association is the method that IPSec uses to track all the particulars concerning a given IPSec communication session. You will need to configure SA parameters and monitor SAs on Cisco routers and the PIX Firewall.

NOTE   The nomenclature gets a little confusing at times, because SAs are used for more than just IPSec. For example, IKE SAs describe the security parameters between two IKE devices.

A separate pair of IPSec SAs are set up for AH and ESP transform. Each IPSec peer agrees to set up SAs consisting of policy parameters to be used during the IPSec session. The SAs are unidirectional for IPSec so that peer 1 will offer peer 2 a policy. If peer 2 accepts this policy, it will send that policy back to peer 1. This establishes two one-way SAs between the peers. Two-way communication consists of two SAs, one for each direction.

Each SA consists of values such as destination address, a security parameter index (SPI), the IPSec transforms used for that session, security keys, and additional attributes such as IPSec lifetime. The SAs in each peer have unique SPI values that will be recorded in the Security Parameter Databases of the devices. The Security Parameter Database is set up in dynamic random-access memory (DRAM) and contains parameter values for each SA. An example of these values is shown in Figure 1-20.

Figure 1-20 *IPSec Security Association*

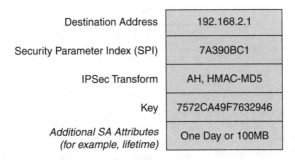

Destination Address	192.168.2.1
Security Parameter Index (SPI)	7A390BC1
IPSec Transform	AH, HMAC-MD5
Key	7572CA49F7632946
Additional SA Attributes (for example, lifetime)	One Day or 100MB

An IPSec transform in Cisco IOS specifies either an AH or an ESP protocol and its corresponding algorithms and mode (transport or tunnel). The Cisco Secure VPN Client uses the concept of security policies to specify the same parameters. Transforms, transform sets, and the corresponding security policies of the Cisco Secure VPN Client are explained in detail in Chapter 12, "Scaling Cisco IPSec-Based VPNs."

Figure 1-21 contains an actual example of SA parameters for two IPSec peers: R1 and R2. Remember that each IPSec SA is unidirectional, and the SA parameters must match on each IPSec peer. The SA parameters are configured by the system administrator and are stored in the SA database. Table 1-1 contains a description of the parameters shown in Figure 1-21.

Figure 1-21 *SA Parameter Example on a Cisco Router*

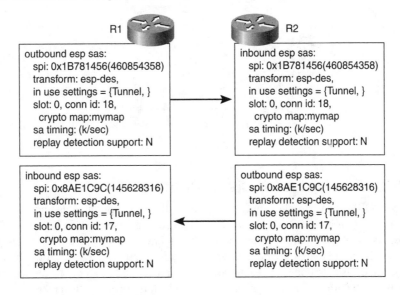

Table 1-1 *SA Parameters*

Parameter	Description
outbound esp sas: spi: 0x1B781456(460854358)	Security parameter index, which matches inbound SPI for that SA
transform: esp-des	IPSec transform
in use settings ={Tunnel, }	IPSec transform mode (tunnel or transport)
slot: 0, conn id: 18, crypto map:mymap	Crypto engine and crypto map information
sa timing: (k/sec)	SA lifetime in KB and seconds
replay detection support: N	Replay detection either on or off

The SAs between IPSec peers enable the configured IPSec policy. When a system sends a packet that requires IPSec protection, it looks up the SA in its database, applies the specified processing, and then inserts the SPI from the SA into the IPSec header. When the IPSec peer receives the packet, it looks up the SA in its database by destination address and SPI, and then processes the packet as required. In summary, the SA is a statement of the negotiated security policy between two devices. Figure 1-22 shows an example of differing policies between peers.

Figure 1-22 *SAs Enable Your Chosen Policy*

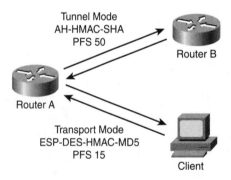

IKE and IPSec Flowchart for Cisco Routers

Cisco IOS software implements and processes IPSec in a predictable and reliable fashion. A summary of how IPSec works in Cisco IOS software is shown in Figure 1-23. The process shown in Figure 1-23 assumes that you have already created your own public and private keys and that at least one access list exists. Figure 1-23 also shows the Cisco IOS commands used to configure each part of the process, although the commands are not shown in the order in which you enter them, which is covered in Chapters 3, "Configuring

Cisco IOS Routers for Preshared Keys Site-to-Site" and 4, "Configuring Cisco IOS Routers for CA Site-to-Site."

Figure 1-23 *IKE and IPSec Flowchart*

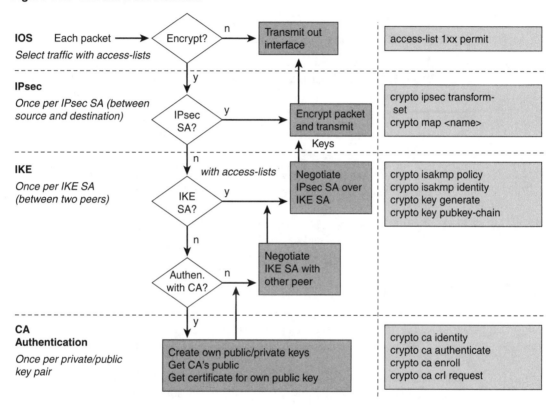

NOTE   Remember, IKE is synonymous with ISAKMP in Cisco router or PIX Firewall configurations.

The following steps describe the IPSec process.

Step 1   Access lists applied to an interface and crypto map are used by Cisco IOS software to select interesting traffic to be encrypted.

Step 2   Cisco IOS software checks to see if IPSec SAs have been established.

Step 3   If the SA has already been established by manual configuration using the **crypto ipsec transform-set** and **crypto map** commands or has been previously set up by IKE, the packet is encrypted based on the policy specified in the crypto map and is transmitted out of the interface.

Step 4   If the SA has not been established, Cisco IOS software checks to see if an IKE SA has been configured and set up.

Step 5   If the IKE SA has been set up, the IKE SA governs negotiation of the IPSec SA as specified in the IKE policy configured by the **crypto isakmp policy** command, the packet is encrypted by IPSec, and it is transmitted.

Step 6   If the IKE SA has not been set up, Cisco IOS software checks to see if certification authority (CA) has been configured to establish an IKE policy.

Step 7   If CA authentication is configured with the various **crypto ca** commands, the router uses public and private keys previously configured, obtains the CA's public certificate, gets a certificate for its own public key, and then uses the key to negotiate an IKE SA, which in turn is used to establish an IPSec SA to encrypt and transmit the packet.

CA Support Overview

With a CA, you do not need to configure keys among all of the encrypting IPSec peers. Instead, you individually enroll each participating peer with the CA and request a certificate. When this has been accomplished, each participating peer can dynamically authenticate all of the other participating routers. To add a new IPSec peer to the network, you only need to configure that new peer to request a certificate from the CA, instead of making multiple key configurations with all the other existing IPSec peers.

This section presents an overview of how CA support works.

CA servers are responsible for managing certificate requests and issuing certificates to participating IPSec network devices. These services provide centralized key management for the participating devices. CAs simplify the administration of IPSec network devices so that IPSec keys do not have to be manually configured on each peer. You can use a CA with a network containing multiple IPSec-compliant devices, such as PIX Firewalls, Cisco routers, the Cisco VPN 3000 Concentrator series, the Cisco Secure VPN Client, and other vendors' IPSec products, as shown in Figure 1-24.

Figure 1-24 *CA Support*

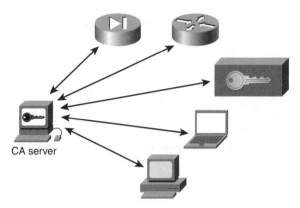

CA server

Digital signatures, enabled by public key cryptography, provide a means to digitally authenticate devices and individual users. In public key cryptography, such as the RSA signature system, each user has a key pair containing both a public and a private key. The keys act as complements, and anything encrypted with one of the keys can be decrypted with the other. An RSA signature is formed when data is encrypted with a user's private key. The receiver verifies the signature by decrypting the message with the sender's public key.

The fact that the message could be decrypted using the sender's public key indicates that the holder of the private key—the sender—must have created the message. This process relies on the receiver having a copy of the sender's public key and knowing with a high degree of certainty that it really does belong to the sender, and not to someone pretending to be the sender.

A digital certificate contains information to identify a user or device, such as the name, serial number, company, department, or IP address. It also contains a copy of the entity's public key. A CA signs the certificate. The CA is a third party that is explicitly trusted by the receiver to validate identities and to create digital certificates.

To validate the CA's signature, the receiver must first know the CA's public key. Normally this is handled out-of-band or through an operation done at installation. For instance, most Web browsers are configured with the public keys of several CAs by default. The IKE, a key component of IPSec, can use digital signatures to authenticate peer devices before setting up SAs, while simultaneously providing scalability.

Without digital signatures, you must manually exchange either public keys or secret keys between each pair of devices that use IPSec to protect communications between them. Without certificates, every new device added to the network requires a configuration change on every other device with which it securely communicates. However, by using digital certificates, each device is enrolled with a CA. When two devices wish to communicate, they exchange certificates and digitally sign data to authenticate each other. When a new device is added to the network, one simply enrolls that device with a CA, and none of the other devices need modification. When the new device attempts an IPSec connection, certificates are automatically exchanged and the device can be authenticated. Without CA interoperability, devices could not use CAs when deploying IPSec. CAs provide a manageable, scaleable solution for IPSec networks.

Digital Signatures

The digital signature provides a form of digital credentials that authenticate the identity of the sending party, whoever that may be. In other words, digital signatures are used to link data with the holder of a specific private key and consist of the following:

- At the local end, a private key is used to encrypt the hash.
- At the remote end:
  - The hash is produced by running the original message through a hash algorithm.
  - The hash that was appended to the original message is decrypted using the sender's public key.
- If the hashes match, the message is signed by a private key.
- Only a specific private key could have produced the digital signature.

Figure 1-25 shows the digital signature process.

Figure 1-25 *Digital Signatures*

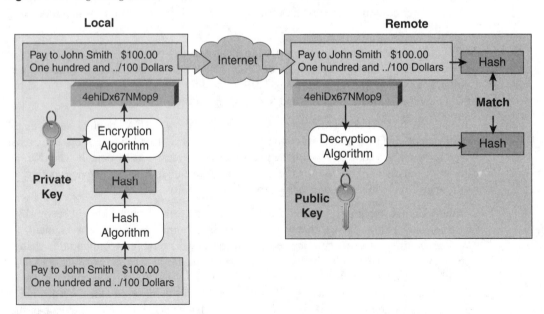

A key pair has no intrinsic ties to any person or entity. It could be sourced from Alice, Tom, or Harry Hacker masquerading as Alice or Tom. A solution is necessary to reliably tie a person or entity to a key pair. Digital signatures provide a way to "guarantee" the source of the message. The solution is digital signatures and digital certificates.

- **Digital signatures**—Tie a message to a sender's private key. The hash can only be decrypted by the sender's public key.

- **Digital certificates**—Bind a person or entity to a private key.

Certificate-Based Authentication

Digital certificates are used to authenticate users. They can be used to identify a person, a company, or a server. They are the equivalent of a digital passport or driver's license. The following example and Figure 1-26 illustrate how this works.

Step 1   Users A and B register separately with the CA.

- Digital certificates are issued by a trusted third party, a CA.

- The CA issues separate certificates and digitally signs them with its private key, thereby certifying the authenticity of the user.

Step 2   User A sends the certificate to User B.

Step 3   User B checks the authenticity of the CA signature on the certificate.

- The CA public key is used to verify the CA signature on the certificate.

- If it passes validation, it is "safe" to assume User A is who he says he is, therefore the message is valid.

Step 4   User B sends the certificate to User A.

- The CA public key is used to verify the CA signature on the certificate.

- Once verified, all subsequent communications can be accepted.

NOTE   Certificates are exchanged during the IPSec negotiations.

Figure 1-26 *Certificate-Based Authentication*

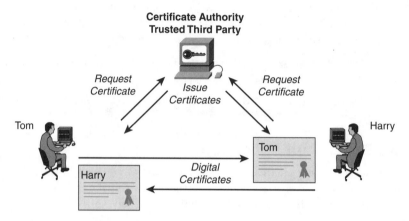

CAs

CAs hold the key to the public key infrastructure (PKI). A CA is a trusted third party whose job is to certify the authenticity of users to ensure that you are who you say you are.

Authenticity is guaranteed by the CA digital signature created with the CA private key. You can verify a digital signature using the CA public key. Only the CA public key can decrypt the digital certificate. The job of a CA is to

- Create certificates
- Administer certificates
- Revoke invalid certificates

The CA can be a corporate network administrator or a recognized third party. Trusted sources supported by the Cisco VPN 3000 Concentrator Series include the following:

- Entrust
- GTE Cybertrust
- Network Associates PGP
- Baltimore
- Microsoft
- Verisign

Some CAs also use a Registration Authority (RA) to provide certificate enrollment services. An RA is server software that acts as a proxy for the CA, providing essential CA functions, such as certificate enrollment and distribution.

PKI

PKI is the set of hardware, software, people, policies, and procedures needed to create, manage, store, distribute, and revoke digital certificates. PKI makes it possible to generate and distribute keys within a secure domain and enables CAs to issue keys and associated certificate and certificate revocation lists (CRLs) in a secure manner. There are two PKI models, as shown in the following list and Figure 1-27.

- Central authority
  - All certificates are signed by a single authority.
  - All certificates can be checked with that CA's public key.
- Hierarchical authority
  - The ability to sign a certificate is delegated through a hierarchy. The top of the hierarchy is the *root CA*. It signs certificates for subordinate authorities.
  - Subordinate CAs sign certificates for lower-level CAs.
  - To validate a user's certificate, the certificate must be validated up through the chain of authority.

Figure 1-27 *PKI*

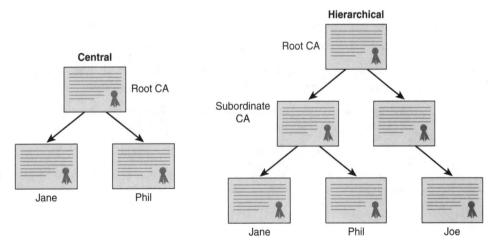

Summary

This chapter provided a very detailed overview of VPNs with a concentration on using IPSec as a VPN technology. It started by covering the various VPN components such as the Cisco Secure PIX Firewall, Cisco routers, and the Cisco VPN Concentrator. It then covered the technicalities of IPSec and the components that make up IPSec.

The chapter covered the five-step process of IPSec VPN establishment that includes IKE phase one and IKE phase two.

The chapter finished by looking at IPSec security associations (SAs) and also provided an overview of the certificate authority (CA) process.

Now that you have a foundation of knowledge on IPSec and VPN terminology, the next chapter looks at the individual VPN components and the configuration challenges that each one brings.

Review Questions

1 What are the three types of VPNs?

2 What type of VPNs link outside customers, suppliers, partners, or communities of interest to an enterprise customer's network over a shared infrastructure using dedicated connections?

3 IPSec consists of which two components?

4 You configure an IPSec transform set to use AH. Is the data payload encrypted?

5 You want to establish an extranet VPN over the Internet. Which type of IPSec mode (transport or tunnel) would be the best solution in this scenario?

6 Which is the most secure encryption algorithm: DES, 3DES, or Diffie-Hellman?

7 Step one of configuring IPSec is defining interesting traffic. What Cisco IOS feature do you use to define this?

8 With preshared keys, can each of the keys be different or must each be the same (have the same value as the other's public key)?

9 What is used to relay the shared key to the VPN peer?

10 IKE peers authenticate themselves using one of four methods. What are these four methods?

PART II

Cisco VPN Family of Products

Chapter 2 Cisco VPN Family of Products

Cisco VPN Family of Products

Chapter 1, "VPNs and VPN Technologies," provides a technical overview of virtual private networks (VPNs) and focuses on IPSec as a VPN technology. This chapter provides an overview of the Cisco VPN family of products, including an overview of each member of the family. Later chapters go into greater product and configuration detail. This chapter concentrates on the Cisco router, Cisco Secure PIX Firewall, and the Cisco VPN Concentrator.

Cisco has embraced VPN technologies throughout its product range. IPSec support has been available in Cisco IOS since 11.3(T) and in the Cisco Secure PIX Firewall since version 5.0. In January 2000, Cisco bought Altiga Networks, and then in March 2000, purchased Compatible Systems Corporation. With these acquisitions came the new VPN Concentrator product range. The VPN Concentrator range consists of the 3000 and 5000 series of dedicated high-speed VPN termination devices. The existing Altiga range became the 3000 series and the Compatible range became the 5000 series.

The VPN Concentrator is a relatively new product from Cisco Systems. This chapter concentrates mainly on the VPN 3000 series.

This chapter covers the following topics:

- Overview of the Cisco VPN product range
- Cisco routers running Cisco IOS software
- Cisco Secure PIX Firewall
- Cisco VPN Concentrator

Overview of the Cisco VPN Product Range

The following main components make up Cisco's VPN offerings:

- **Cisco VPN routers**—Use Cisco IOS software IPSec support to enable a secure VPN. VPN-optimized routers leverage existing Cisco investment, perfect for the hybrid WAN.
- **Cisco Secure PIX Firewall**—Offers a VPN gateway alternative when the security group "owns" the VPN.

- **Cisco VPN Concentrator series**—Offers powerful remote access and site-to-site VPN capability, easy-to-use management interface, and a VPN Client.

- **Cisco Secure VPN Client**—The VPN Client enables secure remote access to Cisco routers and PIX Firewalls and runs on the Windows operating system.

- **Cisco Secure Intrusion Detection System (CSIDS) and Cisco Secure Scanner**—These can be used to monitor and audit the security of the VPN.

- **Cisco Secure Policy Manager and Cisco Works 2000**—These provide VPN-wide system management.

These can all be seen in context in Figure 2-1.

Figure 2-1 *Cisco Secure VPN Components*

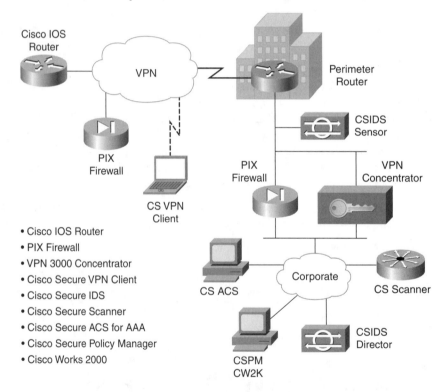

This chapter looks at the VPN offerings on Cisco routers, Cisco Secure PIX Firewall, and the Cisco VPN 3000 Concentrator.

Cisco Routers Running Cisco IOS Software

Cisco IOS software running in Cisco routers combines rich VPN services with industry-leading routing, thus delivering a comprehensive VPN routing solution. Cisco IOS software combines IPSec VPN enhancements with robust firewall, intrusion detection, and secure administration capabilities. The VPN software adds strong triple Data Encryption Standard (3DES) encryption authentication through digital certificates and preshared keys to the baseline Cisco Secure Integrated Software. This Cisco IOS software-based solution fully supports remote access, intranet, and extranet VPN requirements.

VPN Capabilities of Cisco Routers Running Cisco IOS Software

The capability of a router to establish and maintain a VPN is ascertained not by the model of the router but by the software running on the router.

A VPN can be thought of as a way to connect private networks over a public media while offering some sort of security. Therefore you do not require IPSec to establish a VPN. In very simple terms, a VPN can be a connection over a public network using a tunnel interface. This tunnel interface can use Generic Route Encapsulation (GRE) to tunnel the packets over a public network. Users on each private network see the other end of the tunnel (other private network) as one hop. They are unaware of the public infrastructure that is in place between the private routers. Figure 2-2 shows such a scenario.

Figure 2-2   *A Simple VPN Using Two Cisco Routes and a GRE Tunnel*

This book concentrates on IPSec as the VPN protocol of choice. IPSec is explained in Chapter 1. IPSec was adopted by Cisco in IOS version 11.3(T). Specific Cisco IOS versions contain IPSec in addition to DES and 3DES versions. Because of the stringent licensing requirements of 3DES, it is normally sold as an additional product and does not ship as standard—even with the Enterprise IOS feature sets.

Cisco IOS routers support both site-to-site VPNs between IPSec-compliant devices and client-to-site VPNs that terminate VPN sessions from various IPSec operating system-based clients, such as the Cisco VPN Client.

Cisco provides a suite of VPN-optimized routers. These routers run the range of VPN applications, from telecommuter applications with the Cisco 800 for ISDN access to remote-office connectivity with the Cisco 1700, 2600, and 3600 to head-end connectivity with the Cisco 7100, 7200, and 7500 series. Furthermore, Cisco product breadth extends into the new world of broadband telecommuter and small office VPN connectivity with the Cisco UBr900 cable access router/modem and the Cisco 1400 DSL router/modem. Providing DSL and cable solutions is unique to Cisco in the VPN market.

The suite of VPN-optimized routers can be seen in Figure 2-3.

Figure 2-3   *VPN-Optimized Routers*

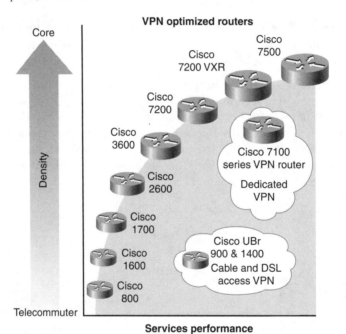

The Cisco 7100 Series VPN Router is an integrated VPN router that provides solutions for VPN-centric environments. VPN-optimized routers provide VPN solutions for hybrid VPN environments where modularity, port density, and flexibility are required for private WAN aggregation and other classic WAN applications. The Cisco 7100 provides solutions where WAN density requirements are lower—where only one or two connections to the VPN cloud are required for VPN connectivity. I/O of the 7100 is focused for this single or dual homing WAN configuration and provides high performance for robust VPN services throughput.

With the quest for higher performing VPN technologies ever expanding, Cisco has recently developed a range of VPN Accelerator Cards (VACs) for Cisco routers. These cards are currently available for the 2600, 3600, 7140, and 7200 series of routers. These VACs perform hardware encryption of DES and 3DES VPNs, greatly improving the throughput of these encryption standards.

Cisco Secure PIX Firewall

The PIX Firewall is the world's leading firewall, providing today's network customers with unmatched speed, reliability, scalability, and functionality. Its integrated appliance design and innovative hybrid security architecture—including stateful and proxy firewalls in addition to IPSec VPN—deliver the highest levels of security and performance, supporting more than a quarter of a million simultaneous connections at over 240 megabits per second (Mbps).

The Cisco Secure PIX Firewall is the dedicated hardware firewall in the Cisco Secure product family. The PIX Firewall is the industry leader in both market share and performance within the firewall market.

The Cisco PIX is designed around a purpose-built, secure, real-time, embedded operating system that leads to excellent performance without compromising security. This high level of performance is indicative of the hardware architecture of the PIX Firewall in relation to other operating system-based appliances.

Currently, there are five versions of the PIX Firewall: PIX 506, PIX 515, PIX 520, PIX 525, and PIX 535. Most of these can be seen in Figure 2-4.

The following list summarizes the PIX Firewall products.

- PIX 506—The PIX 506 is the entry-level firewall designed for high-end small office, home office (SOHO) and remote office, branch office (ROBO) installations. The throughput has been measured at 10 Mbps, which reflects the market to which the product is aimed.

- PIX 515—The PIX 515 is the midrange firewall designed for small to medium businesses and remote office deployments. It occupies only one rack unit and offers a throughput of up to 120 Mbps with a maximum of 125,000 concurrent sessions. The default configuration is two fast Ethernet ports, and it is currently upgradable with two onboard PCI slots.

- PIX 520—The PIX 520 is a high-end firewall designed for enterprise and service provider use. The unit occupies three rack units and offers a throughput of up to 370 Mbps with a maximum of 250,000 concurrent sessions. The default configuration is two fast Ethernet ports, and it is currently upgradable with four onboard PCI slots. The PIX 520 is at end of life and has been replaced by the PIX 525.

- PIX 525—The PIX 525 is intended for enterprise and service provider use. It has a throughput of 370 Mbps with the ability to handle as many as 280,000 simultaneous sessions. The 600 MHz CPU of the PIX 525 can enable it to deliver an additional 25 to 30 percent increase in capacity for firewalling services.

Figure 2-4   *Cisco Secure PIX Firewall Product Range*

- PIX 535—The Cisco Secure PIX 535 is the latest and largest addition to the PIX 500 series. Intended for enterprise and service provider use, it has a throughput of 1.0 Gbps with the ability to handle up to 500,000 concurrent connections. Supporting both site-to-site and remote access VPN applications with 56-bit DES or 168-bit 3DES, the integrated VPN functionality of the PIX 535 can be supplemented with a VPN accelerator card to deliver 100 Mbps throughput and 2,000 IPSec tunnels.

A dedicated PIX Firewall VAC can also be used in the PIX 515, 520, 525, and 535 units. This card performs hardware acceleration of VPN traffic encryption/decryption, providing 100 Mbps IPSec throughput using 168-bit 3DES.

The PIX Firewall is configured using a command-line interface (CLI). The commands are similar to those used in the standard Cisco IOS, but they vary with regard to permitting inbound and outbound traffic.

Further information on the Cisco Secure PIX Firewall can be found at www.cisco.com/go/pix.

VPN Capabilities of Cisco Secure PIX Firewalls

The PIX Firewall uses the industry-standard IPSec protocol suite to enable advanced VPN features. The PIX Firewall IPSec implementation is based on Cisco IOS IPSec that runs in Cisco routers at performance of up to 20 Mbps with 3DES encryption. The configuration of IPSec on the PIX is very similar, but not identical to the configuration of IPSec for Cisco IOS. Later chapters will cover these differences.

This makes the Cisco Secure PIX Firewall an excellent and logical choice to terminate IPSec VPN traffic from other IPSec-compliant network equipment or from Windows clients running a VPN Client.

IPSec within the Cisco Secure PIX Firewall has been available since release 5.0 of the PIX operating system that is called Finesse. Both DES and 3DES encryption standards are supported. DES is included as a no-cost option with the unrestricted versions of the firewalls, although it is not enabled by default: a simple Web-based form has to be filled in with the PIX Serial Number, then somebody from Cisco will e-mail you with the activation key for the DES encryption feature. This can only be performed after an OS upgrade. The configuration is preserved during and after such an upgrade. The process of enabling 3DES encryption is very similar, except you have to purchase a specific license in addition to the PIX Firewall from Cisco.

Cisco Secure PIX Firewalls support both site-to-site VPNs between IPSec-compliant devices and client-to-site VPNs that terminate VPN sessions from various IPSec operating system-based clients, such as the Cisco VPN Client.

PIX OS 5.2 and later also support the Microsoft native Point-to-Point Tunneling Protocol (PPTP) for VPN termination.

A dedicated PIX Firewall VAC can be used in the PIX 515, 520, 525, and 535 units. This card performs hardware acceleration of VPN traffic encryption/decryption, providing 100 Mbps IPSec throughput using 168-bit 3DES.

The older Private Link (PL2) card can also be used for hardware-based VPN acceleration. However, the Private Link card supports only DES and not 3DES encryption. The inclusion of a Private Link card roughly doubles the performance of the DES VPN through the PIX Firewall.

Cisco VPN Concentrator

The Cisco VPN Concentrator series is a family of purpose-built, remote-access VPN platforms and client software that incorporates high availability, high performance, and scalability with the most advanced encryption and authentication techniques available today. With the Cisco VPN Concentrator series, customers can take advantage of the latest VPN technology to vastly reduce their communications expenditures. Unique to the industry, it is the only scalable platform to offer field-swappable and customer-upgradable components. These components, called Scalable Encryption Processing (SEP) modules, enable users to add capacity and throughput easily.

There are currently two main versions of the Cisco VPN Concentrator. These are the VPN 3000 Concentrator and the VPN 5000 Concentrator.

This section covers the VPN capabilities of the various Cisco VPN Concentrators.

VPN 3000 Series

The VPN 3000 Concentrator series includes models to support a range of enterprise customers, from small businesses with 100 or fewer remote access users to large organizations with up to 5000 simultaneous remote users. With all versions of the Cisco VPN 3000 Concentrator, the Cisco VPN 3000 Client is provided at no additional charge and includes unlimited distribution licensing. The Cisco VPN 3000 Concentrator series is available in both nonredundant and redundant configurations, allowing customers to build the most robust, reliable, and cost-effective networks possible. Figure 2-5 shows an example of the VPN 3000 series.

The VPN 3000 Concentrator series supports an easy-to-use management interface accessible with a Web browser.

The Cisco VPN 3000 Concentrator series consists of the following models:

- **VPN 3005**
    - Appropriate for a small branch office
    - Supports up to 100 simultaneous sessions
    - Supports software encryption—up to 100 sessions
    - Not upgradable

Figure 2-5 *Cisco VPN 3000 Series*

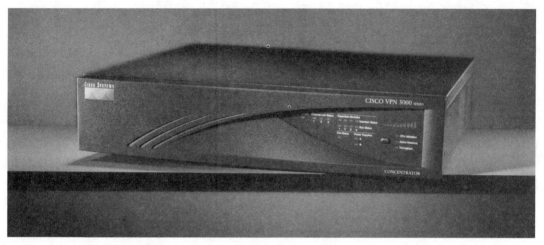

- **VPN 3015**
  - — Appropriate for a small branch office
  - — Supports up to 100 simultaneous sessions
  - — Supports software encryption—up to 100 sessions
  - — Upgradable
- **VPN 3030**
  - — Appropriate for a regional office
  - — Supports up to 1500 simultaneous sessions
  - — Supports one SEP2 hardware module—up to 1500 sessions
  - — Upgradable
- **VPN 3060**
  - — Appropriate for a large central site
  - — Supports up to 5000 simultaneous sessions
  - — Supports two SEP2 hardware modules—up to 5000 sessions
  - — Upgradable
- **VPN 3080**
  - — Appropriate for a large central site or ISP
  - — Supports up to 10,000 simultaneous sessions
  - — Supports four SEP2 hardware modules—up to 10,000 sessions
  - — Upgradable

VPN 3005 Concentrator

Figure 2-6 shows the front and rear panels of the VPN 3005 Concentrator.

Figure 2-6 *The Cisco VPN 3005 Concentrator*

The following hardware features are supported on the Cisco VPN 3005 Concentrator:

* **Height**—1U

* **Memory**—32 MB SRAM standard

* **Encryption**—Software based

* **Scalability**—Up to 100 sessions

* **Network interface**

  — Two autosensing full duplex 10/100BaseT Ethernet interfaces

  — Public to router, private to trusted segment

* **Power supply**—AC operation: 100 to 240V at 50/60 Hz with universal power factor correction

* **Hardware**—Not upgradable

* **Software**—Upgradable

VPN 3015 Concentrator

Figure 2-7 shows the front and rear panels of the VPN 3015 Concentrator.

The following hardware features are supported on the Cisco VPN 3015 Concentrator:

* **Height**—2U

* **Memory**

  — Dual flash image architecture

  — 64 MB SRAM standard

* **Encryption**—Software based

* **Scalability**—Up to 100 simultaneous remote connections

Figure 2-7   *The Cisco VPN 3015 Concentrator*

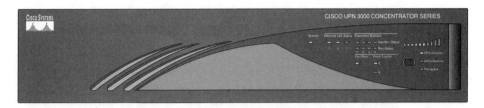

SEP modules
T1/E1 modules
10/100 Ethernet

100-240V power supplies   Private   Public   External
load sharing

- **Network interface**
  - Three autosensing full duplex 10/100BaseT Ethernet interfaces
  - Public to router, private to trusted segment, external to second trusted or DMZ
- **Power supply**
  - AC operation: 100 to 240V at 50/60 Hz with universal power factor correction
  - Replaceable power supply
- **Software**—Upgradable
- **Hardware**—Upgradable

VPN 3030 Concentrator

Figure 2-8 shows the front and rear panels of the VPN 3030 Concentrator.

The following hardware features are supported on the Cisco VPN 3030 Concentrator:

- **Height**—2U
- **Memory**
  - Dual flash image architecture
  - 128 MB SRAM standard

Figure 2-8 *The Cisco VPN 3030 Concentrator*

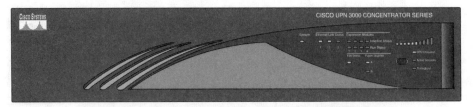

SEP modules
T1/E1 modules
10/100 Ethernet

100-240V power supplies
load sharing

Private   Public   External

- **Encryption**
  - Hardware-based SEP2
  - Programmable DSP-based security accelerator
- **Scalability**—Equipped with one SEP2 module and up to 1500 simultaneous remote connections
- **Network interface**
  - Three autosensing full duplex 10/100BaseT Ethernet interfaces
  - Public to router, private to trusted segment, external to second trusted or DMZ
  - Optional T1 WAN module
- **Power supply**
  - AC operation: 100 to 240V at 50/60 Hz with universal power factor correction
  - Replaceable power supply
  - Hot swappable with optional redundant power supply
- **Software**—Upgradable
- **Hardware**—Upgradable

VPN 3060 Concentrator

Figure 2-9 shows the front and rear panels of the VPN 3060 Concentrator.

Figure 2-9   *The Cisco VPN 3060 Concentrator*

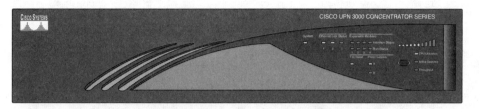

SEP modules
T1/E1 modules
10/100 Ethernet

100-240V power supplies
load sharing

Private   Public   External

The following hardware features are supported on the Cisco VPN 3060 Concentrator:

- **Height**—2U
- **Memory**
  - Dual flash image architecture
  - 256 MB SRAM standard
- **Encryption**
  - Hardware-based SEP2
  - Programmable DSP-based security accelerator
- **Scalability**
  - Equipped with a total of two SEP2 modules, and up to 5000 simultaneous remote connections
- **Network interface**
  - Three autosensing full duplex 10/100BaseT Ethernet interfaces
  - Public to router, private to trusted segment, external to second trusted or DMZ
  - Optional T1 WAN module
- **Power supply**
  - AC operation: 100 to 240V at 50/60 Hz with universal power factor correction
  - Standard hot-swappable redundant power supply
- **Software**—Upgradable
- **Hardware**—Upgradable

VPN 3080 Concentrator

Figure 2-10 shows the front and rear panels of the VPN 3080 Concentrator.

Figure 2-10 *The Cisco VPN 3080 Concentrator*

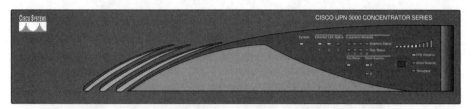

SEP modules
T1/E1 modules
10/100 Ethernet

100-240V power supplies
load sharing

Private   Public   External

The following hardware features are supported on the VPN 3080 Concentrator:

- **Height**—2U
- **Memory**
  - Dual flash image architecture
  - 256 MB SRAM standard
- **Encryption**
  - Hardware-based SEP2
  - Programmable DSP-based security accelerator
- **Scalability**
  - Equipped with four SEP2 modules (two active and two inactive)
  - Up to 10,000 simultaneous remote connections
- **Network interface**
  - Three autosensing full duplex 10/100BaseT Ethernet interfaces
  - Public to router, private to trusted segment, external to second trusted or DMZ
  - Optional T1 WAN module

- **Power supply**
  - AC operation: 100 to 240V at 50/60 Hz with universal power factor correction
  - Standard hot-swappable redundant power supply
- **Migration to 3080**—Factory upgrade

VPN 3000 Concentrator Series LED Indicators (VPN 3015 and Above)

Figure 2-11 shows the front panel from the 3015 to 3080 Concentrators.

Figure 2-11 *VPN 3000 Concentrator Series Front Panel LEDs (VPN 3015 and Above)*

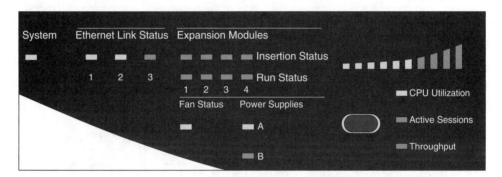

The front LEDs support the indicator lights in Table 2-1.

Table 2-1 *LED Indicator Lights (VPN 3015 and Above)*

LED Indicator	Green	Amber	Off
System	Power on; normal	System has crashed and halted	Power off; all LEDs off
Ethernet Link Status 1 2 3	Connected to network and enabled Blinking indicates connected and configured, but disabled	NA	Not connected to network or not enabled
Expansion Modules Insertion Status	SEP module installed	NA	SEP not installed in system
Expansion Modules Run Status	SEP module operational	NA	If installed, SEP failed diagnostics or encryption not running

continues

Table 2-1   *LED Indicator Lights (VPN 3015 and Above) (Continued)*

LED Indicator	Green	Amber	Off
Fan Status	Operating normally	Not running or below normal RPM	NA
Power Supplies A B	Installed and operating normally	Voltage outside of normal range	Not installed
CPU Utilization	Statistic selected for display	NA	Not selected
Active Sessions	Statistic selected for display	NA	Not selected
Throughput	Statistic selected	NA	Not selected

Figure 2-12 shows the rear panel indicators for the VPN 3015 and above. The model shown has only one SEP, so it is the 3015 that is shown.

Figure 2-12   *VPN 3000 Concentrator Series Rear Panel LEDs (VPN 3015 and Above)*

The rear LEDs support the indicator lights in Table 2-2 and Table 2-3.

Table 2-2   *Ethernet Interfaces Indicator Lights*

LED Indicator	Green	Amber	Off
Link	Carrier detected; normal	NA	No carrier detected; error
Tx	Transmitting data; normal	NA	Not transmitting data; idle
Coll	NA	Data collisions detected	No collisions; normal
100	Speed set to 100 Mbps	NA	Speed set to 10 Mbps

Table 2-3   *SEP Modules Indicator Lights*

LED Indicator	Green	Amber	Off
Power	Power on; normal	NA	Power off; error
Status	Encryption code running	NA	Module failed; diagnostics or encryption code not running

Product Comparison

Table 2-4 can be used to determine which model is best for your environment.

Table 2-4   *Cisco VPN Concentrator Product Comparison*

Feature	3005	3015	3030	3060	3080
Height	1U	2U	2U	2U	2U
Encryption Throughput	4 MBps	4 MBps	50 MBps	100 MBps	100 MBps
Users	100	100	1500	5000	10,000
Encryption	Software	Software	Hardware	Hardware	Hardware
Memory	32 MB	64 MB	128 MB	256 MB	256 MB
Power supplies	1	Up to 2	Up to 2	Up to 2	2
Scalable Encryption Processor Ports	0	0	1	2	4
Hardware Upgradable	No	Yes	Yes	Yes	No

VPN 5000 Series

The Cisco VPN 5000 Concentrator series is a feature-rich, carrier-class VPN product line with support for demanding multiplatform, multiprotocol environments. Utilizing the most advanced high-performance encryption and authentication techniques available, the Cisco VPN 5000 Concentrators include support for the industry's first Layer-3-to-Layer-2 tunnel mapping technology for the utmost flexibility in network design.

Figure 2-13 shows the VPN 5000 Concentrator series.

Figure 2-13 *VPN 5000 Concentrator series*

Deployed at the network edge, the Cisco VPN 5002 and VPN 5008 are designed for medium to large service providers and medium to large enterprise organizations; the Cisco VPN 5001 is designed for small service providers and small- to medium-sized enterprise organizations.

The VPN 5000 series is not covered in this book or the related CSVPN course.

Summary

This chapter provided details about the Cisco VPN family of products. It started by looking at all of the product offerings and then concentrated on the Cisco router, the Cisco Secure PIX Firewall, and the Cisco VPN Concentrator. Most readers of this book will be familiar with Cisco routers and also the Cisco Secure PIX Firewall, but maybe not with the VPN Concentrator. Therefore, this chapter focused on explaining the various models in the VPN 3000 series and the differences among the capabilities of the differing models.

Now that you have learned about IPSec and have looked at the delivery platforms available from Cisco for VPN technologies, the next chapter starts looking at device-specific VPN configuration.

Review Questions

1 VPN Accelerator Cards (VACs) are available for which models of the Cisco Secure PIX Firewall?

2 Which PIX model is predominantly designed for the SOHO or ROBO user?

3 What is the clear text throughput of a Cisco Secure PIX 525 Firewall?

4 What is the lowest specification model in the VPN 3000 Concentrator series?

5 If you had a small branch office that wanted an upgradable VPN solution for up to 100 users at any one time, which model of the VPN Concentrator 3000 series would you choose?

6 Which is the lowest specification router that can perform IPSec VPN termination?

7 If you required a VPN concentrator that could terminate 7500 IPSec tunnels, which model or models could you use?

8 How many IPSec tunnels can the PIX 535 terminate?

9 What is the highest specification model in the VPN 3000 Concentrator Series?

10 Which PIX Firewall boasts 1 Gbps clear text throughput?

PART III

Cisco IOS VPNs

CHAPTER 3

Configuring Cisco IOS Routers for Preshared Keys Site-to-Site

This chapter teaches you how to configure Cisco IOS Internet Protocol Security (IPSec) using preshared keys for authentication. After presenting an overview of the process, the chapter shows you each major step of the configuration.

This chapter covers the following topics:

- Configure IPSec encryption tasks
- Task 1: Prepare for IKE and IPSec
- Task 2: Configure IKE
- Task 3: Configure IPSec
- Task 4: Test and verify IPSec
- Overview of configuring IPSec manually
- Overview of configuring IPSec for RSA encrypted nonces

Configure IPSec Encryption Tasks

The use of Internet Key Exchange (IKE) preshared keys for authentication of IPSec sessions is relatively easy to configure, but it does not scale well for a large number of IPSec clients.

The process for configuring IKE preshared keys in Cisco IOS software for Cisco routers consists of four major tasks. Subsequent sections of this chapter discuss each configuration task in more detail. The four major tasks are as follows:

- **Task 1**: Prepare for IPSec—This task involves determining the detailed encryption policy: identifying the hosts and networks you wish to protect, determining details about the IPSec peers, determining the IPSec features you need, and ensuring existing access control lists (ACLs) are compatible with IPSec.
- **Task 2**: Configure IKE—This task involves enabling IKE, creating the IKE policies, and validating the configuration.
- **Task 3**: Configure IPSec—This task includes defining the transform sets, creating crypto ACLs, creating crypto map entries, and applying crypto map sets to interfaces.

- **Task 4**: Test and verify IPSec—Use **show**, **debug**, and related commands to test and verify that IPSec encryption works and to troubleshoot problems.

Task 1: Prepare for IKE and IPSec

Successful implementation of an IPSec network requires advanced planning before beginning configuration of individual routers.

Configuring IPSec encryption can be complicated. You must plan in advance if you desire to configure IPSec encryption correctly the first time and minimize misconfiguration. You should begin this task by defining the IPSec security policy based on the overall company security policy. Some planning steps are as follows:

Step 1 **Determine IKE (IKE phase one) policy**—Determine the IKE policies between IPSec peers based on the number and location of the peers.

Step 2 **Determine IPSec (IKE phase two) policy**—Identify IPSec peer details such as IP addresses, IPSec transform sets, and IPSec modes. You then configure crypto maps to gather all IPSec policy details together.

Step 3 **Check the current configuration**—Use the **show running-configuration**, **show isakmp** [**policy**], and **show crypto map** commands, and the many other **show** commands to check the current configuration of the router. This is covered later in this chapter.

Step 4 **Ensure that the network operates without encryption**—Ensure that basic connectivity has been achieved between IPSec peers using the desired IP services before configuring IPSec. You can use the **ping** command to check basic connectivity.

Step 5 **Ensure that ACLs are compatible with IPSec**—Ensure that perimeter routers and the IPSec peer router interfaces permit IPSec traffic. In this step, you need to enter the **show access-lists** command.

Step 1: Determine IKE (IKE Phase One) Policy

Configuring IKE is complicated. You should determine the IKE policy details to enable the selected authentication method, then configure it. Having a detailed plan lessens the chances of improper configuration. Some planning steps include the following:

- **Determine the key distribution method**—Determine the key distribution method based on the numbers and locations of IPSec peers. For a small network, you might wish to distribute keys manually. For larger networks, you might wish to use a CA server to support scalability of IPSec peers. You must then configure the Internet Security Association Key Management Protocol (ISAKMP) to support the selected key distribution method.

- **Determine the authentication method**—Choose the authentication method based on the key distribution method. Cisco IOS software supports either preshared keys, Rivest, Shamir, and Adelman (RSA) encrypted nonces, or RSA signatures to authenticate IPSec peers. This chapter focuses on using preshared keys.

- **Identify IPSec peer's IP addresses and host names**—Determine the details of all the IPSec peers that will use ISAKMP and preshared keys for establishing security associations (SAs). You will use this information to configure IKE.

- **Determine ISAKMP policies for peers**—An ISAKMP policy defines a combination, or *suite*, of security parameters to be used during the ISAKMP negotiation. Each ISAKMP negotiation begins by each peer agreeing on a common (shared) ISAKMP policy. The ISAKMP policy suites must be determined in advance of configuration. You must then configure IKE to support the policy details you determined. Some ISAKMP policy details include the following:

  — Encryption algorithm

  — Hash algorithm

  — IKE SA lifetime

  The goal of this planning step is to gather the precise data you will need in later steps to minimize misconfiguration.

An IKE policy defines a combination of security parameters used during the IKE negotiation. A group of policies makes up a *protection suite* of multiple policies that enable IPSec peers to establish IKE sessions and SAs with a minimal configuration. Table 3-1 shows an example of possible combinations of IKE parameters into either a strong or a stronger policy suite.

Table 3-1   *IKE Phase One Policy Parameters*

Parameter	Strong	Stronger
Encryption algorithm	DES	3DES
Hash algorithm	MD5	SHA-1
Authentication method	Preshare	RSA Encryption RSA Signature
Key exchange	D-H Group 1	D-H Group 2
IKE SA lifetime	86,400 seconds	Less than 86,400 seconds

Create IKE Policies for a Purpose

IKE negotiations must be protected, so each IKE negotiation begins by each peer agreeing on a common (shared) IKE policy. This policy states which security parameters will be used to protect subsequent IKE negotiations.

After the two peers agree upon a policy, the security parameters of the policy are identified by an SA established at each peer. These SAs apply to all subsequent IKE traffic during the negotiation.

You can create multiple prioritized policies at each peer to ensure that at least one policy will match a remote peer's policy.

Define IKE Policy Parameters

You can select specific values for each IKE parameter per the IKE standard. You choose one value over another based on the security level you desire and the type of IPSec peer to which you will connect.

There are five parameters to define in each IKE policy, as outlined in Table 3-2. Table 3-1 showed the relative strength of each parameter, and Table 3-2 shows the default values.

Table 3-2 *IKE Policy Parameters*

Parameter	Accepted Values	Keyword	Default
Message encryption algorithm	DES	**des**	DES
	3DES	**3des**	
Message integrity (hash) algorithm	SHA-1 (HMAC variant)	**sha**	SHA-1
	MD5 (HMAC variant)	**md5**	
Peer authentication method	Preshared keys	**pre-share**	RSA signatures
	RSA encrypted nonces	**rsa-encr**	
	RSA signatures	**rsa-sig**	
Key exchange parameters (Diffie-Hellman group identifier)	768-bit Diffie-Hellman or	**1**	768-bit Diffie-Hellman
	1024-bit Diffie-Hellman	**2**	
ISAKMP-established SA's lifetime	Can specify any number of seconds	—	86,400 seconds (one day)

You should determine IKE policy details for each peer before configuring IKE. Figure 3-1 shows a summary of IKE policy details that will be configured in examples contained within this chapter. The authentication method of preshared keys is covered in this chapter.

Figure 3-1   *IKE Policy Example*

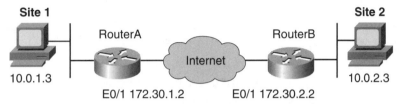

Parameter	Site 1	Site 2
Encryption algorithm	DES	DES
Hash algorithm	MD5	MD5
Authentication method	Preshared keys	Preshared keys
Key exchange	768-bit D-H	768-bit D-H
IKE SA lifetime	86,400 seconds	86,400 seconds
Peer IP address	172.30.2.2	172.30.1.2

Step 2: Determine IPSec (IKE Phase Two) Policy

An IPSec policy defines a combination of IPSec parameters used during the IPSec negotiation. Planning for IPSec (IKE phase two) is another important step you should complete before actually configuring IPSec on a Cisco router. Policy details to determine at this stage include the following:

- **Select IPSec algorithms and parameters for optimal security and performance**— Determine what type of IPSec security to use when securing interesting traffic. Some IPSec algorithms require you to make trade-offs between high performance and stronger security. Some algorithms have import and export restrictions that might delay or prevent implementation of your network.

- **Select transforms and, if necessary, transform sets**—Use the IPSec algorithms and parameters previously decided upon to help select IPSec transforms, transform sets, and modes of operation.

- **Identify IPSec peer details**—Identify the IP addresses and host names of all IPSec peers to which you will connect.

- **Determine IP address and applications of hosts to be protected**—Decide which host IP addresses and applications should be protected at the local and remote peer.

- **Select manual or IKE-initiated SAs**—Choose whether SAs are manually established or are established by IKE.

The goal of this planning step is to gather the precise data you will need in later steps to minimize misconfiguration.

Cisco IOS software supports the following IPSec transforms, shown in Table 3-3 and Table 3-4.

Table 3-3 *Authentication Header*

ah-md5-hmac	AH-HMAC-MD5 transform
ah-sha-hmac	AH-HMAC-SHA transform
ah-rfc1828	AH-MD5 transform (RFC1828) used with older IPSec implementations

NOTE Authentication Header (AH) is rarely used because authentication is now available with the esp-sha-hmac and esp-md5-hmac transforms. AH is also not compatible with Network Address Translation (NAT) or Port Address Translation (PAT).

Table 3-4 *Encapsulating Security Payload (ESP)*

esp-des	ESP transform using DES cipher (56 bits)
esp-3des	ESP transform using 3DES(EDE) cipher (168 bits)
esp-md5-hmac	ESP transform with HMAC-MD5 authentication used with an esp-des or esp-3des transform to provide additional integrity of ESP packet
esp-sha-hmac	ESP transform with HMAC-SHA authentication used with an esp-des or esp-3des transform to provide additional integrity of ESP packet
esp-null	ESP transform without a cipher; can be used in combination with esp-md5-hmac or esp-sha-hmac if one wants ESP authentication with no encryption
esp-rfc1829	ESP-DES-CBC transform (RFC1829) used with older IPSec implementations

NOTE Never use esp-null in a production environment because it does not protect data flows.

Examples of acceptable transforms that can be combined into sets are as follows:

- ah-md5-hmac
- esp-des
- esp-3des and esp-sha-hmac

- ah-sha-hmac and esp-des and esp-sha-hmac
- ah-rfc1828 and esp-rfc1829

The Cisco IOS command parser prevents you from entering invalid combinations; for example, after you specify an AH transform, it does not allow you to specify another AH transform for the current transform set.

Determining network design details includes defining a more detailed IPSec policy for protecting traffic. You can then use the detailed policy to help select IPSec transform sets and modes of operation. Your IPSec policy should answer the following questions:

- What protections are required or are acceptable for the protected traffic?
- Which IPSec transforms or transform sets should be used?
- What are the peer IPSec endpoints for the traffic?
- What traffic should or should not be protected?
- Which router interfaces are involved in protecting internal networks and external networks?
- How are SAs set up (manual or IKE negotiated), and how often should the SAs be renegotiated?

Figure 3-2 shows a summary of IPSec encryption policy details that will be configured in examples in this chapter. Details about IPSec transforms are covered in the next section. The example policy specifies that TCP traffic between the hosts should be encrypted by IPSec using DES.

Figure 3-2   *IPSec Policy Example*

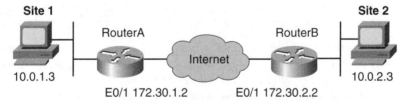

Policy	Site 1	Site 2
Transform set	ESP-DES, tunnel	ESP-DES, tunnel
Peer host name	RouterB	RouterA
Peer IP address	172.30.2.2	172.30.1.2
Hosts to be encrypted	10.0.1.3	10.0.2.3
Traffic (packed) type to be encrypted	TCP	TCP
SA establishment	ipsec-isakmp	ipsec-isakmp

An important part of determining the IPSec policy is to identify the IPSec peer with which the Cisco router will communicate. The peer must support IPSec as specified in the RFCs as supported by Cisco IOS. Many different types of peers are possible. Before configuration, identify all the potential peers and their VPN capabilities. Possible peers include, but are not limited to, the following:

- Other Cisco routers
- The Cisco Secure PIX Firewall
- The Cisco Secure VPN Client
- CA servers, if they are used
- Other vendors' IPSec products that conform to IPSec RFCs

Step 3: Check the Current Configuration

The current Cisco router configuration should be checked to see whether there are any IPSec policies already configured that are useful for, or might interfere with, the IPSec policies you plan to configure. Previously configured IKE and IPSec policies and details can and should be used, if possible, to save configuration time. However, previously configured IKE and IPSec policies and details can make troubleshooting more difficult if problems arise.

You can see whether any IKE policies have been previously configured starting with the **show running-config** command. You can also use the variety of **show** commands specific to IPSec. For example, you can use the **show crypto isakmp policy** command, as shown in Example 3-1, to examine IKE policies. The default protection suite seen here is available for use without modification. You can also use the other available **show** commands covered in other sections of this chapter to view IKE and IPSec configuration.

The **show crypto map** command shown in Example 3-1 is useful for viewing any previously configured crypto maps (crypto maps are covered in detail later in this chapter). Previously configured crypto maps can and should be used to save configuration time. However, previously configured crypto maps can interfere with the IPSec policy you are trying to configure.

You can also use the **show crypto ipsec transform-set** command to view previously configured transform sets. Previously configured transform sets can, and should, be used to save configuration time.

Example 3-1 *Checking the Current Configuration*

```
router# show crypto isakmp policy
Default protection suite
    encryption algorithm:   DES - Data Encryption Standard (56 bit keys)
    hash algorithm:         Secure Hash Standard
    authentication method:  Rivest-Shamir-Adleman Signature
```

Example 3-1 *Checking the Current Configuration (Continued)*

```
      Diffie-Hellman Group:    #1 (768 bit)
      lifetime:                86400 seconds, no volume limit
router# show crypto map
Crypto Map "mymap" 10 ipsec-isakmp
      Peer = 172.30.2.2
      Extended IP access list 102
          access-list 102 permit ip host 172.30.1.2 host 172.30.2.2
      Current peer: 172.30.2.2
      Security association lifetime: 4608000 kilobytes/3600 seconds
      PFS (Y/N): N
    Transform sets={ mine, }
router# show crypto ipsec transform-set mine
Transform set mine: { esp-des }
    will negotiate = { Tunnel, },
```

Step 4: Ensure That the Network Works

Basic connectivity between peers must be checked before you begin configuring IPSec.

The router **ping** command can be used to test basic connectivity between IPSec peers. Although a successful ICMP echo (ping) will verify basic connectivity between peers, you should ensure that the network operates with any other protocols or ports you want to encrypt, such as Telnet, FTP, or SQL*NET, before beginning IPSec configuration.

After IPSec is activated, basic connectivity troubleshooting can be difficult because the security configuration might mask a more fundamental networking problem. Previous security settings could result in no connectivity.

Step 5: Ensure That Access Lists Are Compatible with IPSec

You will need to ensure existing ACLs on perimeter routers, the PIX Firewall, or other routers do not block IPSec traffic. Perimeter routers typically implement a restrictive security policy with ACLs, where only specific traffic is permitted and all other traffic is denied. Such a restrictive policy blocks IPSec traffic, so you need to add specific **permit** statements to the ACL to allow IPSec traffic.

Ensure that your ACLs are configured so that ISAKMP, Encapsulating Security Payload (ESP), and Authentication Header (AH) traffic is not blocked at interfaces used by IPSec. ISAKMP uses UDP port 500. ESP is assigned IP protocol number 50, and AH is assigned IP protocol number 51. In some cases, you might need to add a statement to router ACLs to explicitly permit this traffic. You may need to add the ACL statements to the perimeter router by performing the following steps:

Step 1   Examine the current ACL configuration at the perimeter router and determine whether it will block IPSec traffic:

```
routerA# show access-lists
```

Step 2   Add ACL entries to permit IPSec traffic as follows:

— Copy the existing ACL configuration and paste it into a text editor.

— Add the ACL entries to the top of the list in the text editor.

— Delete the existing ACL with the **no access-list** *access-list number* command.

— Enter configuration mode and copy and paste the new ACL into the router.

— Verify that the ACL is correct with the **show access-list** command.

A concatenated sample showing ACL entries permitting IPSec traffic for RouterA is shown in Example 3-2.

Example 3-2   *ACL Entries Permitting IPSec Traffic for RouterA*

```
RouterA# show running-config
!
interface Ethernet0/1
 ip address 172.30.1.2 255.255.255.0
 ip access-group 102 in
!
access-list 102 permit ahp host 172.30.2.2 host 172.30.1.2
access-list 102 permit esp host 172.30.2.2 host 172.30.1.2
access-list 102 permit udp host 172.30.2.2 host 172.30.1.2 eq isakmp
```

Note that the protocol keyword of **esp** equals the ESP protocol (number 50), the keyword of **ahp** equals the AH protocol (number 51), and the **isakmp** keyword equals UDP port 500. This can be seen in Figure 3-3.

Figure 3-3 *Ensure Access Lists Are Compatible with IPSec*

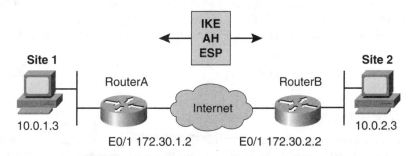

Ensure protocols 50 and 51 and UDP port 500 traffic are
not blocked at interfaces used by IPSec.

Task 2: Configure IKE

The next major task in configuring Cisco IOS IPSec is to configure the IKE parameters
gathered earlier. This section presents the steps used to configure IKE policies.

Configuring IKE consists of the following essential steps and commands:

Step 1   Enable or disable IKE with the **crypto isakmp enable** command.

Step 2   Create IKE policies with the **crypto isakmp policy** commands.

Step 3   Configure preshared keys with the **crypto isakmp key** and associated
commands.

Step 4   Verify the IKE configuration with the **show crypto isakmp policy**
command.

Step 1: Enable or Disable IKE

The first step in configuring IKE is to enable or disable ISAKMP. ISAKMP is globally
enabled and disabled with the **crypto isakmp enable** command. ISAKMP is enabled by
default. Use the **no** form of the command to disable ISAKMP.

ISAKMP does not have to be enabled for individual interfaces, but it is enabled globally for all interfaces at the router. You might choose to block ISAKMP access on interfaces not used for IPSec to prevent possible denial of service attacks by using an ACL statement that blocks UDP port 500 on the interfaces. For example, to enable IKE on your router, you would type

```
Router(config)#crypto isakmp enable
```

Step 2: Create IKE Policies

The next major step in configuring Cisco IOS ISAKMP support is to define a suite of ISAKMP policies. The goal of defining a suite of IKE policies is to establish ISAKMP peering between two IPSec endpoints. Use the IKE policy details gathered during the planning task.

Use the **crypto isakmp policy** command to define an IKE policy. IKE policies define a set of parameters used during the IKE negotiation. Use the **no** form of this command to delete an IKE policy. The command syntax is as follows:

```
crypto isakmp policy priority
```

priority	Uniquely identifies the IKE policy and assigns a priority to the policy. Use an integer from 1 to 10,000, with 1 being the highest priority and 10,000 the lowest.

This command invokes the ISAKMP policy configuration (config-isakmp) command mode.

NOTE   Assign the most secure policy the lowest priority number so that the most secure policy will find a match before any less secure policies are configured. Lower-priority policies are attempted first.

The **crypto isakmp policy** command invokes the ISAKMP policy configuration command mode (config-isakmp) where you can set ISAKMP parameters. If you do not specify one of these commands for a policy, the default value will be used for that parameter.

The following are the options that are available in config-isakmp mode:

```
router (config-isakmp)# ?
ISAKMP commands:
  authentication {rsa-sig | rsa-encr | pre-share}
  default
  encryption {des | 3des}
  exit
```

```
group
hash {md5 | sha}
lifetime seconds
no
```

While in the config-isakmp command mode, the keywords in Table 3-5 are available to specify the parameters in the policy.

Table 3-5   *config-isakmp Command Mode Keywords*

Keyword	Accepted Values	Default Value	Description
des	56-bit DES-CBC	des	Message encryption algorithm.
sha	SHA-1 (HMAC variant)	sha	Message integrity (Hash) algorithm.
md5	MD5 (HMAC variant)		
rsa-sig	RSA signatures	rsa-sig	Peer authentication method.
rsa-encr	RSA encrypted nonces		
pre-share	preshared keys		
1	768-bit Diffie-Hellman or	1	Key exchange parameters (Diffie-Hellman group identifier).
2	1024-bit Diffie-Hellman		
-	Can specify any number of seconds	86,400 seconds (one day)	ISAKMP-established SA's lifetime. You can usually leave this value at the default.
exit			Exits the config-isakmp mode.

You can configure multiple ISAKMP policies on each peer participating in IPSec. ISAKMP peers negotiate acceptable ISAKMP policies before agreeing upon the SA to be used for IPSec.

When the ISAKMP negotiation begins in IKE phase one main mode, ISAKMP looks for an ISAKMP policy that is the same on both peers. The peer that initiates the negotiation sends all its policies to the remote peer, and the remote peer tries to find a match with its policies. The remote peer looks for a match by comparing its own highest priority policy against the other peer's received policies in its ISAKMP policy suite. The remote peer checks each of its policies in order of its priority (highest priority first) until a match is found.

A match is made when both policies from the two peers contain the same encryption, hash, authentication, and Diffie-Hellman parameter values, and when the remote peer's policy specifies a lifetime less than or equal to the lifetime in the policy being compared. (If the lifetimes are not identical, the shorter lifetime from the remote peer's policy is used.) Assign the most secure policy the lowest priority number so that the most secure policy will find a match before any less secure policies are configured.

If no acceptable match is found, ISAKMP refuses negotiation and IPSec is not established. If a match is found, ISAKMP completes the main mode negotiation, and IPSec SAs are created during IKE phase two quick mode.

Consider the sample ISAKMP policies for RouterA and RouterB in Example 3-3. Note that only the first policies match between peers for preshared keys.

Example 3-3 *IKE Policy Configuration Example*

```
routerA(config)#
crypto isakmp policy 100
  hash md5
  authentication pre-share
crypto isakmp policy 200
  authentication rsa-sig
  group 2
  lifetime 5000
crypto isakmp policy 300
  authentication rsa-encr
  lifetime 10000

routerB(config)#
crypto isakmp policy 100
  hash md5
  authentication pre-share
crypto isakmp policy 200
  authentication rsa-sig
  group 2
  lifetime 5000
crypto isakmp policy 300
  authentication rsa-sig
  lifetime 10000
```

Step 3: Configure Preshared Keys

IPSec peers authenticate each other during ISAKMP negotiations using the preshared key and the ISAKMP identity. The identity can be either the router's IP address or its host name. Cisco IOS software uses the IP address identity method by default, therefore, a command indicating the address mode does not appear in the router configuration.

If you choose to use the host name identity method, you must specify the method with the **crypto isakmp identity** global configuration command. Use the **no** form of this command to reset the ISAKMP identity to the default value (address). The command syntax is as follows:

```
crypto isakmp identity {address | hostname}
```

address	Sets the ISAKMP identity to the IP address of the interface that is used to communicate to the remote peer during ISAKMP negotiations.
	The keyword is typically used when there is only one interface that will be used by the peer for ISAKMP negotiations, and the IP address is known.
hostname	Sets the ISAKMP identity to the host name concatenated with the domain name (for example, myhost.domain.com).
	The keyword should be used if there is more than one interface on the peer that might be used for ISAKMP negotiations, or if the interface's IP address is unknown (such as with dynamically assigned IP addresses).

If you use the host name identity method, you may need to specify the host name for the remote peer if a DNS server is not available for name resolution. An example of this follows:

```
RouterA(config)# ip host RouterB.domain.com 172.30.2.1
```

Configure a preshared authentication key with the **crypto isakmp key** global configuration command. You must configure this key whenever you specify preshared keys in an ISAKMP policy. Use the **no** form of this command to delete a preshared authentication key. The command syntax is as follows:

```
crypto isakmp key keystring address peer-address
crypto isakmp key keystring hostname peer-hostname
```

keystring	Specify the preshared key. Use any combination of alphanumeric characters up to 128 bytes. This preshared key must be identical at both peers.
peer-address	Specify the IP address of the remote peer.
hostname	Specify the host name of the remote peer. This is the peer's host name concatenated with its domain name (for example, myhost.domain.com).

NOTE   A given preshared key is shared between two peers. At a given peer, you could specify the same key to share with multiple remote peers; however, a more secure approach is to specify different keys to share between different pairs of peers.

The configuration in Example 3-4 shows ISAKMP and preshared keys for RouterA and RouterB. Note that the keystring of cisco1234 matches. The address identity method is specified. The ISAKMP policies are compatible. Default values do not have to be configured.

Example 3-4   *ISAKMP and Preshared Keys for RouterA and RouterB*

```
RouterA(config)# crypto isakmp key cisco1234 address 172.30.2.1
RouterA(config)# crypto isakmp policy 110
RouterA(config-isakmp)# hash md5
RouterA(config-isakmp)# authentication pre-share
RouterA(config-isakmp)# exit

RouterB(config)# crypto isakmp key cisco1234 address 172.30.1.1
RouterB(config)# crypto isakmp policy 110
RouterB(config-isakmp)# hash md5
RouterB(config-isakmp)# authentication pre-share
RouterB(config-isakmp)# exit
```

Step 4: Verify the IKE Configuration

You can use the **show crypto isakmp policy** command to display configured and default policies. The resultant ISAKMP policy for RouterA is shown in Example 3-5. RouterB's configuration is identical.

Example 3-5   *ISAKMP Policy for RouterA*

```
RouterA# show crypto isakmp policy
Protection suite of priority 110
        encryption algorithm:    DES - Data Encryption Standard (56 bit keys)
        hash algorithm:          Message Digest 5
        authentication method:   Pre-Shared Key
        Diffie-Hellman group:    #1 (768 bit)
        lifetime:                86400 seconds, no volume limit
Default protection suite
        encryption algorithm:    DES - Data Encryption Standard (56 bit keys)
        hash algorithm:          Secure Hash Standard
        authentication method:   Rivest-Shamir-Adelman Signature
        Diffie-Hellman group:    #1 (768 bit)
        lifetime:                86400 seconds, no volume limit
```

Task 3: Configure IPSec

The next major task in configuring Cisco IOS IPSec is to configure the IPSec parameters previously gathered. This section presents the steps used to configure IPSec.

The general tasks and commands used to configure IPSec encryption on Cisco routers are summarized as follows. Subsequent sections of this chapter discuss each configuration step in detail.

Step 1   Configure transform set suites with the **crypto ipsec transform-set** command.

Step 2   Configure global IPSec SA lifetimes with the **crypto ipsec security-association lifetime** command.

Step 3   Configure crypto ACLs with the **access-list** command.

Step 4   Configure crypto maps with the **crypto map** command.

Step 5   Apply the crypto maps to the terminating/originating interface with the **interface** and **crypto map** commands.

Step 1: Configure Transform Set Suites

The first major step in configuring Cisco IOS IPSec is to use the IPSec security policy to define a transform set.

A transform set is a combination of individual IPSec transforms designed to enact a specific security policy for traffic. During the ISAKMP IPSec SA negotiation that occurs in IKE phase two quick mode, the peers agree to use a particular transform set for protecting a particular data flow. Transform sets combine the following IPSec factors:

- Mechanism for payload authentication: AH transform
- Mechanism for payload encryption: ESP transform
- IPSec mode (transport versus tunnel)

Transform sets equal a combination of an AH transform, an ESP transform, and the IPSec mode (either tunnel or transport mode).

Define a transform set with the **crypto ipsec transform-set** global configuration command. To delete a transform set, use the **no** form of the command. The command syntax is as follows:

```
crypto ipsec transform-set transform-set-name transform1
    [transform2 [transform3]]
```

transform-set-name	Specify the name of the transform set to create (or modify).
transform1	Specify up to three transforms. These transforms define the IPSec security protocols and algorithms.
transform2	
transform3	

The command invokes the crypto-transform configuration mode.

You can configure multiple transform sets and then specify one or more of the transform sets in a crypto map entry. The transform set defined in the crypto map entry is used in the IPSec SA negotiation to protect the data flows specified by that crypto map entry's ACL. During the negotiation, the peers search for a transform set that is the same at both peers. When such a transform set is found, it is selected and applied to the protected traffic as part of both peers' IPSec SAs.

When ISAKMP is not used to establish SAs, a single transform set must be used. The transform set is not negotiated.

Transform sets are limited to one AH transform and one or two ESP transforms. Some example combinations follow.

The following example uses ESP encryption with 56-bit DES and tunnel mode (default):

```
crypto ipsec transform-set MINIMAL esp-des
```

The following example uses ESP authentication with MD5, ESP encryption with 56-bit DES, and tunnel mode (default):

```
crypto ipsec transform-set noAH esp-md5-hmac esp-des
```

The following example uses AH authentication with MD5, ESP authentication with MD5, ESP encryption with 56-bit DES, and tunnel mode (default):

```
crypto ipsec transform-set CPUeater ah-md5-hmac esp-md5-hmac esp-des
```

The following example uses AH authentication with SHA and transport mode:

```
crypto ipsec transform-set AUTH  ah-sha-hmac
```

Edit Transform Sets

Use the following steps if you need to change a transform set:

Step 1   Delete the transform set from the crypto map.

Step 2   Delete the transform set from global configuration.

Step 3   Reenter the transform set with corrections.

Step 4   Assign the transform set to a crypto map.

Step 5   Clear the SA database.

Step 6   Observe the SA negotiation and ensure that it works properly.

An alternative method is to reenter the transform set with the new transforms as follows.

The command was the following:

```
crypto ipsec transform-set RouterA esp-MD5-hmac
```

Change it as follows:

```
RouterA(config)# crypto ipsec transform-set RouterA esp-des
RouterA(cfg-crypto-trans)# exit
RouterA(config)#
```

The command is now:

```
crypto ipsec transform-set RouterA esp-des
```

Transform sets are negotiated during quick mode in IKE phase two using the transform sets you previously configured. You can configure multiple transform sets, then specify one or more of the transform sets in a crypto map entry. Configure the transforms from most to least secure as per your policy. The transform set defined in the crypto map entry is used in the IPSec SA negotiation to protect the data flows specified by that crypto map entry's ACL.

During the negotiation, the peers search for a transform set that is the same at both peers. When such a transform set is found, it is selected and applied to the protected traffic as part of both peers' IPSec SAs. IPSec peers agree on one transform proposal per SA (unidirectional).

Figure 3-4 demonstrates transform set negotiation.

Figure 3-4   *Transform Set Negotiation*

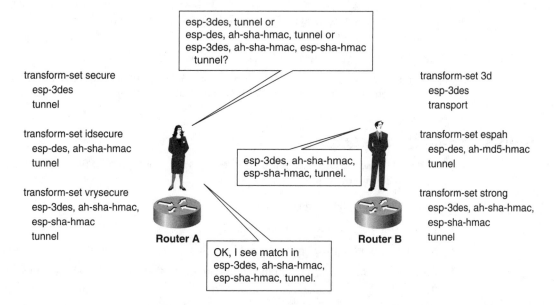

Transform sets are negotiated during IKE phase two.

Step 2: Configure Global IPSec SA Lifetimes

Both global and interface-specific SA lifetimes can be created. This section covers how to configure global SAs.

The IPSec SA lifetime determines how long IPSec SAs remain valid before they are renegotiated. Cisco IOS software supports a global lifetime value that applies to all crypto maps. The global lifetime value can be overridden within a crypto map entry. You can change global IPSec SA lifetime values using the **crypto ipsec security-association lifetime** global configuration command. To reset a lifetime to the default value, use the **no** form of the command. The command syntax is as follows:

```
crypto ipsec security-association lifetime
    {seconds seconds | kilobytes kilobytes}
```

seconds *seconds*	Specifies the number of seconds a SA will live before expiring. The default is 3600 seconds (1 hour).
kilobytes *kilobytes*	Specifies the volume of traffic (in kilobytes) that can pass between IPSec peers using a given SA before that SA expires. The default is 4,608,000 kilobytes.

The following is an example global SA lifetime. In the example, a new SA is renegotiated after 2700 seconds, or 45 minutes. When an SA expires, a new one is negotiated automatically without interrupting the data flow.

```
crypto ipsec security-association lifetime seconds 2700
```

Cisco recommends that you use the default lifetime values. Individual IPSec SA lifetimes can be configured using crypto maps, which are covered in a later section in this chapter.

Step 3: Create Crypto ACLs

Crypto ACLs are used to define which IP traffic is or is not protected by IPSec. This section covers how to configure crypto ACLs.

Crypto ACLs perform the following functions:

- Indicate the data flow to be protected by IPSec
- Select outbound traffic to be protected by IPSec
- Process inbound traffic to filter out and discard traffic that should have been protected by IPSec
- Determine whether or not to accept requests for IPSec SAs for the requested data flows when processing IKE negotiations

You must use extended IP ACLs to create crypto ACLs. The crypto ACLs identify the traffic flows to be protected. Extended IP ACLs select IP traffic to encrypt by protocol, IP address, network, subnet, and port. Although the ACL syntax is unchanged from extended IP ACLs, the meanings are slightly different for crypto ACLs: **permit** specifies that matching packets must be encrypted; and **deny** specifies that matching packets need not be encrypted. Crypto ACLs behave in a way similar to an extended IP ACL applied to outbound traffic on an interface.

The command syntax for the basic form of extended IP access lists is as follows:

```
access-list access-list-number {permit | deny} protocol source source-wildcard
        destination destination-wildcard [precedence precedence] [tos tos] [log]
```

permit	Causes all IP traffic that matches the specified conditions to be protected by crypto, using the policy described by the corresponding crypto map entry.
deny	Instructs the router to route traffic in the clear.
source and d*estination*	These are networks, subnets, or hosts.
protocol	Indicates which IP packet types to encrypt.

NOTE Although the ACL syntax is unchanged, the meanings are slightly different for crypto ACLs: **permit** specifies that matching packets must be encrypted; **deny** specifies that matching packets need not be encrypted.

Any unprotected inbound traffic that matches a *permit* entry in the crypto ACL for a crypto map entry flagged as IPSec will be dropped, because this traffic was expected to be protected by IPSec.

If you want certain traffic to receive one combination of IPSec protection (authentication only) and other traffic to receive a different combination (both authentication and encryption), create two different crypto ACLs to define the two different types of traffic. These different ACLs are then used in different crypto map entries that specify different IPSec policies.

CAUTION Cisco recommends that you avoid using the **any** keyword to specify source or destination addresses. The **permit any any** statement is strongly discouraged, as this will cause all outbound traffic to be protected (and all protected traffic sent to the peer specified in the corresponding crypto map entry) and will require protection for all inbound traffic. Then, all inbound packets that lack IPSec protection will be silently dropped, including packets for routing protocols, NTP, echo, echo response, and so on.

Try to be as restrictive as possible when defining which packets to protect in a crypto ACL. If you must use the **any** keyword in a permit statement, you must preface that statement with a series of **deny** statements to filter out any traffic that would otherwise fall within the permit statement and that you do not want to be protected.

In a later step, you will associate a crypto ACL to a crypto map, which in turn is assigned to a specific interface.

Cisco recommends that you configure "mirror image" crypto ACLs for use by IPSec. Both inbound and outbound traffic is evaluated against the same "outbound" IPSec ACL. The ACL's criteria is applied in the forward direction to traffic exiting your router, and in the reverse direction to traffic entering your router. When a router receives encrypted packets back from an IPSec peer, it uses the same ACL to determine which inbound packets to decrypt by viewing the source and destination addresses in the ACL in reverse order.

The example shown in Figure 3-5 illustrates why symmetrical ACLs are recommended.

Figure 3-5 *Crypto Access Lists*

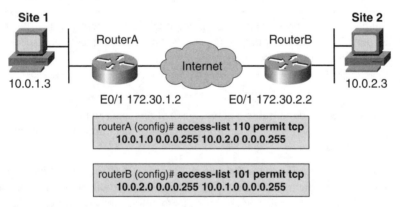

For site 1, IPSec protection is applied to traffic between hosts on the 10.0.1.0 network as the data exits RouterA's s0 interface enroute to site 2 hosts on the 10.0.2.0 network. For traffic from site 1 hosts on the 10.0.1.0 network to site 2 hosts on the 10.0.2.0 network, the ACL entry on RouterA is evaluated as follows:

- source = hosts on 10.0.1.0 network
- dest = hosts on 10.0.2.0 network

For incoming traffic from site 2 hosts on the 10.0.2.0 network to site 1 hosts on the 10.0.1.0 network, that same ACL entry on RouterA is evaluated as follows:

- source = hosts on 10.0.2.0 network
- permit = hosts on 10.0.1.0 network

Step 4: Create Crypto Maps

Crypto map entries must be created for IPSec to set up SAs for traffic flows that must be encrypted. This section looks at the purpose of crypto maps, examines the **crypto map** command, and considers example crypto maps.

Crypto map entries created for IPSec set up SA parameters, tying together the various parts configured for IPSec, including the following:

- Which traffic should be protected by IPSec (crypto ACL)
- The granularity of the traffic to be protected by a set of SAs
- Where IPSec-protected traffic should be sent (who the remote IPSec peer is)
- The local address to be used for the IPSec traffic
- What IPSec security type should be applied to this traffic (transform sets)
- Whether SAs are established manually or are established through IKE
- Other parameters that might be necessary to define an IPSec SA

You can apply only one crypto map set to a single interface. The crypto map set can include a combination of Cisco Encryption Technology (CET), IPSec using IKE, and IPSec with manually configured SA entries. Multiple interfaces can share the same crypto map set if you want to apply the same policy to multiple interfaces.

If you create more than one crypto map entry for a given interface, use the sequence number (*seq-num*) of each map entry to rank the map entries: the lower the *seq-num*, the higher the priority. At the interface that has the crypto map set, traffic is evaluated against higher-priority map entries first.

You must create multiple crypto map entries for a given interface if any of the following conditions exist:

- If different data flows are to be handled by separate IPSec peers.
- If you want to apply different IPSec security to different types of traffic (to the same or separate IPSec peers), for example, if you want traffic between one set of subnets to be authenticated and traffic between another set of subnets to be both authenticated and encrypted. In this case, the different types of traffic should have been defined in two separate ACLs, and you must create a separate crypto map entry for each crypto ACL.
- If you are not using IKE to establish a particular set of SAs, and want to specify multiple ACL entries, you must create separate ACLs (one per permit entry) and specify a separate crypto map entry for each ACL.

You must use the **crypto map** global configuration command to create or modify a crypto map entry and enter the crypto map configuration mode. Set the crypto map entries referencing dynamic maps to be the lowest priority entries in a crypto map set (that is, have the highest sequence numbers). Use the **no** form of this command to delete a crypto map entry or set. The command syntax is as follows:

```
crypto map map-name seq-num cisco
crypto map map-name seq-num ipsec-manual
crypto map map-name seq-num ipsec-isakmp [dynamic dynamic-map-name]
no crypto map map-name [seq-num]
```

cisco	(Default value) Indicates that CET will be used instead of IPSec for protecting the traffic specified by this newly specified crypto map entry.
map-name	The name you assign to the crypto map set.
seq-num	The number you assign to the crypto map entry.
ipsec-manual	Indicates that ISAKMP will not be used to establish the IPSec SAs for protecting the traffic specified by this crypto map entry.
ipsec-isakmp	Indicates that ISAKMP will be used to establish the IPSec SAs for protecting the traffic specified by this crypto map entry.
dynamic	(Optional) Specifies that this crypto map entry references a preexisting static crypto map. If you use this keyword, none of the crypto map configuration commands are available.
dynamic-map-name	(Optional) Specifies the name of the dynamic crypto map set that should be used as the policy template.

When you enter the **crypto map** command, you invoke the crypto map configuration mode with the following available commands:

```
router(config-crypto-map)# help
    match address [access-list-id | name]
    peer [hostname | ip-address]
    transform-set [set_name(s)]
    security-association [inbound|outbound]
    set
    no
    exit
```

The following shows two different crypto maps. One map is called mymap and uses ipsec-manual. The other map is called yourmap and uses ipsec-isakmp. The latter map (using preshared keys) is the correct choice in this chapter:

```
router(config)# crypto map mymap 110 ipsec-manual
router(config)# crypto map yourmap 111 ipsec-isakmp
```

The **crypto map** command has a crypto map configuration mode with the commands and syntax in Table 3-6.

Table 3-6   *Crypto Map Configuration Mode Commands and Syntax*

Syntax	Description
set	Used with the **peer**, **pfs**, **transform-set**, and **security-association** commands.
peer [**hostname**	**ip-address**]	Specifies the allowed IPSec peer by IP address or host name.
pfs [**group1**	**group2**]	Specifies Diffie-Hellman Group 1 or Group 2.
transform-set [*set_name(s)*]	Specify list of transform sets in priority order. For an **ipsec-manual** crypto map, you can specify only one transform set. For an **ipsec-isakmp** or **dynamic** crypto map entry, you can specify up to six transform sets.
security-association lifetime	Sets SA lifetime parameters in seconds or kilobytes.
match address [*access-list-id*	*name*]	Identifies the extended ACL by its name or number. The value should match the *access-list-number* or name argument of a previously defined IP-extended ACL being matched.
no	Used to delete commands entered with the **set** command.
exit	Exits crypto map configuration mode.

After you define crypto map entries, you can assign the crypto map set to interfaces using the **crypto map** (interface configuration) command.

NOTE   ACLs for crypto map entries tagged as *ipsec-manual* are restricted to a single permit entry, and subsequent entries are ignored. The SAs established by that particular crypto map entry are only for a single data flow. To be able to support multiple manually established SAs for different kinds of traffic, define multiple crypto ACLs and then apply each one to a separate ipsec-manual crypto map entry. Each ACL should include one permit statement defining what traffic to protect.

Example 3-6 illustrates a crypto map with two peers specified for redundancy. If the first peer cannot be contacted, the second peer is used. There is no limit to the number of redundant peers that can be configured. Example 3-6 also shows the configuration modes.

Example 3-6 *Crypto Map Example*

```
RouterA(config)# crypto map mymap 10 ipsec-isakmp
RouterA(config-crypto-map)# match address 101
routerA(config-crypto-map)# set peer 172.30.2.1
routerA(config-crypto-map)# set peer 172.30.3.1
routerA(config-crypto-map)# set pfs group1
routerA(config-crypto-map)# set transform-set mytransform
routerA(config-crypto-map)# set security-association lifetime 2700
routerA(config-crypto-map)# exit
```

Step 5: Apply Crypto Maps to Interfaces

The last step in configuring IPSec is to apply the crypto map set to an interface.

Apply the crypto map to the IPSec router's interface connected to the Internet with the **crypto map** command in interface configuration mode. Use the **no** form of the command to remove the crypto map set from the interface. The command syntax is as follows:

crypto map *map-name*

map-name	This is the name that identifies the crypto map set, and it is the name assigned when the crypto map is created.

As soon as you apply the crypto map, the SAs initialize. Only one crypto map set can be assigned to an interface. If multiple crypto map entries have the same *map-name* but a different *seq-num*, they are considered to be part of the same set and are all applied to the interface. The crypto map entry with the lowest *seq-num* is considered the highest priority and is evaluated first.

Example 3-7 illustrates applying a crypto map to the serial (dirty) interface. Be aware that applying the crypto map to the interface you are using terminates your session to the router if you do not have IPSec configured on your system. Because of this fact, Telnet sessions to configure IPSec should be used with caution, as it is possible to cut yourself off from Telnet access to the router if you apply the crypto map to the wrong interface.

Example 3-7 *Crypto Map Interface Examples*

```
RouterA(config)# interface serial 0
RouterA(config-if)# crypto map mymap
RouterA(config-if)# exit
RouterA(config)#
```

Consider the configuration examples shown in Figure 3-6 for RouterA and RouterB. The examples in Figure 3-6 are concatenated to show only commands related to what has been covered in this chapter to this point.

Figure 3-6   *IPSec Configuration Example*

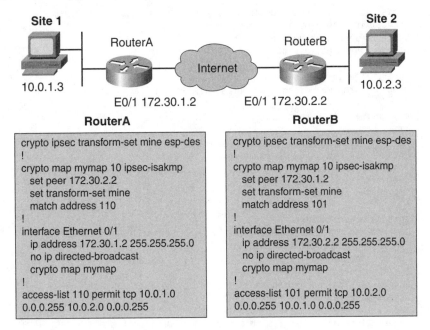

Example 3-8 has additional commands, such as a generic ACL on the serial interface.

Example 3-8   *IPSec Configuration*

```
RouterA# show running-config
crypto isakmp policy 100
 hash md5
 authentication pre-share
crypto isakmp key cisco1234 address 172.30.2.1
!
crypto ipsec transform-set mine esp-des
!
 !
 crypto map mymap 110 ipsec-isakmp
 set peer 172.30.2.1
 set transform-set mine
 match address 110
!
interface Ethernet0/1
 ip address 172.30.1.1 255.255.255.0
 ip access-group 101 in
 crypto map mymap
!
access-list 101 permit ahp host 172.30.2.1 host 172.30.1.1
access-list 101 permit esp host 172.30.2.1 host 172.30.1.1
access-list 101 permit udp host 172.30.2.1 host 172.30.1.1 eq isakmp
```

continues

Example 3-8 *IPSec Configuration (Continued)*

```
access-list 110 permit tcp 10.0.1.0 0.0.0.255 10.0.2.0 0.0.0.255
access-list 110 deny ip any any
RouterB# show running-config
crypto isakmp policy 100
 hash md5
 authentication pre-share
crypto isakmp key cisco1234 address 172.30.1.1
!
crypto ipsec transform-set mine esp-des
!
 !
 crypto map mymap 100 ipsec-isakmp
 set peer 172.30.1.1
 set transform-set mine
 match address 102
!
interface Ethernet0/1
 ip address 172.30.2.1 255.255.255.0
 ip access-group 101 in
 crypto map mymap
!
access-list 101 permit ahp host 172.30.1.1 host 172.30.2.1
access-list 101 permit esp host 172.30.1.1 host 172.30.2.1
access-list 101 permit udp host 172.30.1.1 host 172.30.2.1 eq isakmp
access-list 102 permit tcp 10.0.2.0 0.0.0.255 10.0.1.0 0.0.0.255
access-list 102 deny ip any any
```

Task 4: Test and Verify IPSec

Cisco IOS software contains a number of **show**, **clear**, and **debug** commands useful for testing and verifying IPSec and ISAKMP, which are considered in this section.

You can perform the following actions to test and verify that you have correctly configured the VPN using Cisco IOS:

- Display your configured IKE policies using the **show crypto isakmp policy** command.
- Display your configured transform sets using the **show crypto ipsec transform set** command.
- Display the current state of your IPSec SAs with the **show crypto ipsec sa** command.
- View your configured crypto maps with the **show crypto map** command.
- Debug IKE and IPSec traffic through the Cisco IOS with the **debug crypto ipsec** and **debug crypto isakmp** commands.

ISAKMP show Command

Use the **show crypto isakmp policy** EXEC command to view the parameters for each ISAKMP policy, as shown in Example 3-9 for RouterA.

Example 3-9 **show crypto isakmp policy** *Command*

```
RouterA# show crypto isakmp policy
Protection suite of priority 110
        encryption algorithm:   DES - Data Encryption Standard (56 bit keys)
        hash algorithm:         Message Digest 5
        authentication method:  Rivest-Shamir-Adelman Encryption
        Diffie-Hellman group:   #1 (768 bit)
        lifetime:               86400 seconds, no volume limit
Default protection suite
        encryption algorithm:   DES - Data Encryption Standard (56 bit keys)
        hash algorithm:         Secure Hash Standard
        authentication method:  Rivest-Shamir-Adelman Signature
        Diffie-Hellman group:   #1 (768 bit)
        lifetime:               86400 seconds, no volume limit
```

IPSec show Commands

Use the **show crypto ipsec transform-set** EXEC command to view the configured transform sets. The command has the following syntax:

```
show crypto ipsec transform-set [tag transform-set-name]
```

tag *transform-set-name*	(Optional) Shows only the transform sets with the specified transform-set-name

If no keyword is used, all transform sets configured at the router are displayed. Output from this command can be seen in Example 3-10.

Example 3-10 **show crypto ipsec transform-set** *Output*

```
router# show crypto ipsec transform-set
Transform set mine: { esp-des }
  will negotiate = { Tunnel, },
```

Use the **show crypto ipsec sa** EXEC command to view the settings used by current SAs. If no keyword is used, all SAs are displayed. The command syntax is as follows:

```
show crypto ipsec sa [map map-name | address | identity] [detail]
```

Output from this command can be seen in Example 3-11.

Example 3-11 show crypto ipsec sa *Output*

```
routerA# show crypto ipsec sa
interface: Ethernet0/1
        Crypto map tag: mymap, local addr. 172.30.1.2
        local ident (addr/mask/prot/port): (172.30.1.2/255.255.255.255/0/0)
       remote ident (addr/mask/prot/port): (172.30.2.2/255.255.255.255/0/0)
      current_peer: 172.30.2.2
        PERMIT, flags={origin_is_acl,}
       #pkts encaps: 21, #pkts encrypt: 21, #pkts digest 0
       #pkts decaps: 21, #pkts decrypt: 21, #pkts verify 0
       #send errors 0, #recv errors 0
        local crypto endpt.: 172.30.1.2, remote crypto endpt.: 172.30.2.2
        path mtu 1500, media mtu 1500
        current outbound spi: 8AE1C9C
```

Use the **show crypto map** EXEC command to view the crypto map configuration. If no
keywords are used, all crypto maps configured at the router will be displayed. The
command syntax is as follows:

```
show crypto map [interface interface | tag map-name]
```

interface *interface*	(Optional) Shows only the crypto map set applied to the specified interface
tag *map-name*	(Optional) Shows only the crypto map set with the specified map-name

Output from this command can be seen in Example 3-12.

Example 3-12 show crypto map *Output*

```
routerA# show crypto map
Crypto Map "mymap" 10 ipsec-isakmp
        Peer = 172.30.2.2
        Extended IP access list 102
            access-list 102 permit ip host 172.30.1.2 host
        172.30.2.2
        Current peer: 172.30.2.2
        Security association lifetime: 4608000 kilobytes/3600 seconds
        PFS (Y/N): N
        Transform sets={ mine, }
```

IPSec debug Commands

Use the **debug crypto ipsec** EXEC and the **debug crypto isakmp** commands to display
IPSec and ISAKMP events. The **no** form of these commands disables debugging output.

Because these commands generate a significant amount of output for every IP packet processed, use them only when traffic on the IP network is low, so other activity on the system is not adversely affected.

Example 3-13 of ISAKMP and IPSec debugging shows normal IPSec setup messages. Note the inline comments.

Example 3-13 *ISAKMP and IPSec Debugging*

```
RouterA# debug crypto ipsec
Crypto IPSEC debugging is on
RouterA# debug crypto isakmp
Crypto ISAKMP debugging is on
RouterA#
*Feb 29 08:08:06.556 PST: IPSEC(sa_request): ,
  (key eng. msg.) src= 172.30.1.2, dest= 172.30.2.2,
    src_proxy= 10.0.1.0/255.255.255.0/0/0 (type=4),
    dest_proxy= 10.0.2.0/255.255.255.0/0/0 (type=4),
    protocol= ESP, transform= esp-des esp-md5-hmac ,
    lifedur= 3600s and 4608000kb,
    spi= 0x0(0), conn_id= 0, keysize= 0, flags= 0x4004
! Interesting traffic from Site1 to Site2 triggers ISAKMP Main Mode.
*Feb 29 08:08:06.556 PST: ISAKMP (4): beginning Main Mode exchange
*Feb 29 08:08:06.828 PST: ISAKMP (4): processing SA payload. message ID = 0
*Feb 29 08:08:06.828 PST: ISAKMP (4): Checking ISAKMP transform 1
    against priority 100 policy
*Feb 29 08:08:06.828 PST: ISAKMP:       encryption DES-CBC
*Feb 29 08:08:06.828 PST: ISAKMP:       hash MD5
*Feb 29 08:08:06.828 PST: ISAKMP:       default group 1
*Feb 29 08:08:06.832 PST: ISAKMP:       auth pre-share
*Feb 29 08:08:06.832 PST: ISAKMP (4): atts are acceptable. Next payload is 0
! The IPSec peers have found a matching ISAKMP policy
*Feb 29 08:08:06.964 PST: ISAKMP (4): SA is doing pre-shared key authentication
! Pre-shared key authentication is identified
*Feb 29 08:08:07.368 PST: ISAKMP (4): processing KE payload. message ID = 0
*Feb 29 08:08:07.540 PST: ISAKMP (4): processing NONCE payload. message ID = 0
*Feb 29 08:08:07.540 PST: ISAKMP (4): SKEYID state generated
*Feb 29 08:08:07.540 PST: ISAKMP (4): processing vendor id payload
*Feb 29 08:08:07.544 PST: ISAKMP (4): speaking to another IOS box!
*Feb 29 08:08:07.676 PST: ISAKMP (4): processing ID payload. message ID = 0
*Feb 29 08:08:07.676 PST: ISAKMP (4): processing HASH payload. message ID = 0
*Feb 29 08:08:07.680 PST: ISAKMP (4): SA has been authenticated with
172.30.2.2
! Main mode is complete. The peers are authenticated, and secret
! keys are generated. On to Quick Mode!
*Feb 29 08:08:07.680 PST: ISAKMP (4): beginning Quick Mode exchange,
    M-ID of -1079597279
*Feb 29 08:08:07.680 PST: IPSEC(key_engine): got a queue event...
*Feb 29 08:08:07.680 PST: IPSEC(spi_response): getting spi 3658276911d for SA
        from 172.30.2.2      to 172.30.1.2      for prot 3
*Feb 29 08:08:08.424 PST: ISAKMP (4): processing SA payload.
    message ID = -1079597279
*Feb 29 08:08:08.424 PST: ISAKMP (4): Checking IPSec proposal 1
```

continues

Example 3-13 *ISAKMP and IPSec Debugging (Continued)*

```
*Feb 29 08:08:08.424 PST: ISAKMP: transform 1, ESP_DES
*Feb 29 08:08:08.424 PST: ISAKMP:    attributes in transform:
*Feb 29 08:08:08.424 PST: ISAKMP:       encaps is 1
*Feb 29 08:08:08.424 PST: ISAKMP:       SA life type in seconds
*Feb 29 08:08:08.424 PST: ISAKMP:       SA life duration (basic) of 3600
*Feb 29 08:08:08.428 PST: ISAKMP:       SA life type in kilobytes
*Feb 29 08:08:08.428 PST: ISAKMP:       SA life duration (VPI) of
    0x0 0x46 0x50 0x0
*Feb 29 08:08:08.428 PST: ISAKMP:       authenticator is HMAC-MD5
*Feb 29 08:08:08.428 PST: ISAKMP (4): atts are acceptable.
*Feb 29 08:08:08.428 PST: IPSEC(validate_proposal_request): proposal part #1,
  (key eng. msg.) dest= 172.30.2.2, src= 172.30.1.2,
    dest_proxy= 10.0.2.0/255.255.255.0/0/0 (type=4),
    src_proxy= 10.0.1.0/255.255.255.0/0/0 (type=4),
    protocol= ESP, transform= esp-des esp-md5-hmac ,
    lifedur= 0s and 0kb,
    spi= 0x0(0), conn_id= 0, keysize= 0, flags= 0x4
*Feb 29 08:08:08.432 PST: ISAKMP (4): processing NONCE payload. message ID = -10
79597279
*Feb 29 08:08:08.432 PST: ISAKMP (4): processing ID payload.
    message ID = -1079597279
*Feb 29 08:08:08.432 PST: ISAKMP (4): processing ID payload.
    message ID = -1079597279
! A matching IPSec policy has been negotiated and authenticated.
! Next the SAs are set up.
*Feb 29 08:08:08.436 PST: ISAKMP (4): Creating IPSec SAs
*Feb 29 08:08:08.436 PST:           inbound SA from 172.30.2.2      to 172.30.1.2
    (proxy 10.0.2.0     to 10.0.1.0   )
*Feb 29 08:08:08.436 PST:           has spi 365827691 and conn_id 5 and flags 4
*Feb 29 08:08:08.436 PST:           lifetime of 3600 seconds
*Feb 29 08:08:08.440 PST:           lifetime of 4608000 kilobytes
*Feb 29 08:08:08.440 PST:           outbound SA from 172.30.1.2      to 172.30.2.2
    (proxy 10.0.1.0     to 10.0.2.0   )
*Feb 29 08:08:08.440 PST:           has spi 470158437 and conn_id 6 and flags 4
*Feb 29 08:08:08.440 PST:           lifetime of 3600 seconds
*Feb 29 08:08:08.440 PST:           lifetime of 4608000 kilobytes
*Feb 29 08:08:08.440 PST: IPSEC(key_engine): got a queue event...
*Feb 29 08:08:08.440 PST: IPSEC(initialize_sas): ,
  (key eng. msg.) dest= 172.30.1.2, src= 172.30.2.2,
    dest_proxy= 10.0.1.0/255.255.255.0/0/0 (type=4),
    src_proxy= 10.0.2.0/255.255.255.0/0/0 (type=4),
    protocol= ESP, transform= esp-des esp-md5-hmac ,
    lifedur= 3600s and 4608000kb,
    spi= 0x15CE166B(365827691), conn_id= 5, keysize= 0, flags= 0x4
*Feb 29 08:08:08.444 PST: IPSEC(initialize_sas): ,
  (key eng. msg.) src= 172.30.1.2, dest= 172.30.2.2,
    src_proxy= 10.0.1.0/255.255.255.0/0/0 (type=4),
    dest_proxy= 10.0.2.0/255.255.255.0/0/0 (type=4),
```

Example 3-13 *ISAKMP and IPSec Debugging (Continued)*

```
        protocol= ESP, transform= esp-des esp-md5-hmac ,
        lifedur= 3600s and 4608000kb,
        spi= 0x1C060C65(470158437), conn_id= 6, keysize= 0, flags= 0x4
*Feb 29 08:08:08.444 PST: IPSEC(create_sa): sa created,
  (sa) sa_dest= 172.30.1.2, sa_prot= 50,
    sa_spi= 0x15CE166B(365827691),
    sa_trans= esp-des esp-md5-hmac , sa_conn_id= 5
*Feb 29 08:08:08.444 PST: IPSEC(create_sa): sa created,
  (sa) sa_dest= 172.30.2.2, sa_prot= 50,
    sa_spi= 0x1C060C65(470158437),
    sa_trans= esp-des esp-md5-hmac , sa_conn_id= 6
! IPSec SAs are set up and data can be securely exchanged.
RouterA#
```

Crypto System Error Messages for ISAKMP

Cisco IOS software can generate many useful system error messages for ISAKMP. Two of the error messages follow:

- **%CRYPTO-6-IKMP_SA_NOT_AUTH: Cannot accept Quick Mode exchange from %15i if SA is not authenticated!**—The ISAKMP SA with the remote peer was not authenticated, yet the peer attempted to begin a Quick Mode exchange. This exchange must be done only with an authenticated SA. The recommended action is to contact the remote peer's administrator to resolve the improper configuration.

- **%CRYPTO-6-IKMP_SA_NOT_OFFERED**: **Remote peer %15i responded with attribute [chars] not offered or changed**—ISAKMP peers negotiate policy by the initiator, offering a list of possible alternate protection suites. The responder responded with an ISAKMP policy that the initiator did not offer. The recommended action is to contact the remote peer's administrator to resolve the improper configuration.

Troubleshooting Cisco IOS IPSec VPNs are covered in more detail in Chapter 5, "Troubleshooting Cisco IOS VPNs."

Overview of Configuring IPSec Manually

You can configure your keys manually. This section provides a brief discussion of how this is done and also details why manual key use is not generally recommended.

Use the **security-association** command in crypto map configuration mode to manually specify the IPSec session keys within a crypto map entry. Use the **no** form of this command to remove IPSec session keys from a crypto map entry. This command is only available for **ipsec-manual** crypto map entries. The command has the following syntax:

```
set security-association {inbound | outbound} ah spi hex-key-string
set security-association {inbound | outbound} esp spi cipher hex-key-string
[authenticator hex-key-string]
```

inbound	Sets the inbound IPSec session key. (You must set both inbound and outbound keys.)
outbound	Sets the outbound IPSec session key.
ah	Sets the IPSec session key for the AH protocol. Use when the crypto map entry's transform set includes an AH transform.
esp	Sets the IPSec session key for the ESP protocol. Use when the crypto map entry's transform set includes an ESP transform.
spi	Specifies the security parameter index (SPI), a number that is used to identify uniquely an SA. The SPI is an arbitrary number you assign in the range of 256 to 4,294,967,295 (FFFF FFFF).
hex-key-string	Specifies the session key entered in hexadecimal format. It is an arbitrary string of 8, 16, or 20 bytes. The crypto map's transform set includes: • A DES algorithm, specify at least 8 bytes per key • An MD5 algorithm, specify at least 16 bytes per key • An SHA algorithm, specify 20 bytes per key Keys longer than the previous sizes ae simply truncated.
cipher	Indicates that the key string is to be used with the ESP encryption transform.
authentic ator	(Optional) Indicates that the key string is to be used with the ESP authentication transform. This argument is required only when the crypto map entry's transform set includes an ESP authentication transform.

If the crypto map's transform set includes an AH or ESP protocol, you must define IPSec AH or ESP keys for both inbound and outbound traffic. If your transform set includes an ESP authentication protocol, you must define IPSec keys for ESP authentication for inbound and outbound traffic.

When you define multiple IPSec session keys within a single crypto map, you can assign the same security parameter index (SPI) number to all the keys. The SPI is used to identify the SA used with the crypto map. However, not all peers have the same flexibility in SPI assignment. You should coordinate SPI assignment with your peer's operator, making certain that the same SPI is not used more than once for the same destination address and protocol combination.

SAs established with this command do not expire, unlike SAs established with ISAKMP.

Session keys at one peer must match the session keys at the remote peer. If you change a session key, the SA using the key is deleted and reinitialized.

Configuring IPSec Manually Is Not Recommended

You can configure IPSec SAs manually and not use ISAKMP to set up the SA. Cisco recommends that you use ISAKMP to set up the SAs because it is very difficult to ensure that the SA values match between peers, and D-H is a more secure method to generate secret keys between peers. Other reasons not to configure IPSec manually include the following:

- Manual keying does not scale well and is often insecure because of difficulty in manually creating secure keying material.
- Manually established SAs do not expire.
- ACLs for crypto map entries tagged as **ipsec-manual** are restricted to a single permit entry, and subsequent entries are ignored.
- The SAs established by a manual crypto map entry are only for a single data flow.

Overview of Configuring IPSec for RSA Encrypted Nonces

This section provides a brief overview of configuring IPSec for RSA encrypted nonces.

RSA encrypted nonces provide a strong method of authenticating the IPSec peers and the Diffie-Hellman key exchange. RSA encrypted nonces provide repudiation—a quality that prevents a third party from being able to trace your activities over a network. A drawback is that they are somewhat more difficult to configure and, therefore, are more difficult to scale to a large number of peers. RSA encrypted nonces require that peers possess each other's public keys but do not use a certificate authority (CA). Instead, there are two ways for peers to get each other's public keys:

- You manually configure and exchange RSA keys.
- You use RSA signatures previously used during a successful ISAKMP negotiation with a remote peer.

NOTE	RSA encrypted nonces must initially be exchanged by some out-of-band method. This can lead to security vulnerabilities.

The IPSec configuration process for RSA encryption is very similar to preshared keys with some notable exceptions, summarized as follows:

- Task 1: Prepare for IPSec to determine a detailed security policy for RSA encryption to include how to distribute the RSA public keys.

- Task 2: Configure RSA keys manually.

- Task 3: Configure ISAKMP for IPSec to select RSA encryption as the authentication method in an ISAKMP policy.

- Task 4: Configure IPSec, which is typically done the same as in pre-share.

- Task 5: Test and verify IPSec and exercise additional commands to view and manage RSA public keys.

This chapter has already covered most of the tasks in the previous list, with the exception of Task 2. The following section covers Task 2.

Task 2: Configure RSA Keys

NOTE   For a complete discussion of all the tasks and steps necessary to configure RSA encrypted nonces, see the "Configuring IKE Security Protocol" chapter in the Cisco IOS Security Configuration Guide, release 12.1. This section provides only a brief overview of the commands used for Task 2, as it is unique to RSA encrypted nonces.

Configuring RSA keys involves the following six steps:

Step 1   Plan for RSA keys.

Step 2   Configure the router's host name and domain name (if they have not already been configured).

Step 3   Generate the RSA keys.

Step 4   Enter peer RSA public keys. There are several substeps necessary to enter the peer's public keys. Attention to detail is important, as any mistakes made entering the keys will cause them not to work.

Step 5   Verify the key configuration. It is easy for mistakes to be made when copying and pasting the RSA keys. Verifying the keys ensures that they match.

Step 6   Manage RSA keys. Removing old keys is part of the configuration process. Old keys can consume much unnecessary space.

Summary

This chapter focused on the configuration of an IPSec VPN on Cisco IOS routers using preshared keys. The chapter identified the four tasks that are required to configure IPSec:

- Prepare for IKE and IPSec
- Configure IKE
- Configure IPSec
- Test and verify IPSec

The chapter covered each individual task and identified the steps that are required to perform each task. Each task was explained in great detail, along with configuration examples that will empower you to implement these technologies in your place of work.

The chapter briefly covered the use of RSA encrypted nonces; more information on this can be found from the Cisco IOS configuration guide for the relevant release of IOS you are using.

Review Questions

1   How many tasks are involved in configuring IPSec?

2   Do you configure IKE phase one or IKE phase two first?

3   What command is used to display information about the crypto map?

4   How do you apply a crypto map to an interface?

5   With Diffie-Hellman, there are two options, which are group 1 and 2. Group 1 uses 768-bit encryption: what does group 2 use?

6   What port does ISAKMP use?

7   To allow ISAKMP, ESP, and AH through an access list, what would you have to allow?

8   What command would create a transform set that uses ESP authentication with MD5, ESP encryption with 56-bit DES, and tunnel mode?

9   What command globally enables ISAKMP?

10   IPSec peers authenticate each other during ISAKMP negotiations using the preshared key and the ISAKMP identity. The identity can be either the router's IP address or what other method?

CHAPTER 4

Configuring Cisco IOS Routers for CA Site-to-Site

This chapter introduces configuration of Cisco IOS Internet Protocol Security (IPSec) using a certificate authority (CA). After presenting an overview of the configuration process, the chapter shows you each major step of the configuration that is unique to CA support. It includes the following topics:

- Configure CA support tasks
- Task 1: Prepare for Internet Key Exchange (IKE) and IPSec
- CA support overview
- Task 2: Configure CA support
- Task 3: Configure IKE
- Task 4: Configure IPSec
- Task 5: Test and verify IPSec

Configure CA Support Tasks

This section presents an overview of the CA support tasks you will perform in this chapter.

The configuration process for Rivest, Shamir, and Adelman (RSA) signatures consists of five major tasks. This chapter discusses the CA configuration tasks and steps in detail. Tasks and steps identical to preshared keys are not covered in detail in this chapter. Refer to Chapter 7, "Configuring the Cisco PIX Firewall for CA Site-to-Site," for a detailed explanation of these steps. The items covered in this chapter are in bold as follows:

- **Task 1: Prepare for IPSec**—Preparing for IPSec involves determining the detailed encryption policy: identifying the hosts and networks you wish to protect, determining IPSec peer details, determining the IPSec features you need, and ensuring existing access lists are compatible with IPSec.

- **Task 2: Configure CA support**—This involves setting the router's host name and domain name, generating the keys, declaring a CA, and authenticating and requesting your own certificates.

- **Task 3: Configure IKE for IPSec**—Configuring IKE involves enabling IKE, creating the IKE policies, and validating the configuration.

- **Task 4: Configure IPSec**—IPSec configuration includes defining the transform sets, creating crypto access lists, creating crypto map entries, and applying crypto map sets to interfaces.

- **Task 5: Test and verify IPSec**—Use **show, debug,** and related commands to test and verify that IPSec encryption works and to troubleshoot problems.

Task 1: Prepare for IKE and IPSec

Successful implementation of an IPSec network requires advance planning before beginning configuration of individual routers. Configuring IPSec encryption can be complicated. Having a detailed plan lessens the chances of improper configuration.

You must plan in advance if you desire to configure IPSec encryption correctly the first time and minimize misconfiguration. You should begin this task by defining the IPSec security policy based on the overall company security policy. Some planning steps follow:

NOTE   Step 1 and Step 2 are covered in detail in this chapter. The other steps in the list are presented for review purposes and are not covered in this chapter. Refer to the previous chapter for a detailed explanation of Steps 3 through 6.

Step 1   **Plan for CA support**—Determine the CA server details. This includes variables such as the type of CA server to be used, the IP address, and the CA administrator contact information.

Step 2   **Determine IKE (IKE phase one) policy**—Determine the IKE policies between IPSec peers based on the number and location of the peers.

Step 3   **Determine IPSec (IKE phase two) policy**—Identify IPSec peer details such as IP addresses and IPSec modes. You then configure crypto maps to gather all IPSec policy details together.

Step 4   **Check the current configuration**—Use the **write terminal, show isakmp [policy]**, and **show crypto map** commands, and the many other **show** commands that are covered later in this chapter.

Step 5   **Ensure the network works without encryption**—Ensure that basic connectivity has been achieved between IPSec peers using the desired IP services before configuring IPSec. You can use the **ping** command to check basic connectivity.

Step 6   **Ensure access lists are compatible with IPSec**—Ensure that perimeter routers and the IPSec peer router interfaces permit IPSec traffic. In this step, you need to enter the **show access-lists** command.

Step 1: Plan for CA Support

Successful implementation of an IPSec network requires advance planning before beginning configuration of individual routers. This section outlines how to prepare for IKE and CA support.

Configuring CA is complicated. Having a detailed plan lessens the chances of improper configuration. Some planning steps include the following:

- **Determine the type of CA server to use**—CA servers come in a multitude of configurations and capabilities. You must determine which one fits your needs in advance of configuration. Requirements include (but are not limited to), the RSA key type required, Certificate Revocation List (CRL) capabilities, and support for registration authority (RA) mode.

- **Identify the CA server's IP address, host name, and URL**—This information is necessary if you use Lightweight Directory Protocol (LDAP).

- **Identify the CA server administrator contact information**—You need to arrange for your certificates to be validated if the process is not automatic.

The goal is to be ready for CA support configuration.

Figure 4-1 illustrates the minimum information needed to configure a CA server on a Cisco router. Depending on the CA server chosen, other variables might also have to be identified and resolved.

Figure 4-1 *Determine CA Server Details*

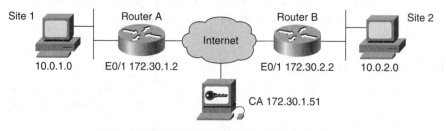

Parameter	CA Server
Type of CA server	Entrust
Host name	entrust-ca
IP address	172.30.1.51
URL	www.ca.com
Administrator contact	1-800-555-1212

Step 2: Determine IKE (IKE Phase One) Policy

In order to configure IKE, you have to ensure that you have the correct information before you start any configuration. You should determine the IKE policy details to enable the selected authentication method, then configure it. Having a detailed plan lessens the chances of improper configuration. Some planning steps include the following:

- **Determine the key distribution method**—Determine the key distribution method based on the numbers and locations of IPSec peers. For small networks, you might wish to distribute keys manually. For larger networks, you might wish to use a CA server to support scalability of IPSec peers. You must then configure Internet Security Association Key Management Protocol (ISAKMP) to support the selected key distribution method.

- **Determine the authentication method**—Choose the authentication method based on the key distribution method. Cisco IOS software supports either preshared keys, RSA encrypted nonces, or RSA signatures to authenticate IPSec peers. This chapter focuses on using RSA signatures.

- **Identify IPSec peer's IP addresses and host names**—Determine the details of all the IPSec peers that will use ISAKMP and RSA signature keys for establishing security associations (SAs). You will use this information to configure IKE.

- **Determining ISAKMP policies for peers**—An ISAKMP policy defines a combination, or *suite*, of security parameters to be used during the ISAKMP negotiation. Each ISAKMP negotiation begins by each peer agreeing on a common (shared) ISAKMP policy. The ISAKMP policy suites must be determined in advance of configuration. You must then configure IKE to support the policy details you determined. Some ISAKMP policy details include:

— Encryption algorithm

— Hash algorithm

— IKE SA lifetime

The goal of this planning step is to gather the precise data you will need in later steps to minimize misconfiguration.

An IKE policy defines a combination of security parameters used during the IKE negotiation. A group of policies makes up a *protection suite* of multiple policies that enable IPSec peers to establish IKE sessions and establish SAs with a minimal configuration.

Creating IKE Policies for a Purpose

IKE negotiations must be protected, so each IKE negotiation begins by each peer agreeing on a common (shared) IKE policy. This policy states which security parameters are used to protect subsequent IKE negotiations.

After the two peers agree upon a policy, the security parameters of the policy are identified by an SA established at each peer, and these SAs apply to all subsequent IKE traffic during the negotiation.

You can create multiple prioritized policies at each peer to ensure that at least one policy will match a remote peer's policy.

Defining IKE Policy Parameters

You can select specific values for each IKE parameter per the IKE standard. You choose one value over another based on the security level you desire and the type of IPSec peer to which you will connect.

There are five parameters to define in each IKE policy, as outlined in Table 4-1.

Table 4-1   *IKE Policy Parameters*

Parameter	Accepted Values	Keyword	Default
Message encryption algorithm	DES	**des**	DES
	3DES	**3des**	
Message integrity (hash) algorithm	SHA-1 (HMAC variant)	**sha**	SHA-1
		md5	
	MD5 (HMAC variant)		

continues

Table 4-1   *IKE Policy Parameters (Continued)*

Parameter	Accepted Values	Keyword	Default
Peer authentication method	Preshared keys RSA encrypted nonces RSA signatures	**pre-share** **rsa-encr** **rsa-sig**	RSA signatures
Key exchange parameters (Diffie-Hellman group identifier)	768-bit Diffie-Hellman or 1024-bit Diffie-Hellman	**1** **2**	768-bit Diffie-Hellman
ISAKMP-established security association's lifetime	Can specify any number of seconds	—	86,400 seconds (one day)

You can select specific values for each ISAKMP parameter per the ISAKMP standard. You choose one value over another based on the security level you desire and the type of IPSec peer to which you will connect. There are five parameters to define in each IKE policy, as presented in Table 4-2. The table shows the relative strength of each parameter.

Table 4-2   *ISAKMP Parameters*

Parameter	Strong	Stronger
Message encryption algorithm	DES	3DES
Message integrity (hash) algorithm	MD5	SHA-1
Peer authentication method	Preshare	RSA Encryption RSA Signature
Key exchange parameters (Diffie-Hellman group identifier)	D-H Group 1	D-H Group 2
ISAKMP-established security association's lifetime	86,400 seconds	<86,400 seconds

You should determine IKE policy details for each peer before configuring IKE. Figure 4-2 shows a summary of IKE policy details that will be configured in examples and in labs for this chapter. The authentication method of RSA signature keys is covered in this chapter.

Figure 4-2 *IKE Policy Example*

Parameter	Site 1	Site 2
Encryption Algorithm	DES	DES
Hash Algorithm	MD5	MD5
Authentication Method	RSA Signatures	RSA Signatures
Key Exchange	768-bit D-H	768-bit D-H
IKE SA Lifetime	86,400 seconds	86,400 seconds
Peer IP Address	172.30.2.2	172.30.1.2

NOTE   Refer to the previous chapter for a detailed explanation of Steps 3 through 6. After the "CA Support Overview" section, this chapter covers Task 2.

CA Support Overview

This section presents an overview of Cisco IOS CA support.

Cisco IOS supports the following open CA standards:

- **IKE**—A hybrid protocol that implements Oakley and Skeme key exchanges inside the ISAKMP framework. Although IKE can be used with other protocols, its initial implementation is with the IPSec protocol. IKE provides authentication of the IPSec peers, negotiates IPSec keys, and negotiates IPSec security associations.

- **Public-Key Cryptography Standard #7 (PKCS #7)**—A standard from RSA Security Inc. used to encrypt, sign, and package certificate enrollment messages.

- **Public-Key Cryptography Standard #10 (PKCS #10)**—A standard syntax from RSA Security Inc. for certificate requests.

- **RSA keys**—RSA is the public key cryptographic system developed by Ronald Rivest, Adi Shamir, and Leonard Adelman. RSA keys come in pairs: one public key and one private key.

- **X.509v3 certificates**—Certificate support that allows the IPSec-protected network to scale by providing the equivalent of a digital ID card to each device. When two devices wish to communicate, they exchange digital certificates to prove their identity (thus removing the need to manually exchange public keys with each peer or to manually specify a shared key at each peer). These certificates are obtained from a CA. X.509 is part of the X.500 standard.

• **CA interoperability**—CA interoperability permits Cisco IOS devices and CAs to communicate so that your Cisco IOS device can obtain and use digital certificates from the CA. Although IPSec can be implemented on your network without the use of a CA, using a CA with Simple Certificate Enrollment Protocol (SCEP) provides manageability and scalability for IPSec.

The SCEP is an initiative of Cisco, VeriSign, Entrust, Microsoft, Netscape, and Sun Microsystems that provides a standard way of managing the certificate life cycle.

NOTE   The Certificate Enrollment Protocol (CEP) terminology used in older documentation is the same as the SCEP terminology presently used.

This initiative is important for driving open development for certificate handling protocols that can be interoperable with many vendors' devices.

PKCS #7 and #10 are acronyms for the Public-Key Cryptography Standards #7 and #10. These are standards from RSA Security Inc. used to encrypt and sign certificate enrollment messages.

SCEP is described in the Internet Engineering Task Force (IETF) draft filename *draft-nourse-scep-04.txt* that you can find at http://www.ietf.org/.

The Manual Enrollment Process

SCEP provides two authentication methods: manual authentication and authentication based on preshared secret. In the manual mode, the end entity submitting the request is required to wait until the CA operator, using any reliable out-of-band method, can verify its identity. An MD5 "fingerprint" generated on the PKCS# must be compared out-of-band between the server and the end entity. SCEP Clients and CAs (or RAs, if appropriate) must display this fingerprint to a user to enable this verification, if manual mode is used. When using a preshared secret scheme, the server should distribute a shared secret to the end entity that can uniquely associate the enrollment request with the given end entity. The distribution of the secret must be private: only the end entity should know this secret. When creating the enrollment request, the end entity is asked to provide a challenge password. When using the preshared secret scheme, the end entity must type in the redistributed secret as the password. In the manual authentication case, the challenge password is also required, because the server might challenge an end entity with the password before any certificate can be revoked. Later on, this challenge password is included as a PKCS#10 attribute and is sent to the server as encrypted data. The PKCS#7 envelope protects the privacy of the challenge password with Data Encryption Standard (DES) encryption.

CA Servers Interoperable with Cisco Routers

There are several other CA vendors that interoperate with Cisco IOS software on Cisco routers as follows:

- **Entrust Technologies, Inc.**—Entrust/PKI 4.0
- **VeriSign**—OnSite 4.5
- **Baltimore Technologies**—UniCERT v3.05
- **Microsoft Corporation**—Windows 2000 Certificate Services 5.0

Each of the CA vendors supports the SCEP for enrolling Cisco routers. Cisco is using the Cisco Security Associate Program to test new CA and Public Key Infrastructure (PKI) solutions with the Cisco Secure family of products. More information on the Security Associate Program can be found at the following URL: www.cisco.com/warp/public/cc/so/neso/sqso/csap/index.shtml.

Entrust Technologies

The Entrust CA server is one of the servers that is interoperable with Cisco. One of the major differences among CA servers is the question of who administers it.

Entrust is software that is installed and administered by the user. The Cisco IOS interoperates with the Entrust/PKI 4.0 CA server. Entrust/PKI delivers the ability to issue digital IDs to any device or application supporting the X.509 certificate standard, meeting the need for security, flexibility, and low cost by supporting all devices and applications from one PKI. Entrust/PKI offers the following features:

- **Requirements**—Entrust runs on the Windows NT 4.0 (required for Cisco interoperability), Solaris 2.6, HP-UX 10.20, and AIX 4.3 operating systems. It requires RSA usage keys on the routers and must use Cisco IOS release 11.(3)5T and later.
- **Standards supported**—Entrust supports CA services, and RA capability, SCEP, and PKCS#10.

Refer to the Entrust Web site at www.entrust.com for more information.

VeriSign OnSite 4.5

The VeriSign OnSite CA server is interoperable with Cisco routers. VeriSign administers the CA, providing the certificates as a service.

VeriSign's OnSite 4.5 solution delivers a fully integrated enterprise PKI to control, issue, and manage IPSec certificates for PIX Firewalls and Cisco routers. VeriSign OnSite is a service administered by VeriSign. VeriSign OnSite offers the following features:

- **Requirements**—There are no local server requirements. Configure the router for CA mode with a high (greater than 60 seconds) retry count. It must use Cisco IOS release 12.0(6.0.1)T and later. Cisco IOS 12.0(5)T is not supported because of a known bug in that release.

- **Standards supported**—Supports SCEP, x509 certificate format, and PKCS# 7, 10, 11, and 12.

Refer to the VeriSign Web site at www.verisign.com for more information.

Baltimore Technologies

Baltimore Technologies has implemented support for SCEP in UniCERT (Baltimore's CA server) and the PKI Plus toolkit; these make it easy for customers to enable certificates within their environments.

- **Requirements**—The current release of the UniCERT CA module is available for Windows NT. It must use Cisco IOS release 12.0(5)T and later.

- **Standards supported**—The following standards are supported with this CA server: X509 v3, X.9.62, X.9.92, X9.21-2; CRL v2; RFC 2459; PKCS# 1,7,10,11,12; RFC 2510, RFC 2511; SCEP; LDAP v2, LDAP v3; DAP; SQL; TCP/IP; POP3; SMTP; HTTP; OCSP; FIPS 186-1, FIPS 180-1, FIPS 46-3, and FIPS 81 CBC.

Refer to the Baltimore Web site at www.baltimore.com for more information.

Microsoft Windows 2000 Certificate Services 5.0

Microsoft has integrated SCEP support into the Windows 2000 CA server through the Security Resource Kit for Windows 2000. This support lets customers use SCEP to obtain certificates and certificate revocation information from Microsoft Certificate Services for all of Cisco's VPN security solutions.

- **Requirements**—Compatible PC capable of running Windows 2000 Server. It must use Cisco IOS release 12.0(5)T and above.

- **Standards supported**—The following standards are supported with this CA server: X.509 version 3, CRL version 2, PKCS family (PKCS #7, #10, #12), PKIX, SSL version 3, Kerberos v5 RFC 1510, 1964 tokens, SGC, IPSec, PKINIT, PC/SC, and IETF 2459.

The SCEP tool is not installed by the Windows 2000 Resource Kit Setup. You must install the SCEP tool separately. To install it, use the following procedure:

1 Before you start, you must install the SCEP Add-on for Certificate Services on a root CA. Both enterprise root CAs and standalone root CAs are supported.

2 Log on with the appropriate administrative privileges to the server on which the root CA is installed.

3 Run the **cepsetup.exe** file located on the Windows 2000 Resource Kit CD.

4 In the SCEP Add-on for Certificate Services Setup wizard, perform the following steps:

 — Select whether or not you want to require a challenge phrase for certificate enrollment. You might wish to use a challenge phrase for added security, especially if you configure the CA to grant certificates automatically. You later obtain the challenge phrase immediately before enrolling the IPSec Client by accessing the CA's URL, http://URLHostName/certsrv/mscep/mscep.dll, and copying the phrase. The phrase is then entered upon IPSec client enrollment.

 — Enter information about who is enrolling for the RA certificate, which will later allow certificates to be requested from the CA on behalf of the router.

 — (Optional) Select Advanced Enrollment Options if you want to specify the cryptographic service provider (CSP) and key lengths for the RA signature and encryption keys.

5 The URL http://URLHostName/certsrv/mscep/mscep.dll is displayed when the SCEP Setup wizard finishes and confirms a successful installation. URLHostName is the name of the server that hosts the CA's enrollment Web pages (also referred to as Certificate Services Web pages).

You might need to update the **mscep.dll** with a later version.

Refer to the Microsoft Web site at www.microsoft.com for more information.

Enroll a Device with a CA

The typical process for enrolling in a CA follows and is shown in Figure 4-3:

Step 1 Configure the router for CA support.

Step 2 Generate a public and private key pair on the router.

Step 3 The router authenticates the CA server.

Step 4 The router sends a certificate request to the CA.

Step 5 The CA creates and signs an identity (ID) and root certificate and, optionally, an RA certificate.

Step 6 The CA sends the certificates to the router and posts the certificates in its public repository (directory).

Figure 4-3 *Enroll a Device with a CA*

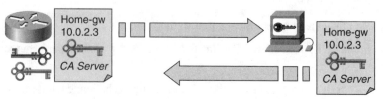

- Configure CA support on the IPSec peer.
- Generate public and private keys.
- Authenticate the CA server.
- Send a certificate request to the CA.
- The CA signs the certificate.
- Retrieve the certificate from the CA.

Most of these steps have been automated by Cisco and the SCEP protocol that is supported by many CA server vendors. Each vendor determines how long certificates are valid. Contact the relevant vendor to determine how long the certificates will be valid in your particular case.

Task 2: Configure CA Support

This section presents a detailed explanation of the steps necessary to configure CA support on Cisco routers.

Configuring Cisco IOS CA support is complicated. Having a detailed plan lessens the chances of improper configuration. Some planning steps and their associated commands include the following:

Step 1 **Manage the non-volatile RAM (NVRAM) memory usage (optional)**—In some cases, storing certificates and CRLs locally does not present a problem. However, in other cases, memory might become an issue, particularly if your CA supports an RA, and a large number of CRLs end up being stored on your router.

Step 2 **Set the router's time and date**—The router must have an accurate time and date to enroll with a CA server.

Step 3   **Configure the router's host name and domain name**—The host name is used in prompts and default configuration filenames. The domain name is used to define a default domain name that the Cisco IOS software uses to complete unqualified host names.

Step 4   **Generate an RSA key pair**—RSA keys are used to identify the remote VPN peer. You can generate one general purpose key or two special purpose keys.

Step 5   **Declare a CA**—To declare the CA that your router should use, use the **crypto ca identity** global configuration command. Use the **no** form of this command to delete all identity information and certificates associated with the CA.

Step 6   **Authenticate the CA**—The router needs to authenticate the CA. It does this by obtaining the CA's self-signed certificate that contains the CA's public key.

Step 7   **Request your own certificate**—Complete this step to obtain your router's certificate from the CA.

Step 8   **Save the configuration**—After configuring the router for CA support, the configuration should be saved.

Step 9   **Monitor and maintain CA interoperability (optional)**—The following steps are optional, depending on your particular requirements:

   — Request a CRL.

   — Delete your router's RSA keys.

   — Delete both public and private certificates from the configuration.

   — Delete peer's public keys.

Step 10   **Verify the CA support configuration**—The commands detailed in this section allow you to view your own and any other configured CA certificates.

Step 1: Manage NVRAM Memory Usage (Optional)

In some cases, storing certificates and CRLs locally will not present a problem. However, in other cases, memory might become an issue, particularly if your CA supports an RA, and a large number of CRLs end up being stored on your router. These certificates and CRLs can consume a large amount of NVRAM space.

To save NVRAM space, you can specify that certificates and CRLs should not be stored locally but should be retrieved from the CA when needed. This will save NVRAM space but could have a slight performance impact.

To specify that certificates and CRLs should not be stored locally on your router, but should be retrieved when required, turn on query mode by using the **crypto ca certificate query** command in global configuration mode.

Step 2: Set the Router's Time and Date

Ensure that the router's time zone, time, and date have been accurately set with the **show clock** commands in privileged exec mode. The clock must be accurately set before generating RSA key pairs and enrolling with the CA server because the keys and certificates are time-sensitive.

To specify the router's time zone, use the **clock timezone** global configuration command. The command sets the time zone and an offset from Universal Time Code (UTC, displayed by the router). The command syntax is as follows:

```
clock timezone zone hours [minutes]
```

zone	Name of the time zone to be displayed when standard time is in effect
hours	Hours offset from UTC
minutes	(Optional) Minutes offset from UTC

The following example sets the time zone to central standard time (CST) in the United States:

```
RouterA(config)# clock timezone cst -6
```

To set the router's time and date, use the **clock set** privileged EXEC command. The command syntax is as follows:

```
clock set hh:mm:ss day month year
clock set hh:mm:ss month day year
```

hh:mm:ss	Current time in hours (military format), minutes, and seconds
day	Current day (by date) in the month
month	Current month (by name)
year	Current year (no abbreviation)

The following example sets the time to one second before midnight, December 31, 2000:

```
RouterA(config)# clock set 23:59:59 31 december 2000
```

You can also optionally set your router to automatically update the calendar and time from a Network Time Protocol (NTP) server with the **ntp** series of commands.

NOTE	Cisco recommends using an NTP server to set the router's time on routers that do not have a clock circuit chip. Further information on the configuration of NTP can be found by visiting the following URL: www.cisco.com/univercd/cc/td/doc/product/software/ios121/121cgcr/fun_c/fcprt3/fcd303.htm#xtocid2708216.

Step 3: Configure the Router's Host Name and Domain Name

If the router's host name and domain name have not previously been configured, you will need to configure them for CA support to work correctly.

To specify or modify the host name for the network server, use the **hostname** global configuration command. The host name is used in prompts and default configuration filenames. The setup command facility also prompts for a host name at startup. The command syntax is as follows:

```
hostname name
```

name	New host name for the network server

To define a default domain name that the Cisco IOS software uses to complete unqualified host names (names without a dotted-decimal domain name), use the **ip domain-name** global configuration command. To disable use of the DNS, use the **no** form of this command. The command syntax is as follows:

```
ip domain-name name
```

name	Default domain name used to complete unqualified host names. Do not include the initial period that separates an unqualified name from the domain name.

Use the **ip host** global configuration command to define a static host name-to-address mapping in the host cache. To remove the name-to-address mapping, use the **no** form of this command. The command syntax is as follows:

```
ip host name address1 [address2...address8]
```

name	Name of the host. The first character can be either a letter or a number.
address1	Associated IP address.
address2...address8	(Optional) Additional associated IP address. You can bind up to eight addresses to a host name.

Step 4: Generate RSA Key Pair

NOTE Before issuing the command to generate RSA keys, make sure your router has a host name and IP domain name configured (with the **hostname** and **ip domain-name** commands). You will be unable to complete the **crypto key generate rsa** command without a host name and IP domain name.

Use the **crypto key generate rsa** global configuration command to generate RSA key pairs. The command syntax is as follows:

```
crypto key generate rsa [usage-keys]
```

usage-keys	(Optional) Specifies that two RSA special usage key pairs should be generated (that is, one encryption pair and one signature pair) instead of one general purpose key pair

By default, RSA key pairs do not exist. If *usage-keys* is not used in the command, general purpose keys are generated. RSA keys are generated in pairs: one public RSA key and one private RSA key. If your router already has RSA keys when you issue this command, you are warned and prompted to replace the existing keys with new keys.

The keys generated by the **generate RSA keys** command are saved in the private configuration in NVRAM, which is never displayed to the user or backed up to another device.

There are two mutually exclusive types of RSA key pairs: special usage keys and general purpose keys. When you generate RSA key pairs, you can indicate whether to generate special usage keys or general purpose keys.

Special Usage Keys

If you generate special usage keys, two pairs of RSA keys are generated. One pair is used with any IKE policy that specifies RSA signatures as the authentication method, and the other pair is used with any IKE policy that specifies RSA encrypted nonces as the authentication method.

If you plan to have both types of RSA authentication methods in your IKE policies, you might prefer to generate special usage keys. With special usage keys, each key is not unnecessarily exposed. (Without special usage keys, one key is used for both authentication methods, increasing that key's exposure.)

General Purpose Keys

If you generate general purpose keys, only one pair of RSA keys is generated. This pair is used with IKE policies, specifying either RSA signatures or RSA encrypted nonces. Therefore, a general purpose key pair might get used more frequently than a special usage key pair.

Key generation can be very time consuming based on the router and length of the key chosen. Example 4-1 shows an example of generating a general key pair.

Example 4-1 *Key Generation*

```
RouterA(config)# crypto key generate rsa
The name for the keys will be: router.cisco.com
Choose the size of the key modulus in the range of 360 to 2048 for your
Signature Keys. Choosing a key modulus greater than 512 may take a few minutes.

How many bits in the modulus [512]: 512
Generating RSA keys ...
[OK]


RouterA# show crypto key mypubkey rsa
% Key pair was generated at: 23:58:59 UTC Dec 31 2000
Key name: RouterA.cisco.com
 Usage: General Purpose Key
 Key Data:
  305C300D 06092A86 4886F70D 01010105 00034B00 30480241 00A9443B 62FDACFB
  CCDB8784 19AE1CD8 95B30953 1EDD30D1 380219D6 4636E015 4D7C6F33 4DC1F6E0
  C929A25E 521688A1 295907F4 E98BF920 6A81CE57 28A21116 E3020301 0001
```

Modulus Length

When you generate RSA keys, you are prompted to enter a modulus length. A longer modulus could offer stronger security, but it takes longer to generate and takes longer to use. A modulus below 512 is normally not recommended. Cisco recommends using a minimum modulus of 1024. Table 4-3 shows examples of how long it takes to generate keys of different modulus lengths.

Table 4-3 *Modulus Lengths and Processing Time*

Router	Modulus Length			
	360 bits	**512 bits**	**1024 bits**	**2048 bits**
Cisco 2500	11 seconds	20 seconds	4 minutes, 38 seconds	Longer than 1 hour
Cisco 4700	Less than 1 second	1 second	4 seconds	50 seconds

Step 5: Declare a CA

Use the **crypto ca identity** global configuration command to declare what CA your router will use. Use the **no** form of this command to delete all identity information and certificates associated with the CA. The command syntax is as follows:

```
crypto ca identity name
```

name	Create a name for the CA. (If you previously declared the CA and just want to update its characteristics, specify the name you previously created.) The CA might require a particular name, such as its domain name.

NOTE   The **crypto ca identity** is only significant locally. It does not have to match the identity defined on any of the VPN peers.

Performing the **crypto ca identity** command puts you into the ca-identity configuration mode, where you can specify characteristics for the CA with the commands displayed in Table 4-4.

Table 4-4   *ca-identity Configuration Mode Commands*

Command	Description
enrollment url	Specify the URL of the CA—Always required
enrollment mode ra	Specify the RA mode—Required only if your CA system provides an RA
query url	Specify the URL of the LDAP server—Required only if your CA supports an RA and the LDAP protocol
enrollment retry-period	(Optional) Specify a period of time the router should wait between sending certificate request retries
enrollment retry-count	(Optional) Specify how many certificate request retries your router will send before giving up
crl optional	(Optional) Specify that your router can still accept other peers' certificates if the CRL is not accessible

The configuration shown in Example 4-2 declares an Entrust CA and identifies characteristics of the CA. In this example, the name mycaserver is created for the CA, which is located at http://vpnca. The example also declares a CA using an RA. The CA's scripts are stored in the default location, and the CA uses SCEP instead of LDAP. This is the minimum possible configuration required to declare a CA that uses an RA.

Example 4-2   *CA Declaration Example*

```
router(config)# crypto ca identity mycaserver
router(ca-identity)# enrollment url http://vpnca
router(ca-identity)# enrollment mode ra
router(ca-identity)# exit
```

Notice the following about Example 4-2:

- This specifies the URL for the CA server.
- This is the minimum configuration to declare a CA.
- An RA acts as a proxy for a CA.

Example 4-3 declares a Microsoft Windows 2000 CA. Note that the enrollment URL points to the MSCEP DLL.

Example 4-3   *Declaring a Windows 2000 CA*

```
Router#show running-config
crypto ca identity labca
 enrollment mode ra
 enrollment url http://vpnca/certsrv/mscep/mscep.dll
 crl optional
```

Step 6: Authenticate the CA

The router needs to authenticate the CA to verify that it is valid. The router does this by obtaining the CA's self-signed certificate that contains the CA's public key. Because the CA's certificate is self-signed (the CA signs its own certificate), the CA's public key should be manually authenticated by contacting the CA administrator to compare the CA certificate's fingerprint when you perform this step. To get the CA's public key, use the **crypto ca authenticate** *name* command in global configuration mode. Use the same name that you used when declaring the CA with the **crypto ca identity** command.

If you are using RA mode (using the **enrollment mode ra** command) when you issue the **crypto ca authenticate** command, the RA signing and encryption certificates are returned from the CA and the CA certificate.

Example 4-4 shows a CA authentication.

Example 4-4   *CA Authentication*

```
r1(config)# crypto ca authenticate labca
Certificate has the following attributes:
Fingerprint: 93700C31 4853EC4A DED81400 43D3C82C
% Do you accept this certificate? [yes/no]: y
```

Step 7: Request Your Own Certificate

To obtain your router's certificate from the CA, use the **crypto ca enroll** global configuration command. Use the **no** form of this command to delete a current enrollment request.

crypto ca enroll *name*

name	Specify the name of the CA. Use the same name as when you declared the CA using the **crypto ca identity** command.

This command requests certificates from the CA for all of your router's RSA key pairs. This task is also known as *enrolling* with the CA.

During the enrollment process, you are prompted for a challenge password, which can be used by the CA administrator to validate your identity. Do not forget the password you use. (Technically, enrolling and obtaining certificates are two separate events, but they both occur when the **crypto ca enroll** command is issued.)

Your router needs a signed certificate from the CA for each of your router's RSA key pairs; if you previously generated general purpose keys, this command obtains the one certificate corresponding to the one general purpose RSA key pair. If you previously generated special usage keys, this command obtains two certificates corresponding to each of the special usage RSA key pairs.

If you already have a certificate for your keys, you will be unable to complete this command; instead, you are prompted to remove the existing certificate first. (You can remove existing certificates with the **no certificate** command.)

Example 4-5 shows a CA enrollment.

Example 4-5   *CA Enrollment*

```
r1(config)# crypto ca enroll labca
% Start certificate enrollment ..
% Create a challenge password. You will need to verbally provide this
    password to the CA Administrator in order to revoke your certificate.
    For security reasons, your password will not be saved in the configuration.
    Please make a note of it.

Password: <password>
Re-enter password: <password>

% The subject name in the certificate will be: r1.cisco.com
% Include the router serial number in the subject name? [yes/no]: no
% Include an IP address in the subject name? [yes/no]: no
Request certificate from CA? [yes/no]: yes
% Certificate request sent to Certificate Authority
% The certificate request fingerprint will be displayed.
% The 'show crypto ca certificate' command will also show the fingerprint.
```

Example 4-5   *CA Enrollment (Continued)*

```
r1(config)#
   Signing Certificate Request Fingerprint:
   0EE481F1 CBB4AF30 5D757610 6A4CF13D
Encryption Certificate Request Fingerprint:
   710281D4 4DE854C7 AA61D953 CC5BD2B9
```

CAUTION   The **crypto ca enroll** command is not saved in the router configuration. If your router reboots after you issue the **crypto ca enroll** command but before you receive the certificate or certificates, you must reissue the command.

Step 8: Save the Configuration

After configuring the router for CA support, the configuration should be saved using the **copy running-config startup-config** command.

Step 9: Monitor and Maintain CA Interoperability

The following steps are optional, depending on your particular requirements:

- **Request a Certificate Revocation List (CRL)**—A CRL is not always required. If the CA server requires a CRL, you need to request one from the CA server. To request immediate download of the latest CRL, use the following command in global configuration mode:

```
crypto ca crl request name
```

name	Specify the name of the CA. Use the same name as when you declared the CA using the **crypto ca identity** command.

When your router receives a certificate from a peer, it will download a CRL from either the CA or a CRL distribution point as designated in the peer's certificate. Your router then checks the CRL to make sure the certificate the peer sent has not been revoked. (If the certificate appears on the CRL, your router will not accept the certificate and will not authenticate the peer.)

With CA systems that support RAs, multiple CRLs exist, and the peer's certificate will indicate which CRL applies and should be downloaded by your router. If your router does not have the applicable CRL and is unable to obtain one, your router will reject the peer's certificate, unless you include the **crl optional** command in your configuration. If you use the **crl optional** command, your router will still try to obtain a CRL, but if it cannot obtain a CRL it can still accept the peer's certificate.

When your router receives additional certificates from peers, your router will continue to attempt to download the appropriate CRL, even if it was previously unsuccessful and even if the **crl optional** command is enabled. The **crl optional** command only specifies that when the router cannot obtain the CRL, the router is not forced to reject a peer's certificate outright.

- **Delete your router's RSA keys**—There might be circumstances where you would want to delete your router's RSA keys. For example, if you believe the RSA keys were compromised in some way and should no longer be used, you should delete the keys. To delete all of your router's RSA keys, use the following command in global configuration mode: **crypto key zeroize rsa**.

- **Delete certificates from the configuration**—After you delete a router's RSA keys, you should also delete the certificates from the configuration. Follow these steps to accomplish this:

  — Ask the CA administrator to revoke your router's certificates at the CA; you must supply the challenge password you created when you originally obtained the router's certificates with the **crypto ca enroll** command.

  — Manually remove the router's certificates from the router configuration. To delete your router's certificate or RA certificates from your router's configuration, use the following commands in global configuration mode:

    — **show crypto ca certificates**—View the certificates stored on your router. Note the serial number of the certificate you wish to delete.

    — **crypto ca certificate chain** *name*—Enter the certificate chain configuration mode.

    — **no certificate** *certificate-serial-number*—Delete the certificate. Use the serial number you noted in the first bullet.

NOTE   To delete the CA's certificate, you must remove the entire CA identity, which also removes all certificates associated with the CA: your router's certificate, the CA certificate, and any RA certificates. To remove a CA identity, use the following command in global configuration mode: **no crypto ca identity name**.

- **Delete peer's public keys**—There might be circumstances where you would want to delete other peers' RSA public keys from your router's configuration. For example, if you no longer trust the integrity of a peer's public key, you should delete the key. To delete the peer's public keys, use the following commands:

  — **crypto key pubkey-chain rsa**—Enter the public key chain configuration mode.

  — **no named-key** *key-name* [**encryption** | **signature**] or **no addressed-key** *key-address* [**encryption** | **signature**]—Delete a remote peer's RSA public key. Specify the peer's fully qualified domain name (FQDN) or the remote peer's IP address. You can optionally delete just the encryption key or the signature key by using the *encryption* or *signature* keywords.

Step 10: Verify the CA Support Configuration

Example 4-6 illustrates the result of the **show crypto ca certificates** command.

Example 4-6   **show crypto ca certificates**

```
router# show crypto ca certificates

Certificate
  Subject Name
    Name: myrouter.xyz.com
        IP Address: 172.30.1.2
    Status: Available
  Certificate Serial Number: 0123456789ABCDEF0123456789ABCDEF
  Key Usage: General Purpose

CA Certificate
  Status: Available
  Certificate Serial Number: 3051DF7123BEE31B8341DFE4B3A338E5F
  Key Usage: Not Set
```

Example 4-7 shows sample output from the **show crypto key mypubkey rsa** command. Special usage RSA keys were previously generated for this router using the **crypto key generate rsa** command.

Example 4-7   **show crypto key mypubkey rsa**

```
% Key pair was generated at: 23:57:50 UTC Dec 31 2000
Key name: myrouter.xyz.com
  Usage: Signature Key
  Key Data:
    005C300D 06092A86 4886F70D 01010105 00034B00 30480241 00C5E23B 55D6AB22
    04AEF1BA A54028A6 9ACC01C5 129D99E4 64CAB820 847EDAD9 DF0B4E4C 73A05DD2
    BD62A8A9 FA603DD2 E2A8A6F8 98F76E28 D58AD221 B583D7A4 71020301 0001
% Key pair was generated at: 23:58:59 UTC Dec 31 2000
Key name: myrouter.xyz.com
```

continues

Example 4-7 **show crypto key mypubkey rsa** *(Continued)*

```
Usage: Encryption Key
 Key Data:
 00302017 4A7D385B 1234EF29 335FC973 2DD50A37 C4F4B0FD 9DADE748 429618D5
 18242BA3 2EDFBDD3 4296142A DDF7D3D8 08407685 2F2190A0 0B43F1BD 9A8A26DB
 07953829 791FCDE9 A98420F0 6A82045B 90288A26 DBC64468 7789F76E EE21
```

Example 4-8 shows sample output from the **show crypto key pubkey-chain rsa** command.

Example 4-8 **show crypto key pubkey-chain rsa**

```
Codes: M - Manually Configured, C - Extracted from certificate
 Code     Usage        IP-address      Name
 M        Signature    10.0.0.1        myrouter.domain.com
 M        Encryption   10.0.0.1        myrouter.domain.com
 C        Signature    172.30.1.2      routerA.domain.com
 C        Encryption   172.30.1.2      routerA.domain.com
 C        General      172.30.2.2      routerB.domain1.com
```

Example 4-8 shows manually configured special usage RSA public keys for the peer somerouter. This sample also shows three keys obtained from peers' certificates: special usage keys for peer routerA and a general purpose key for peer routerB.

Certificate support is used in the previous example; if certificate support was not in use, none of the peers' keys would show C in the code column, but would all have to be manually configured.

CA Support Configuration Example

Example 4-9 displays the running-config of a router properly configured for CA support.

Example 4-9 *CA Support Configuration Example*

```
RouterA# show running-config
!
hostname RouterA
!
ip domain-name cisco.com
!
crypto ca identity mycaserver
 enrollment mode ra
 enrollment url http://vpnca:80
 query url ldap://vpnca
 crl optional
crypto ca certificate chain entrust
 certificate 37C6EAD6
  30820299 30820202 A0030201 02020437 C6EAD630 0D06092A
  864886F7 0D010105
  (certificates concatenated)
```

Task 3: Configure IKE

The next major task in configuring Cisco IOS IPSec is to configure IKE parameters gathered earlier. This section presents the steps used to configure IKE policies.

Configuring IKE consists of the following essential steps and commands:

Step 1   Enable or disable IKE with the **crypto isakmp enable** command.

Step 2   Create IKE policies with the **crypto isakmp policy** command.

Step 3   Set the IKE identity to address or host name with the **crypto isakmp identity** command.

Step 4   Test and verify the IKE configuration with the **show crypto isakmp policy** and **show crypto isakmp sa** commands.

Step 2: Create IKE Policies

The **crypto isakmp policy** command invokes the ISAKMP policy configuration command mode (config-isakmp) where you can set ISAKMP parameters. If you do not specify one of these commands for a policy, the default value is used for that parameter. While in the config-isakmp command mode, the keywords in Table 4-5 are available to specify the parameters in the policy.

Table 4-5   *ISAKMP Values*

Keyword	Accepted Values	Default Value	Description
des	56-bit DES-CBC	des	Message encryption algorithm.
3des	168-bit DES		
sha	SHA-1 (HMAC variant)	sha	Message integrity (hash) algorithm.
md5	MD5 (HMAC variant)		
rsa-sig	RSA signatures	rsa-sig	Peer authentication method.
rsa-encr	RSA encrypted nonces		
pre-share	preshared keys		

continues

Table 4-5 *ISAKMP Values (Continued)*

Keyword	Accepted Values	Default Value	Description
1 2	768-bit Diffie-Hellman or 1024-bit Diffie-Hellman	1	Key exchange parameters (Diffie-Hellman group identifier).
—	Can specify any number of seconds	86,400 seconds (one day)	ISAKMP-established SA's lifetime. You can usually leave this value at the default.
exit			Exits the config-isakmp mode.

You can configure multiple ISAKMP policies on each peer participating in IPSec. ISAKMP peers negotiate acceptable ISAKMP policies before agreeing upon the SA to be used for IPSec.

Task 4: Configure IPSec

The next major task in configuring Cisco IOS IPSec is to configure the IPSec parameters previously gathered. This section presents the steps used to configure IPSec.

NOTE   The following steps are identical to those for configuring preshared keys. Refer to the previous chapter for the detailed explanation of each step.

The general tasks and commands used to configure IPSec encryption on Cisco routers are summarized as follows.

Step 1   Configure transform set suites with the **crypto ipsec transform-set** command.

Step 2   Configure global IPSec security association lifetimes with the **crypto ipsec security-association lifetime** command.

Step 3   Configure crypto access lists with the **access-list** command.

Step 4   Configure crypto maps with the **crypto map** command.

Step 5   Apply the crypto maps to the terminating or originating interface with the **interface** and **crypto map** commands.

Task 5: Test and Verify IPSec

Cisco IOS software contains a number of **show**, **clear**, and **debug** commands useful for testing and verifying IPSec and ISAKMP, which are considered in this section.

NOTE   Although many of the test and verify commands are used the same way as when configuring preshared keys, there are some commands unique to RSA signatures.

You can perform the following actions to test and verify that you have correctly configured VPN using Cisco IOS:

- Display your configured IKE policies using the **show crypto isakmp policy** command.
- Display your configured transform sets using the **show crypto ipsec transform set** command.
- Display the current state of your IPSec SAs with the **show crypto ipsec sa** command.
- View your configured crypto maps with the **show crypto map** command.
- Debug IKE and IPSec traffic through the Cisco IOS with the **debug crypto ipsec** and **debug crypto isakmp** commands.
- Debug CA events through the Cisco IOS with the **debug crypto key-exchange** and **debug crypto pki** commands.

Summary

This chapter provided detailed information on how to configure a Cisco IOS router to use a CA for IPSec VPNs. It started by looking at the tasks involved in configuring CA support for IPSec encryption. Many of these tasks are the same as those in Chapter 3, which looked at preshared key support for Cisco IOS-based VPNs. This chapter provided an overview of CAs and their related technologies. Following this overview, it looked at the configuration steps involved in configuring CA support for a Cisco IOS router. After the CA was configured, the chapter continued with the rest of the IPSec configuration tasks until the VPN was established.

Now you have configured both preshared keys and CA support on Cisco IOS routers. Next you will look at the troubleshooting tools that are available to troubleshoot Cisco IOS-based IPSec VPNs.

Review Questions

1 What command displays the configured access lists on a router that is part of an IPSec VPN?

2 Currently, which CA servers can be used by Cisco IOS devices?

3 To use the Entrust PKI CA Server, what version of Cisco IOS is required?

4 When you generate an RSA key pair on an IOS router, what are you prompted for?

5 What command displays your configured IKE policies?

6 Before you can generate an RSA key pair, what two items must be set on the IOS router?

7 How do you globally enable IKE?

8 What command generates the RSA key pair?

9 To use the Microsoft 2000 CA, what version of IOS is required?

10 How do you view the certificates that are stored on your router?

CHAPTER 5

Troubleshooting Cisco IOS VPNs

Chapter 3, "Configuring Cisco IOS Routers for Preshared Keys Site-to-Site," and Chapter 4, "Configuring Cisco IOS Routers for CA Site-to-Site," cover the configuration of Internet Protocol Security (IPSec) virtual private networks (VPNs) on Cisco routers that run Cisco IOS. Basic troubleshooting scenarios are presented within those chapters. This chapter presents a sample network and explains some basic troubleshooting that can alleviate common problems when configuring a Cisco IOS-based IPSec VPN. The chapter provides the sample IPSec configurations for the Cisco IOS routers and then displays the various **show** and **debug** output related to the common problems that are covered.

This chapter covers the following topics:

- Sample IPSec network configuration

- Configuring IPSec

- Troubleshooting the IPSec configuration

Sample IPSec Network Configuration

Figure 5-1 shows the sample network referred to in this troubleshooting chapter. The diagram presents two hosts (Host A and Host B) that are connected over the public Internet. The requirement of the network configuration is for a VPN to be established between Router A and Router B to facilitate the protected connection from Host A to Host B.

Figure 5-1   *Sample IPSec Network*

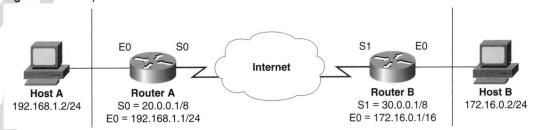

Host A	Router A		Router B	Host B
192.168.1.2/24	S0 = 20.0.0.1/8		S1 = 30.0.0.1/8	172.16.0.2/24
	E0 = 192.168.1.1/24		E0 = 172.16.0.1/16	

Host A and Host B are both using RFC 1918-compliant private addresses that are not routable on the Internet.

The initial configurations are shown in Example 5-1 and Example 5-2.

Example 5-1   *Router A Initial Configuration*

```
Building configuration...

Current configuration:
!
version 12.0
service timestamps debug uptime
service timestamps log uptime
no service password-encryption
!
hostname RouterA
!
!
ip subnet-zero
!
!
interface Ethernet0
 ip address 192.168.1.1 255.255.255.0
 no ip directed-broadcast
!
interface Serial0
 ip address 20.0.0.1 255.0.0.0
 no ip directed-broadcast
 no ip mroute-cache
!
interface Serial1
 no ip address
 no ip directed-broadcast
 shutdown
!
ip classless
ip route 0.0.0.0 0.0.0.0 Serial0
!
!
!
line con 0
 exec-timeout 0 0
 transport input none
line aux 0
line vty 0 4
!
end
```

Example 5-2 shows the Router B initial configuration.

Example 5-2   *Router B Initial Configuration*

```
Building configuration...

Current configuration:
!
version 12.0
service timestamps debug uptime
service timestamps log uptime
no service password-encryption
!
hostname RouterB
!
!
ip subnet-zero
!
!
!
!
!
interface Ethernet0
 ip address 172.16.0.1 255.255.0.0
 no ip directed-broadcast
!
interface Ethernet1
 no ip address
 no ip directed-broadcast
 shutdown
!
interface Serial0
 no ip address
 no ip directed-broadcast
 no ip mroute-cache
 shutdown
 no fair-queue
!
interface Serial1
 ip address 30.0.0.1 255.0.0.0
 no ip directed-broadcast
!
ip classless
ip route 0.0.0.0 0.0.0.0 Serial1
!
!
!
line con 0
 exec-timeout 0 0
 transport input none
line aux 0
line vty 0 4
!
end
```

Because both of these routers also provide access to the public Internet and act as the single egress point from the network, they both have static default routes pointing to their respective Serial interfaces.

Both of the routers' Serial interfaces are publicly addressed and connected. Before starting the IPSec configuration, you have to ensure that these routers can communicate with each other. For the IPSec peer relationship to be formed, Layer 3 communication must be established between both peers. The best way to check this is to ping the remote IPSec peer from the local IPSec peer at each end. This is shown in Example 5-3.

Example 5-3   *Pinging the Remote IPSec Peer from the Local IPSec Peer at Each End*

```
RouterA#ping 30.0.0.1

Type escape sequence to abort.
Sending 5, 100-byte ICMP Echos to 30.0.0.1, timeout is 2 seconds:
!!!!!
Success rate is 100 percent (5/5), round-trip min/avg/max = 4/6/8 ms

RouterB#ping 20.0.0.1

Type escape sequence to abort.
Sending 5, 100-byte ICMP Echos to 20.0.0.1, timeout is 2 seconds:
!!!!!
Success rate is 100 percent (5/5), round-trip min/avg/max = 4/5/8 ms
```

You can see from the results in Example 5-3 that Router A can ping the Serial interface of Router B and vice versa. This confirms that communication between these peers exists.

Configuring IPSec

Now that you have a working routing configuration, you will need to add the IPSec components to get to a stage where you have a fully working IPSec configuration. Once you have reached this point in this example, you will introduce errors to the configuration and compare the results.

The IPSec configurations are as shown in Example 5-4 and Example 5-5.

Example 5-4   *Router A IPSec Configuration*

```
crypto isakmp policy 10
 authentication pre-share
crypto isakmp key thisisaverysecurekey address 30.0.0.1
!
!
crypto ipsec transform-set MySet esp-des esp-md5-hmac
!
!
crypto map MyMap 10 ipsec-isakmp
 set peer 30.0.0.1
```

Example 5-4 *Router A IPSec Configuration (Continued)*

```
 set transform-set MySet
 match address 100
 !
interface Serial0
 ip address 20.0.0.1 255.0.0.0
 no ip directed-broadcast
 no ip mroute-cache
 crypto map MyMap
 !
access-list 100 permit ip 192.168.1.0 0.0.0.255 172.16.0.0 0.0.255.255
```

Example 5-5 shows the Router B IPSec configuration.

Example 5-5 *Router B IPSec Configuration*

```
crypto isakmp policy 10
 authentication pre-share
crypto isakmp key thisisaverysecurekey address 20.0.0.1
 !
 !
crypto ipsec transform-set MySet esp-des esp-md5-hmac
 !
 !
crypto map MyMap 10 ipsec-isakmp
 set peer 20.0.0.1
 set transform-set MySet
 match address 100
 !
interface Serial1
 ip address 30.0.0.1 255.0.0.0
 no ip directed-broadcast
 crypto map MyMap
 !
access-list 100 permit ip 172.16.0.0 0.0.255.255 192.168.1.0 0.0.0.255
```

Refer to Chapters 3 and 4 on how to configure IPSec on Cisco IOS if you require an explanation of any of the configuration lines.

With this configuration in the routers, you can now verify that Host A can successfully ping Host B using the VPN over the public Internet.

show Commands

In this working state, you will need to look at the output of a few **show** commands to ascertain what a normal configuration will show.

There are numerous **show** commands that can be used to verify IPSec operation. These **show** commands can be split into two sections:

- **Display show commands**—Display information about the IPSec configuration
- **Information show commands**—Display information about the state of the IPSec connections on the router

Display **show** Commands

In this section you will look at the output of three display **show** commands. These are **show crypto ipsec transform-set**, **show crypto map**, and **show crypto isakmp policy**. The output shown is from Router A. The output from Router B is identical for the **show crypto ipsec transform-set** and **show crypto isakmp policy** commands; it must be in order for an IPSec peer to be established. The **show crypto map** output for Router B will reflect Router A as its peer.

The **show** command in Example 5-6 displays the configured IPSec transform set. Note that the example is using esp-des and esp-md5-hmac within the transform set. The default mode for IPSec is tunnel.

Example 5-6   **show crypto ipsec transform-set** *Output*

```
RouterA#show crypto ipsec transform-set
Transform set MySet: { esp-des esp-md5-hmac  }
   will negotiate = { Tunnel,  },
```

The output in Example 5-7 shows the configured crypto map that is called MyMap. The information here appertains to the remote IPSec peer and also to the access list that controls the encryption of the IPSec traffic.

Example 5-7   **show crypto map** *Output*

```
RouterA#show crypto map
Crypto Map "MyMap" 10 ipsec-isakmp
        Peer = 30.0.0.1
        Extended IP access list 100
            access-list 100 permit ip 192.168.1.0 0.0.0.255 172.16.0.0 0.0.255.255
        Current peer: 30.0.0.1
        Security association lifetime: 4608000 kilobytes/3600 seconds
        PFS (Y/N): N
        Transform sets={ MySet, }
```

In Example 5-8, you can see the default policy (priority 65535) and the configured ISAKMP policy of 10. You can see that the example uses preshared keys and Diffie-Hellman group 1.

Example 5-8   **show crypto isakmp policy** *Output*

```
RouterA#show crypto isakmp policy
Protection suite of priority 10
        encryption algorithm:   DES - Data Encryption Standard (56 bit keys).
        hash algorithm:         Secure Hash Standard
        authentication method:  Pre-Shared Key
        Diffie-Hellman group:   #1 (768 bit)
        lifetime:               86400 seconds, no volume limit
Default protection suite
        encryption algorithm:   DES - Data Encryption Standard (56 bit keys).
        hash algorithm:         Secure Hash Standard
        authentication method:  Rivest-Shamir-Adleman Signature
        Diffie-Hellman group:   #1 (768 bit)
        lifetime:               86400 seconds, no volume limit
```

Information **show** Commands

Once data that matches the IPSec access list has passed the interface with the crypto map applied to it, the VPN will be established. At this point, some additional commands can be entered that show various states of the IPSec components. The commands covered in this section are **show crypto engine connections active** and **show crypto ipsec sa**. For this test, you will initiate a ping from Host A to Host B and look at the commands on Router B.

The output in Example 5-9 shows the two IPSec connections, one inbound (Decrypt) and one outbound (Encrypt). These are linked with the security associations (SAs) that can be seen in the output from the **show crypto ipsec sa** command. Seven hundred and forty-nine packets have been both encrypted and decrypted. This will be the ICMP echo and echo replies that the hosts originated.

Example 5-9   **show crypto engine connections active** *Output*

```
RouterB#show crypto engine connections active

  ID Interface      IP-Address     State  Algorithm          Encrypt  Decrypt
   1 <none>         <none>         set    DES_56_CBC               0        0
   8 Serial1        30.0.0.1       set    HMAC_MD5+DES_56_CB       0      749
   9 Serial1        30.0.0.1       set    HMAC_MD5+DES_56_CB     749        0

Crypto adjacency count : Lock: 0, Unlock: 0
```

Example 5-10 displays the output of the **show crypto ipsec sa** command. Quite a lot of information is presented by this command. The start of the command shows the interface and crypto map name that is associated with the interface. Then the inbound and outbound SAs are shown. These are either Authentication Header (AH) or Encapsulating Security

Payload (ESP) SAs. In this case, because only ESP is used, there are no AH inbound or outbound SAs.

Example 5-10 show crypto ipsec sa *Output*

```
RouterB#show crypto ipsec sa

interface: Serial1
    Crypto map tag: MyMap, local addr. 30.0.0.1

   local  ident (addr/mask/prot/port): (172.16.0.0/255.255.0.0/0/0)
   remote ident (addr/mask/prot/port): (192.168.1.0/255.255.255.0/0/0)
   current_peer: 20.0.0.1
     PERMIT, flags={origin_is_acl,}
    #pkts encaps: 1248, #pkts encrypt: 1248, #pkts digest 1248
    #pkts decaps: 1248, #pkts decrypt: 1248, #pkts verify 1248
    #send errors 1, #recv errors 0

    local crypto endpt.: 30.0.0.1, remote crypto endpt.: 20.0.0.1
    path mtu 1500, media mtu 1500
    current outbound spi: 1DE813F8

    inbound esp sas:
     spi: 0x107624CB(276178123)
       transform: esp-des esp-md5-hmac ,
       in use settings ={Tunnel, }
       slot: 0, conn id: 8, crypto map: MyMap
       sa timing: remaining key lifetime (k/sec): (4607912/3423)
       IV size: 8 bytes
       replay detection support: Y


    inbound ah sas:


    outbound esp sas:
     spi: 0x1DE813F8(501748728)
       transform: esp-des esp-md5-hmac ,
       in use settings ={Tunnel, }
       slot: 0, conn id: 9, crypto map: MyMap
       sa timing: remaining key lifetime (k/sec): (4607912/3423)
       IV size: 8 bytes
       replay detection support: Y


    outbound ah sas:
```

You can also see next to the PERMIT statement that it was a condition met by an access control list (ACL) that initiated the IPSec connection.

Troubleshooting the IPSec Configuration

In the previous section, you saw how to successfully configure an IPSec VPN between Router A and Router B. This was to provide a connection between Host A and Host B over the public Internet. You then ran various **show** commands and saw what to look for in a working configuration. Now that you have a working configuration, you have a platform to introduce planned errors and watch the results.

This section first covers the most common errors associated with the configuration of IPSec on Cisco IOS.

- Incompatible Internet Security Association Key Management Protocol (ISAKMP) policies
- Differing preshared keys between the IPSec peers
- Incorrect IPSec access lists
- Wrong crypto map placement
- Routing issues

Incompatible ISAKMP Policies

The ISAKMP policy on each of the IPSec peers must match in order for the IPSec VPN to be established.

Take a look at the ISAKMP policies for Router A and Router B. The command to display the ISAKMP policy is **show crypto isakmp policy**. Example 5-11 shows the ISAKMP policies for Router A.

Example 5-11 *ISAKMP policies for Router A*

```
RouterA#show crypto isakmp policy
Protection suite of priority 10
        encryption algorithm:   DES - Data Encryption Standard (56 bit keys).
        hash algorithm:         Secure Hash Standard
        authentication method:  Pre-Shared Key
        Diffie-Hellman group:   #1 (768 bit)
        lifetime:               86400 seconds, no volume limit
Default protection suite
        encryption algorithm:   DES - Data Encryption Standard (56 bit keys).
        hash algorithm:         Secure Hash Standard
        authentication method:  Rivest-Shamir-Adleman Signature
        Diffie-Hellman group:   #1 (768 bit)
        lifetime:               86400 seconds, no volume limit
```

Example 5-12 shows the ISAKMP policies for Router B.

Example 5-12 *ISAKMP policies for Router B*

```
RouterB#show crypto isakmp policy
Protection suite of priority 10
        encryption algorithm:    DES - Data Encryption Standard (56 bit keys).
        hash algorithm:          Secure Hash Standard
        authentication method:   Pre-Shared Key
        Diffie-Hellman group:    #1 (768 bit)
        lifetime:                86400 seconds, no volume limit
Default protection suite
        encryption algorithm:    DES - Data Encryption Standard (56 bit keys).
        hash algorithm:          Secure Hash Standard
        authentication method:   Rivest-Shamir-Adleman Signature
        Diffie-Hellman group:    #1 (768 bit)
        lifetime:                86400 seconds, no volume limit
```

You can see from the output in Example 5-11 and Example 5-12 that both of these routers have two ISAKMP policies, or protection suites. The first has a priority of 10, and the default has a priority of 65535, although this value is not shown. You can also see that the values for the priority 10 suite all match between Routers A and B. This is essential for ISAKMP negotiation.

The values controlled by the ISAKMP policy are

- Encryption algorithm
- Hash algorithm
- Authentication method
- Diffie-Hellman group
- SA lifetime

All of these values can be set from the ISAKMP configuration mode on the Cisco IOS router. The output in Example 5-13 shows you the available commands from the ISAKMP configuration mode on the router.

Example 5-13 *ISAKMP Commands*

```
RouterA(config)# crypto isakmp policy 10
RouterA(config-isakmp)#?
ISAKMP commands:
  authentication  Set authentication method for protection suite
  default         Set a command to its defaults
  encryption      Set encryption algorithm for protection suite
  exit            Exit from ISAKMP protection suite configuration mode
  group           Set the Diffie-Hellman group
  hash            Set hash algorithm for protection suite
  lifetime        Set lifetime for ISAKMP security association
  no              Negate a command or set its defaults
```

Like the preceding **show** commands, the command **debug crypto isakmp** is of great use when troubleshooting ISAKMP issues. This command actually displays the full ISAKMP exchange as it occurs in the router. The full debug output for a ping from the E0 Interface of Router A to the E0 interface of Router B is shown in Example 5-14.

Example 5-14 *Output of* **debug crypto isakmp**

```
00:42:43: ISAKMP (4): beginning Main Mode exchange
00:42:43: ISAKMP (4): sending packet to 30.0.0.1 (I) MM_NO_STATE.
00:42:44: ISAKMP (4): received packet from 30.0.0.1 (I) MM_NO_STATE
00:42:44: ISAKMP (4): processing SA payload. message ID = 0
00:42:44: ISAKMP (4): Checking ISAKMP transform 1 against priority 10 policy
00:42:44: ISAKMP:       encryption DES-CBC
00:42:44: ISAKMP:       hash SHA
00:42:44: ISAKMP:       default group 1
00:42:44: ISAKMP:       auth pre-share
00:42:44: ISAKMP (4): atts are acceptable. Next payload is 0
00:42:46: ISAKMP (4): SA is doing pre-shared key authentication using id
      type ID_IPV.4_ADDR
00:42:46: ISAKMP (4): sending packet to 30.0.0.1 (I) MM_SA_SETUP.
00:42:48: ISAKMP (4): received packet from 30.0.0.1 (I) MM_SA_SETUP
00:42:48: ISAKMP (4): processing KE payload. message ID = 0
00:42:50: ISAKMP (4): processing NONCE payload. message ID = 0
00:42:50: ISAKMP (4): SKEYID state generated
00:42:50: ISAKMP (4): processing vendor id payload
00:42:50: ISAKMP (4): speaking to another IOS box!
00:42:50: ISAKMP (4): ID payload
        next-payload : 8
        type         : 1
        protocol     : 17
        port         : 500
        length       : 8
00:42:50: ISAKMP (4): Total payload length: 12
00:42:50: ISAKMP (4): sending packet to 30.0.0.1 (I) MM_KEY_EXCH
00:42:50: ISAKMP (4): received packet from 30.0.0.1 (I) MM_KEY_EXCH
00:42:50: ISAKMP (4): processing ID payload. message ID = 0
00:42:50: ISAKMP (4): processing HASH payload. message ID = 0
00:42:50: ISAKMP (4): SA has been authenticated with 30.0.0.1
00:42:50: ISAKMP (4): beginning Quick Mode exchange, M-ID of 1397342770
00:42:50: ISAKMP (4): sending packet to 30.0.0.1 (I) QM_IDLE
00:42:51: ISAKMP (4): received packet from 30.0.0.1 (I) QM_IDLE
00:42:51: ISAKMP (4): processing SA payload. message ID = 1397342770
00:42:51: ISAKMP (4): Checking IPSec proposal 1
00:42:51: ISAKMP: transform 1, ESP_DES
00:42:51: ISAKMP:    attributes in transform:
00:42:51: ISAKMP:        encaps is 1
00:42:51: ISAKMP:        SA life type in seconds
00:42:51: ISAKMP:        SA life duration (basic) of 3600
00:42:51: ISAKMP:        SA life type in kilobytes
00:42:51: ISAKMP:        SA life duration (VPI) of  0x0 0x46 0x50 0x0
00:42:51: ISAKMP:        authenticator is HMAC-MD5
00:42:51: ISAKMP (4): atts are acceptable.
00:42:51: ISAKMP (4): processing NONCE payload. message ID = 1397342770
```

continues

Example 5-14 *Output of* **debug crypto isakmp** *(Continued)*

```
00:42:51: ISAKMP (4): processing ID payload. message ID = 1397342770
00:42:51: ISAKMP (4): unknown error extracting ID
00:42:51: ISAKMP (4): processing ID payload. message ID = 1397342770
00:42:51: ISAKMP (4): unknown error extracting ID
00:42:51: ISAKMP (4): Creating IPSec SAs
00:42:51:           inbound SA from 30.0.0.1        to 20.0.0.1
        (proxy 172.16.0.0      to 192.168.1.0    )
00:42:51:           has spi 167445490 and conn_id 5 and flags 4
00:42:51:           lifetime of 3600 seconds
00:42:51:           lifetime of 4608000 kilobytes
00:42:51:           outbound SA from 20.0.0.1        to 30.0.0.1
        (proxy 192.168.1.0     to 172.16.0.0     )
00:42:51:           has spi 102963262 and conn_id 6 and flags 4
00:42:51:           lifetime of 3600 seconds
00:42:51:           lifetime of 4608000 kilobytes
00:42:51: ISAKMP (4): sending packet to 30.0.0.1 (I) QM_IDLE
```

From the output in Example 5-14, notice the shaded portion. This shaded portion shows that the ISAKMP values are acceptable, and then the router continues with the ISAKMP negotiation process.

So this is what the debug output looks like in a working configuration. But what if you change a value in the ISAKMP policy?

In this example, you will change the hash value from the default SHA to MD5 on Router A and observe the output from the **debug crypto isakmp** command.

First, look at the newly configured ISAKMP policy on Router A. This can be seen in Example 5-15.

Example 5-15 **show crypto isakmp policy**

```
RouterA#show crypto isakmp policy
Protection suite of priority 10
        encryption algorithm:   DES - Data Encryption Standard (56 bit keys).
        hash algorithm:         Message Digest 5
        authentication method:  Pre-Shared Key
        Diffie-Hellman group:   #1 (768 bit)
        lifetime:               86400 seconds, no volume limit
Default protection suite
        encryption algorithm:   DES - Data Encryption Standard (56 bit keys).
        hash algorithm:         Secure Hash Standard
        authentication method:  Rivest-Shamir-Adleman Signature
        Diffie-Hellman group:   #1 (768 bit)
        lifetime:               86400 seconds, no volume limit
```

The shaded portion shows that the hash algorithm has been changed from SHA to MD5. Now if you carry out the same ping, router to router, as before, the debug output will look like that shown in Example 5-16.

Example 5-16 *ISAKMP Debug Output*

```
01:43:48: ISAKMP (7): beginning Main Mode exchange
01:43:48: ISAKMP (7): sending packet to 30.0.0.1 (I) MM_NO_STATE
01:43:48: ISAKMP (7): received packet from 30.0.0.1 (I) MM_NO_STATE
01:43:48: %CRYPTO-6-IKMP_MODE_FAILURE: Processing of Informational
    mode failed with peer at 30.0.0.1
```

You can clearly see from this debug output that there was a failure in the ISAKMP negotiation.

Differing Preshared Keys Between the IPSec Peers

The preshared secret keys must be *exactly* the same on both of the IPSec peers. These keys are compared during the ISAKMP phase one authentication. There are two steps to check for here. The first step is to ensure that both routers are using preshared authentication in their ISAKMP policies. The second step is to ensure that the preshared keys match.

You can ensure that both routers are using preshared authentication in their ISAKMP policies with the **show crypto isakmp** command. The output in Example 5-17 and Example 5-18 is the result of the aforementioned command on both Routers A and B.

Example 5-17 show crypto isakmp *Output for Router A*

```
RouterA#show crypto isakmp policy
Protection suite of priority 10
        encryption algorithm:   DES - Data Encryption Standard (56 bit keys).
        hash algorithm:         Secure Hash Standard
        authentication method:  Pre-Shared Key
        Diffie-Hellman group:   #1 (768 bit)
        lifetime:               86400 seconds, no volume limit
Default protection suite
        encryption algorithm:   DES - Data Encryption Standard (56 bit keys).
        hash algorithm:         Secure Hash Standard
        authentication method:  Rivest-Shamir-Adleman Signature
        Diffie-Hellman group:   #1 (768 bit)
        lifetime:               86400 seconds, no volume limit
```

Example 5-18 shows the **show crypto isakmp** output for Router B.

Example 5-18 show crypto isakmp *Output for Router B*

```
RouterB#show crypto isakmp policy
Protection suite of priority 10
        encryption algorithm:   DES - Data Encryption Standard (56 bit keys).
        hash algorithm:         Secure Hash Standard
        authentication method:  Pre-Shared Key
        Diffie-Hellman group:   #1 (768 bit)
        lifetime:               86400 seconds, no volume limit
Default protection suite
        encryption algorithm:   DES - Data Encryption Standard (56 bit keys).
        hash algorithm:         Secure Hash Standard
        authentication method:  Rivest-Shamir-Adleman Signature
        Diffie-Hellman group:   #1 (768 bit)
        lifetime:               86400 seconds, no volume limit
```

Check that the authentication method on both of the routers is set to Preshared Key; you can see from Example 5-17 and Example 5-18 that it is. If the authentication methods do not match between the routers, then the ISAKMP negotiation will fail, as outlined in the previous section.

You know that the routers are both using preshared keys as their authentication method. Now look at the preshared keys on both routers with the **show crypto isakmp key** command, as shown in Example 5-19 and Example 5-20.

Example 5-19 show crypto isakmp key *Output for Router A*

```
RouterA#show crypto isakmp key
Hostname/Address        Preshared Key
30.0.0.1                thisisaverysecurekey
```

Example 5-20 shows the output for Router B.

Example 5-20 show crypto isakmp key *Output for Router B*

```
RouterB#show crypto isakmp key
Hostname/Address        Preshared Key
20.0.0.1                thisisaverysecurekey
```

Example 5-19 and Example 5-20 show the preshared keys for both Router A and Router B. You can see that both of these match. Now change the key value for Router A to wrongkey. Example 5-21 is the new output on Router A of the **show crypto isakmp key** command.

Example 5-21 show crypto isakmp key

```
RouterA#show crypto isakmp key
Hostname/Address        Preshared Key
30.0.0.1                wrongkey
```

Example 5-21 shows that the preshared key for the IPSec peer 30.0.0.1 is now wrongkey.

After this configuration change, when you try to ping from Host A to Host B, Router A will display the following debug message:

```
%CRYPTO-4-IKMP_BAD_MESSAGE: IKE message from 30.0.0.1 failed its
    sanity check or is malformed
```

This informs you that the preshared keys have not matched.

Incorrect IPSec Access Lists

The IPSec access list triggers the VPN to be set up between the IPSec peers. This access list operates in a very similar manner to an access list that is used for dial-on-demand routing (DDR). With DDR, interesting traffic (as defined by the access list) causes the BRI interface to be raised and the ISDN call to be placed. The same is true for the IPSec access list. In the initial state, traffic that meets the access list initiates the IPSec process. Once the IPSec connection is established, only traffic that meets the IPSec access list will be encrypted and delivered through the IPSec tunnel. This is a very important point to remember. It is where the IPSec access list differs from the DDR access list.

In the example used in this chapter, you have an access list on both Router A and Router B. These access lists are mirrors of each other. The source in the Router A access list is the destination on the Router B access list, and vice versa. The access lists encrypt anything from the local Ethernet network to the remote Ethernet network.

To introduce an error, you could change the IPSec access list on Router A to have an incorrect source address. Then if you ping from Host A to Host B, the traffic will not kick off the IPSec process and will not be routable to the destination.

The current IPSec access list on Router A is as follows:

```
RouterA#show ip access-list
Extended IP access list 100
    permit ip 192.168.1.0 0.0.0.255 172.16.0.0 0.0.255.255
```

This access lists encrypts traffic from the 192.168.1.0/24 network that is destined for the 172.16.0.0/16 network. If you make a subtle change to this access list, you will break the IPSec process. Remove the existing access list and add the following line of configuration:

```
RouterA(config)#access-list 100 permit ip 192.168.2.0 0.0.0.255 172.16.0.0
    0.0.255.255
```

Note that this will encrypt traffic from the 192.168.2.0/24 network and not the original 192.168.1.0/24 network. After making this change, Host A attempts to ping Host B. Obviously, this fails.

If you are ever faced with a real-world problem similar to this, the first step should always be to ascertain whether the VPN is established between the IPSec peers. There are various ways to accomplish this on a Cisco IOS router, but the easiest way is to use the **show crypto engine connections active** command. This command displays the current state of the IPSec connections, if any. Running this command on Router A has the following result:

```
RouterA#show crypto engine connections active

  ID Interface      IP-Address      State  Algorithm       Encrypt  Decrypt

Crypto adjacency count : Lock: 0, Unlock: 0
```

You can see from the preceding output that there are no active IPSec connections. If you can ascertain that relevant traffic has passed the connection that should start the IPSec process, the problem points to the IPSec access list. A simple sanity check of the IPSec access list should be enough to remedy the problem.

Wrong Crypto Map Placement

On the VPN terminating interface, you have to apply the crypto map. For example, to apply crypto map MyMap to the Serial 0 interface, the command would be:

```
RouterA(config-if)#crypto map mymap
```

This command will make the interface a VPN termination point. Any traffic leaving this interface will be checked against the IPSec access list. If the traffic matches the IPSec access list, it will be encrypted to the standard defined in the related transform set and delivered to the IPSec peer as defined in the crypto map. A useful command for looking at the crypto map applied to an interface is **show crypto map interface serial 0**. The output in Example 5-22 shows this command run on Router A.

Example 5-22 show crypto map interface serial 0 *Output for Router A*

```
RouterA#show crypto map interface serial 0
Crypto Map "MyMap" 10 ipsec-isakmp
        Peer = 30.0.0.1
        Extended IP access list 100
            access-list 100 permit ip 192.168.1.0 0.0.0.255 172.16.0.0 0.0.255.255
        Current peer: 30.0.0.1
        Security association lifetime: 4608000 kilobytes/3600 seconds
        PFS (Y/N): N
        Transform sets={ MySet, }
```

You can see from the output in Example 5-22 that crypto map MyMap is applied to the Serial 0 interface. The output of this command also shows you the IPSec access list, the IPSec peer, the SA settings, the perfect forward secrecy (PFS) status, and the related transform set.

If there is a problem with IPSec traffic, and you have confirmed that the IPSec access list is correct, the crypto map placement is a good next step to check. If the crypto map is not applied to the outbound interface, traffic will never get encrypted for IPSec to forward it to its peer.

NOTE	If there are physical as well as logical interfaces involved in carrying outgoing traffic, the crypto map needs to be applied to both.

Routing Issues

There are two routing issues that have to be addressed. Both of these issues can cause problems that result in the failure of the IPSec process. The first routing issue concerns routing to the IPSec peer. The second routing issue concerns routing the required packets to the interface with the crypto map applied.

Layer 3 communications have to be established between the IPSec peers. This was covered earlier in this chapter; you saw that a simple ping between the IPSec peers is adequate to confirm this. If the IPSec peers cannot establish Layer 3 communications, the IPSec process will never be complete and the peers will never be adjacent to each other. In the example based on Figure 5-1, there are two routers that are publicly addressed and connected over the public Internet. In this instance, both peers should be able to ping each other on the outside (Internet-connected) interface.

The other routing issue is related to the delivery of the packets from the local router to the remote network over the IPSec tunnel. Take Figure 5-1 as an example. You can see that Host A is on network 192.168.1.0/24 and Host B is on the 172.16.0.0/16 network. For Host A to communicate to Host B, a valid route has to exist in the IP routing table of Router A to the Host B network address. This follows basic IP routing principles. Looking at the IP routing table in Example 5-23, you can see that a default route exists out of the Serial 0 interface.

Example 5-23 *show ip route*

```
RouterA#show ip route
Codes: C - connected, S - static, I - IGRP, R - RIP, M - mobile, B - BGP
       D - EIGRP, EX - EIGRP external, O - OSPF, IA - OSPF inter area
       N1 - OSPF NSSA external type 1, N2 - OSPF NSSA external type 2
       E1 - OSPF external type 1, E2 - OSPF external type 2, E - EGP
       i - IS-IS, L1 - IS-IS level-1, L2 - IS-IS level-2, * - candidate default
       U - per-user static route, o - ODR

Gateway of last resort is 0.0.0.0 to network 0.0.0.0

C    20.0.0.0/8 is directly connected, Serial0
C    192.168.1.0/24 is directly connected, Ethernet0
S*   0.0.0.0/0 is directly connected, Serial0
```

Because you are using a static default route, this should not cause a problem with the routing of the packets. Host A will send a packet with source address of 192.168.1.2 and the destination address of 172.16.0.2. Router A does not have a specific route for the 172.16.0.0/16 network, but the default route will direct it at the Serial 0 interface. The crypto map is applied to the Serial 0 interface, and the traffic matches the IPSec access list so it gets encrypted and tunneled to the destination.

The important part to remember is that you have to ensure the router will forward the packet to the interface where the crypto map exists. A default route or a specific route for the remote network will normally suffice in this situation.

Summary

This chapter covered basic implementation of IPSec on Cisco IOS between two sites over the Internet. You saw how to get the VPN working, and then, by introducing errors into the configuration, you saw common problems that can occur. The chapter covered the relevant commands that can be used on the router to troubleshoot the problems that were introduced. These troubleshooting commands and techniques can be used in real-world troubleshooting scenarios.

Review Questions

1   What command will display the configured ISAKMP preshared keys on the Cisco IOS router?

2   Which values are compared during the main mode exchange?

3   You are using IPSec over a GRE Tunnel. The GRE Tunnel has the Serial 0 interface set as the tunnel source. Where do you have to apply the relevant crypto map?

4   You apply a crypto map to an interface. What happens to traffic that does not match the IPSec access list associated with the crypto map?

5   What is the priority value of the default ISAKMP policy?

6   You have a problem with the VPN establishment on a Cisco router where the error message mentions that the sanity check has failed. What is the probable cause of this?

7   Within the ISAKMP policy, what is the default hash algorithm?

8   How do you display real-time information on your router about the state of the ISAKMP negotiation?

9 What command would apply the crypto map called MyMap to the Serial 0 interface? Assume you are in interface configuration mode.

10 Which command produces the following output?

```
ID Interface        IP-Address        State  Algorithm              Encrypt  Decrypt
   1 <none>          <none>            set    DES_56_CBC                   0        0
   8 Serial1         30.0.0.1          set    HMAC_MD5+DES_56_CB           0      749
   9 Serial1         30.0.0.1          set    HMAC_MD5+DES_56_CB         749        0

Crypto adjacency count : Lock: 0, Unlock: 0
```

Cisco PIX Firewall VPNs

CHAPTER 6

Configuring the Cisco PIX Firewall for Preshared Keys Site-to-Site

This chapter covers how to configure a Cisco Secure PIX Firewall using preshared key support for Internet Protocol Security (IPSec). After presenting an overview of the configuration process, the chapter shows you each major step of the configuration.

This chapter includes the following topics:

- Configuring IPSec encryption tasks
- Task 1: Prepare for IPSec
- Task 2: Configure IKE
- Task 3: Configure IPSec
- Task 4: Test and verify VPN configuration

Configuring IPSec Encryption Tasks

This chapter covers configuring the PIX Firewall for IPSec to use preshared keys for authentication. This section presents an overview of the major tasks you will have to perform to configure a PIX Firewall for IPSec preshared keys.

To provide more detail, the overall tasks used to configure preshared key support for IPSec encryption on the PIX Firewall are summarized here. Subsequent sections of this chapter discuss each configuration task in greater detail. The following are the major tasks:

- **Task 1: Prepare for configuring virtual private network (VPN) support**—This task consists of five steps to determine IPSec policies, ensure that the network works, and ensure that the PIX Firewall can support IPSec.

- **Task 2: Configure Internet Key Exchange (IKE) parameters**—This task consists of several configuration steps that ensure that IKE can set up secure channels to desired IPSec peers. Then IKE can set up IPSec security associations (SAs), enabling IPSec sessions.

- **Task 3: Configure IPSec parameters**—This task consists of several configuration steps that specify IPSec SA parameters between peers and set global IPSec values.

- **Task 4: Test and verify VPN configuration**—After you configure IPSec, you will need to verify that you have configured it correctly and ensure that it works.

Task 1: Prepare for IPSec

Successful implementation of an IPSec network requires advance preparation before beginning configuration of individual PIX Firewalls. This section outlines how to determine network design details to configure a PIX Firewall for IPSec preshared key support.

Configuring IPSec encryption can be complicated. You must plan in advance if you desire to configure IPSec encryption correctly the first time and minimize misconfiguration. You should begin this task by defining the IPSec security policy based on the overall company security policy. Some planning steps follow:

Step 1   **Determine IKE (IKE phase one) policy**—Determine the IKE policies between peers based on the number and location of IPSec peers.

Step 2   **Determine IPSec (IKE phase two) policy**—Identify IPSec peer details, such as IP addresses and IPSec modes. You then configure crypto maps to gather all IPSec policy details.

Step 3   **Check the current configuration**—Use the **write terminal**, **show isakmp [policy]**, **show crypto map**, and many other **show** commands, which are covered later in this chapter.

Step 4   **Ensure that the network works without encryption**—Ensure that basic connectivity has been achieved between IPSec peers using the desired IP services before configuring PIX Firewall IPSec. You can use the **ping** command to check basic connectivity.

Step 5   **Ensure access lists are compatible with IPSec**—Ensure that perimeter routers and the PIX Firewall outside interfaces permit IPSec traffic. Implicitly permit IPSec packets to bypass PIX Firewall access lists and conduits. In this step, you need to enter the **show access-lists** command.

These steps for the Cisco Secure PIX Firewall are identical to the configuration for the Cisco IOS Firewall, as outlined in Chapter 3, "Configuring Cisco IOS Routers for Preshared Keys Site-to-Site."

Task 2: Configure IKE

The next major task in configuring the PIX Firewall is to configure the IKE parameters gathered earlier. This section presents the steps used to configure IKE policies.

Configuring IKE consists of the following essential steps and commands:

Step 1   Enable or disable IKE with the **isakmp enable** command.

Step 2   Create IKE policies with the **isakmp policy** command.

Step 3   Configure preshared keys with the **isakmp key** command.

Step 4   Verify IKE configuration with the **show isakmp** [**policy**] command.

Step 1: Enable or Disable IKE

Enable or disable IKE (Internet Security Association Key Management Protocol [ISAKMP]) negotiation for authentication and key exchange:

```
pixfirewall(config)# isakmp enable interface-name
```

Specify the PIX Firewall interface on which the IPSec peer will communicate. IKE is enabled by default and for individual PIX Firewall interfaces.

Use the **no isakmp enable** *interface-name* command to disable IKE.

You might wish to disable IKE on interfaces that do not terminate IKE and IPSec to prevent possible denial-of-service attacks on those interfaces.

NOTE   PIX Firewall version 5.0 software supports IPSec termination on the outside interface only. PIX Firewall version 5.1 and later software supports IPSec termination on any interface.

Step 2: Create IKE Policies

The next major step in configuring Cisco IOS ISAKMP support is to define a suite of IKE policies. The goal of defining a suite of IKE policies is to establish ISAKMP peering between two IPSec endpoints. Use the IKE policy details gathered during the planning task.

Use the **isakmp policy** command to define an IKE policy. IKE policies define a set of parameters used during the IKE negotiation.

Step 1   Identify the policy with a unique priority number.

```
pixfirewall(config)# isakmp policy priority
```

Step 2   Specify the encryption algorithm. The default is **des**.

```
pixfirewall(config)# isakmp policy priority encryption [des | 3des]
```

Step 3   Specify the hash algorithm. The default is **sha**.

```
pixfirewall(config)# isakmp policy priority hash [md5 | sha]
```

Step 4   Specify the authentication method.

```
pixfirewall(config)# isakmp policy priority authentication [pre-share |
rsa-sig]
```

NOTE   If you wish to specify authentication using preshared keys, you must use the **preshare**
        authentication method.

        Step 5 Specify the Diffie-Hellman group identifier. The default is **group 1**.

           `pixfirewall(config)# `**`isakmp policy `**`priority `**`group 1 | 2`**

        Step 6 Specify the IKE SA's lifetime. The default is **86400**.

           `pixfirewall(config)# `**`isakmp policy `**`priority `**`lifetime `**`seconds`

NOTE   PIX Firewall software has preset default values. If you enter a default value for a given
        policy parameter, it will not be written in the configuration. If you do not specify a value
        for a given policy parameter, the default value is assigned. You can observe configured and
        default values with the **show isakmp policy** command.

Step 3: Configure Preshared Keys

IPSec peers authenticate each other during ISAKMP negotiations using the preshared key
and the ISAKMP identity. The identity can be either the PIX Firewall's IP address or its
host name. Configure the IKE preshared key by completing the following substeps:

        Step 1 Specify the ISAKMP identity mode as either *address* or *hostname*
(optional).

           `pixfirewall(config)# `**`isakmp identity {address | hostname}`**

           The default value is to use the IP address of the peer as the identity.

           Choose **hostname** if the host name is specified in the **isakmp key**
command.

           Use this setting consistently across peers using preshared keys.

        Step 2 Specify name-to-address mapping (optional).

           `pixfirewall(config)# `**`name `**`ip_address name`

           The **name** command defines name-to-address mapping.

           This command is not necessary if the destination host names are already
mapped in a Domain Name System (DNS) server.

        Step 3 Specify the preshared key.

           `pixfirewall(config)# `**`isakmp key `**`keystring `**`address `**`peer-address `[`netmask`]

The **isakmp key** command assigns a keystring and the peer address.

The preshared key string must be identical at both peers.

You can specify the peer address as the host or wildcard address.

keystring is any combination of alphanumeric characters up to 128 bytes. This preshared key must be identical at both peers.

peer-address and *netmask* should point to the IP address of the IPSec peer. A wildcard peer address and netmask of 0.0.0.0 0.0.0.0 can be configured to share the preshared key among many peers. However, Cisco strongly recommends using a unique key for each peer.

You can also use the peer's host name for the preshared key.

Preshared keys are easy to configure, yet are not scalable.

Step 4: Verify IKE Phase One Policies

The **write terminal** command displays configured policies. A concatenated example is shown in Example 6-1 and Example 6-2. Note that the preshared key is cisco1234 and the peer is PIX2 at 192.168.2.2.

Example 6-1 *IKE Policies*

```
pix1# write terminal
hostname pix1
isakmp enable outside
isakmp key cisco1234 address 192.168.2.2 netmask 255.255.255.255
isakmp policy 10 authentication pre-share
isakmp policy 10 encryption des
isakmp policy 10 hash sha
isakmp policy 10 group 1
isakmp policy 10 lifetime 86400
```

The **show isakmp policy** command displays configured and default policies, as shown in Example 6-2. Note that the default isakmp protection suite is designed for CA support.

Example 6-2 **show isakmp policy** *Command*

```
pix1# show isakmp policy

Protection suite of priority 10
        encryption algorithm:   DES - Data Encryption Standard (56 bit keys)
        hash algorithm:         Message Digest 5
        authentication method:  Pre-Shared Key
        Diffie-Hellman group:   #1 (768 bit)
        lifetime:               86400 seconds, no volume limit
Default protection suite
        encryption algorithm:   DES - Data Encryption Standard (56 bit keys)
        hash algorithm:         Secure Hash Standard
```

continues

Example 6-2   show isakmp policy *Command (Continued)*

```
              authentication method:  Rivest-Shamir-Adleman Signature
              Diffie-Hellman group:   #1 (768 bit)
              lifetime:               86400 seconds, no volume limit
```

The **show isakmp** command displays configured policies much as they would appear with
the **write terminal** command, as shown in Example 6-3.

Example 6-3   *IKE Policy*

```
pix1(config)# show isakmp
isakmp enable outside
isakmp key cisco1234 address 192.168.2.2 netmask 255.255.255.255
isakmp policy 10 authentication pre-share
isakmp policy 10 encryption des
isakmp policy 10 hash md5
isakmp policy 10 group 1
isakmp policy 10 lifetime 86400
```

Task 3: Configure IPSec

The next major task in configuring PIX Firewall IPSec is to configure IPSec parameters that
you previously determined. This section presents the steps used to configure IPSec
parameters for IKE preshared keys.

The general tasks and commands used to configure IPSec encryption on the PIX Firewall
are summarized as follows. Subsequent sections of this chapter discuss each configuration
step in detail.

Step 1   Configure crypto access lists with the **access-list** command.

Step 2   Configure transform set suites with the **crypto ipsec transform-set**
command.

Step 3   Configure global IPSec SA lifetimes with the **crypto ipsec security-
association lifetime** command (optional).

Step 4   Configure crypto maps with the **crypto map** command.

Step 5   Apply crypto maps to the terminating/originating interface with the
crypto map *map-name* **interface** command.

Step 6   Verify IPSec configuration with the variety of available **show** commands.

Use the **sysopt connection permit-ipsec** command in IPSec configurations to permit IPSec
traffic to pass through the PIX Firewall without a check of **conduit** or **access-list** command
statements. An **access-list** or **conduit** command statement must be available for inbound
sessions.

By default, any inbound session must be explicitly permitted by a **conduit** or **access-list** command statement. With IPSec protected traffic, the secondary access list check could be redundant. To enable IPSec authenticated/cipher inbound session to be always permitted, enable **sysopt connection permit-ipsec**.

The **no sysopt connection permit-ipsec** command disables the option.

Step 1: Configure Crypto Access Lists

The first major step in configuring PIX Firewall IPSec is to configure the crypto access lists to select interesting traffic.

Crypto access lists are traffic selection access lists. They are used to define which IP traffic is interesting and will be protected by IPSec and which traffic will not be protected by IPSec. Crypto access lists perform the following functions:

- Indicate the data flow to be protected by IPSec

- Process inbound traffic to filter out and discard traffic that should have been protected by IPSec

- Determine whether or not to accept requests for IPSec SAs for the requested data flows when processing IKE negotiations

Configure interesting traffic with crypto access lists. Define a crypto access list with the **access-list** global configuration command. To delete an access list, use the **no** form of the command. The command syntax is as follows:

```
access-list access-list-name {deny | permit} protocol source source-netmask
    [operator port [port]] destination destination-netmask
    [operator port [port]]
```

access-list-name	Name or number of an access list.
deny	Does not select a packet for IPSec protection. Prevents traffic from being protected by crypto in the context of that particular crypto map entry.
permit	Selects a packet for IPSec protection. Causes all IP traffic that matches the specified conditions to be protected by crypto, using the policy described by the corresponding crypto map entry.
protocol	Name or number of an IP protocol. It can be one of the keywords **icmp**, **ip**, **tcp**, or **udp**, or an integer representing an IP protocol number. To match any Internet protocol, use the keyword **ip**. The **icmp** keyword cannot be used for IPSec because IKE does not negotiate ICMP in PIX Firewall release 5.1.

continues

source *destination*	Address of the network or host where the packet is being sent or from where the packet was received. There are three other ways to specify the source or destination: Use a 32-bit quantity in four-part, dotted-decimal format. Use the keyword **any** as an abbreviation for a source and source-netmask or destination and destination-netmask of 0.0.0.0 0.0.0.0. This keyword is normally not recommended for use with IPSec. Use host source or host destination as an abbreviation for a source and source-netmask of 255.255.255.255 or a destination and destination-netmask of destination 255.255.255.255.
source-netmask *destination-* *netmask*	Netmask bits (mask) to be applied to source or destination. There are three other ways to specify the source- or destination-netmask: Use a 32-bit quantity in four-part, dotted-decimal format. Place zeroes in the bit positions you want to ignore. Use the keyword **any** as an abbreviation for a source and source-netmask or destination and destination-netmask of 0.0.0.0 0.0.0.0. This keyword is not recommended. Use host source or host destination as an abbreviation for a source and source-netmask of source 255.255.255.255 or a destination and destination-netmask of destination 255.255.255.255.
operator	(Optional) Compares source or destination ports. Possible operands include **lt** (less than), **gt** (greater than), **eq** (equal), **neq** (not equal), and **range** (inclusive range). The range operator requires two port numbers. All other operators require one port number.
port	IP services you permit based on TCP or UDP protocol. Specify ports by either a literal name or a number in the range of 0 to 65,535. You can specify all ports by not specifying a port value.

Some additional details for access lists are as follows:

- *protocol* indicates which IP packet type to encrypt.
- The use of port ranges can dramatically increase the number of IPSec tunnels that the PIX Firewall can originate or terminate. A new tunnel is created for each port.

NOTE   PIX Firewall version 5.0 supports the IP protocol only with granularity to the network, subnet, and host level.

NOTE   Although the access list syntax is unchanged from access lists applied to PIX Firewall interfaces, the meanings are slightly different for crypto access lists: **permit** specifies that matching packets must be encrypted; **deny** specifies that matching packets need not be encrypted.

Any unprotected inbound traffic that matches a permit entry in the crypto access list for a crypto map entry flagged as IPSec is dropped.

If you want certain traffic to receive one combination of IPSec protection (for example, authentication only) and other traffic to receive a different combination of IPSec protection (for example, both authentication and encryption), you need to create two different crypto access lists to define the two different types of traffic.

WARNING   Cisco recommends that you avoid using the **any** keyword to specify source or destination addresses. The **permit any any** statement is strongly discouraged, as this causes all outbound traffic to be protected (and all protected traffic sent to the peer specified in the corresponding crypto map entry) and requires protection for all inbound traffic. Then all inbound packets that lack IPSec protection are silently dropped.

Try to be as restrictive as possible when defining which packets to protect in a crypto access list. If you must use the **any** keyword in a permit statement, you must preface that statement with a series of deny statements to filter out any traffic that would otherwise fall within that permit statement and that you do not want to be protected.

Use the **show access-list** command to display currently configured access lists. Figure 6-1 contains a sample access list for each of the peer PIX Firewalls. Each PIX Firewall in this example has static mapping of a global IP address to an inside host. The access list *source* field is configured for the global IP address of the local PIX Firewall's static, the *destination* field for the peer PIX Firewall's global IP address. The access lists are symmetrical.

You can also use the **nat** [(*if_name*)] **0 access-list** *acl_name* command to exempt the range of addresses specified in the crypto access list from being translated while being encrypted by IPSec. Traffic is still protected by the Adaptive Security Algorithm. With this command, you do not have to configure corresponding statics.

Figure 6-1   **show access-list** *Example*

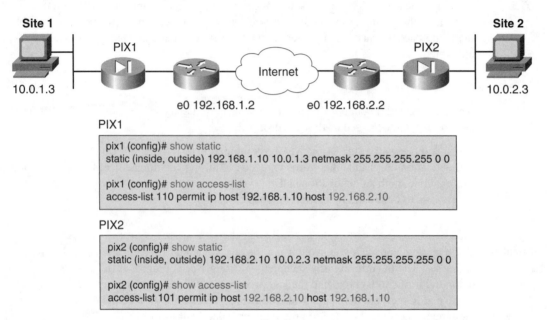

Step 2: Configure Transform Set Suites

The next major step in configuring PIX Firewall IPSec is to use the IPSec security policy to define a transform set.

An IPSec transform specifies a single IPSec security protocol, either Authentication Header (AH) or Encapsulating Security Payload (ESP), with its corresponding security algorithms and mode. The AH transform is a mechanism for payload authentication. The ESP transform is a mechanism for payload encryption.

Some example transforms include the following:

- The AH protocol with the hashed message authentication code (HMAC) with MD5 authentication algorithm in tunnel mode is used for authentication.

- The ESP protocol with the triple Data Encryption Standard (3DES) encryption algorithm in transport mode is used for confidentiality of data.

- The ESP protocol with the 56-bit DES encryption algorithm and the HMAC with Secure Hash Algorithm (SHA) authentication algorithm in tunnel mode is used for authentication and confidentiality.

Figure 6-2 shows a graphical representation of these combinations.

Figure 6-2   *IPSec Transforms*

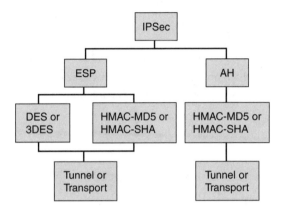

Transform Set Configuration

A transform set is a combination of individual IPSec transforms designed to enact a specific security policy for traffic. During the ISAKMP IPSec SA negotiation that occurs in IKE phase two quick mode, the peers agree to use a particular transform set for protecting a particular data flow. Transform sets combine the following IPSec factors:

- Mechanism for payload authentication: AH transform
- Mechanism for payload encryption: ESP transform
- IPSec mode (transport versus tunnel)

Transform sets equal a combination of an AH transform, an ESP transform, and the IPSec mode (either tunnel or transport mode).

Define a transform set with the **crypto ipsec transform-set** global configuration command. To delete a transform set, use the **no** form of the command. The command syntax is as follows:

```
crypto ipsec transform-set transform-set-name transform1
    [transform2 transform3]]
```

transform-set-name	Specifies the name of the transform set to create (or modify).
transform1	Specifies up to three IPSec transforms. These transforms define the IPSec security protocol and algorithm.
transform2	
transform3	

Some additional details for transform sets are as follows:

- Sets are limited to up to one AH and up to two ESP transforms.
- The default mode is tunnel.
- Configure matching transform sets between IPSec peers.
- If you specify an ESP protocol in a transform set, you can specify just an ESP encryption transform, or both an ESP encryption transform and an ESP authentication transform.

The PIX Firewall supports the following IPSec transforms:

- AH
  - ah-md5-hmac—AH-HMAC-MD5 transform
  - ah-sha-hmac—AH-HMAC-SHA transform
- ESP
  - esp-des—ESP transform using DES cipher (56 bits)
  - esp-3des—ESP transform using 3DES(EDE) cipher (168 bits)
  - esp-md5-hmac—ESP transform with HMAC-MD5 authentication used with an esp-des or esp-3des transform to provide additional integrity of ESP packet
  - esp-sha-hmac—ESP transform with HMAC-SHA authentication used with an esp-des or esp-3des transform to provide additional integrity of ESP packet

---

NOTE   AH is rarely used because authentication is now available with the esp-sha-hmac and esp-md5-hmac transforms. AH is also not compatible with Network Address Translation (NAT) or Port Address Translation (PAT).

Transform Set Examples

Choosing IPSec transform combinations can be complex. The following tips might help you select transforms that are appropriate for your situation:

- Include an ESP encryption transform if you want to provide data confidentiality.
- Include an ESP authentication transform or an AH transform to provide authentication services for the transform set.
- Include an AH transform to ensure data authentication for the outer IP header and the data.

Choose from the MD5 or SHA (HMAC keyed hash variants) authentication algorithms to ensure data authentication (using either ESP or AH). The SHA algorithm is generally considered stronger than MD5, but it is slower. The following are examples of acceptable transform combinations:

- esp-des for high performance encryption
- ah-md5-hmac for authenticating packet contents with no encryption
- esp-3des and esp-md5-hmac for strong encryption and authentication
- ah-sha-hmac and esp-3des and esp-sha-hmac for strong encryption and authentication

Some example combinations follow.

The following example uses AH authentication with MD5, ESP encryption with 56-bit DES, tunnel mode (default):

```
crypto ipsec transform-set SECURE ah-md5-hmac esp-des
```

The following example uses ESP authentication with MD5, ESP encryption with 56-bit DES, tunnel mode (default):

```
crypto ipsec transform-set noAH esp-md5-hmac esp-des
```

The following example uses AH authentication with MD5, ESP authentication with MD5, ESP encryption with 168-bit triple DES, tunnel mode (default):

```
crypto ipsec transform-set CPUeater ah-md5-hmac esp-md5-hmac esp-3des
```

The following example uses AH authentication with SHA, transport mode:

```
crypto ipsec transform-set AUTH  ah-sha-hmac
```

Transform Set Negotiation

Transform sets are negotiated during quick mode in IKE phase two using the transform sets you previously configured. You can configure multiple transform sets and then specify one or more of the transform sets in a crypto map entry. Configure the transforms from most to least secure using your policy. The transform set defined in the crypto map entry is used in the IPSec SA negotiation to protect the data flows specified by that crypto map entry's access list.

During the negotiation, the peers search for a transform set that is the same at both peers, as illustrated in Figure 6-3. When such a transform set is found, it is selected and applied to the protected traffic as part of both peers' IPSec SAs. IPSec peers agree on one transform proposal per SA (unidirectional).

Figure 6-3 shows this transform set negotiation.

Figure 6-3   *Transform Set Negotiation*

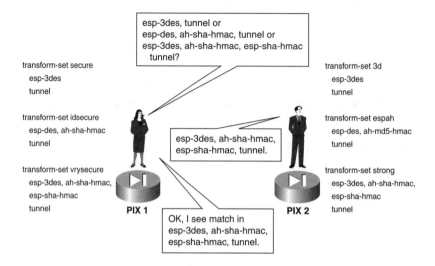

Step 3: Configure Global IPSec SA Lifetimes

The IPSec SA lifetime determines how long IPSec SAs remain valid before they are renegotiated. The PIX Firewall supports a global lifetime value that applies to all crypto maps. The global lifetime value can be overridden within a crypto map entry. You can change global IPSec SA lifetime values using the **crypto ipsec security-association lifetime** global configuration command. To reset a lifetime to the default value, use the **no** form of the command. The command syntax is as follows:

```
crypto ipsec security-association lifetime {seconds seconds |
    kilobytes kilobytes}
```

seconds *seconds*	Specifies the number of seconds an SA lives before expiring. The default is 28,800 seconds (8 hours).
kilobytes *kilobytes*	Specifies the volume of traffic (in kilobytes) that can pass between IPSec peers using a given SA before that SA expires. The default is 4,608,000 kilobytes (approximately 10 Mbps of traffic for 1 hour).

Some additional details about global SA lifetimes are as follows:

- Global IPSec SA lifetime is used by all crypto maps.
- IPSec SA lifetimes are negotiated during IKE phase two.

- You can optionally configure IPSec SA lifetimes in crypto maps.
- Crypto map IPSec SA lifetimes override global IPSec SA lifetimes.

The following is an example global SA lifetime. In the example, a new SA is renegotiated after 900 seconds, or 15 minutes. When an SA expires, a new one is negotiated automatically without interrupting the data flow.

```
pixfirewall(config)#crypto ipsec security-association lifetime kilobytes 1382400
pixfirewall(config)#crypto ipsec security-association lifetime seconds 900
```

Cisco recommends that you use the default lifetime values (28,800 seconds; 4,608,000 kbps). Individual IPSec SA lifetimes can be configured using crypto maps, which are covered in the section, "Crypto Map Commands," later in this chapter.

Step 4: Configure Crypto Maps

Crypto maps entries must be created for IPSec to set up SAs for traffic flows that must be encrypted. This section looks at the purpose of crypto maps, examines the **crypto map** command, and considers example crypto maps.

Crypto map entries created for IPSec set up SA parameters, tying together the various parts required to set up IPSec SAs, including:

- Which traffic should be protected by IPSec (using crypto access list)
- The granularity of the traffic to be protected by a set of SAs (specified by the crypto access list)
- Where IPSec-protected traffic should be sent (who the remote IPSec peer is)
- The local address to be used for the IPSec traffic
- What IPSec security type should be applied to this traffic (transform sets)
- Whether SAs are manually established or are established with ISAKMP
- The IPSec SA lifetime
- Other parameters that might be necessary to define an IPSec SA

Crypto Map Parameters

You can apply only one crypto map set to a single interface. The crypto map set can include a combination of Cisco Encryption Technology (CET), IPSec using IKE, and IPSec with manually configured SA entries. Multiple interfaces can share the same crypto map set if you want to apply the same policy to multiple interfaces.

If you create more than one crypto map entry for a given interface, use the sequence number (*seq-num*) of each map entry to rank the map entries: the lower the *seq-num*, the higher the priority. At the interface that has the crypto map set, traffic is evaluated against higher-priority map entries first.

You must create multiple crypto map entries for a given interface if any of the following conditions exist:

- If different data flows are to be handled by separate IPSec peers.

- If you want to apply different IPSec security to different types of traffic (to the same or separate IPSec peers); for example, if you want traffic between one set of subnets to be authenticated, and traffic between another set of subnets to be both authenticated and encrypted. In this case, the different types of traffic should be defined in two separate access lists, and you must create a separate crypto map entry for each crypto access list.

- If you are not using IKE to establish a particular set of SAs and want to specify multiple access list entries, you must create separate access lists (one per permit entry) and specify a separate crypto map entry for each access list.

Crypto Map Commands

Configure the crypto map with the **crypto map** command as follows:

Step 1   Create a crypto map entry in IPSec ISAKMP mode.

```
pixfirewall(config)# crypto map map-name seq-num ipsec-isakmp
```

Identify the crypto map with a unique crypto map name and sequence number.

Use **ipsec-isakmp** for CA server support.

Step 2   Assign an access list to the crypto map entry.

```
pixfirewall(config)# crypto map map-name seq-num match address access-
list-name
```

Step 3   Specify the peer to which the IPSec protected traffic can be forwarded.

```
pixfirewall(config)# crypto map map-name seq-num set peer hostname | ip-
address
```

Set the peer host name or IP address.

Specify multiple peers by repeating this command.

The peer is the terminating interface of the IPSec peer.

Step 4   Specify which transform sets are allowed for this crypto map entry.

```
pixfirewall(config)# crypto map map-name seq-num set transform-set
        transform-set-name1 [transform-set-name2, transform-set-name9]
```

List multiple transform sets in order of priority (highest priority first).

The most secure transforms should be the highest priority.

You can specify up to nine transform sets.

IPSec peers negotiate a matching set during IKE phase two.

Step 5   (Optional) Specify that IPSec should ask for perfect forward secrecy (PFS) when requesting new SAs for this crypto map entry, or should require PFS in requests received from the peer.

```
pixfirewall(config)# crypto map map-name seq-num set pfs [group1 | group2]
```

NOTE   PFS provides additional security for Diffie-Hellman key exchanges at the cost of additional processing.

Step 6   (Optional) Specify SA lifetime for the crypto map entry if you want the SAs for this entry to be negotiated using IPSec SA lifetimes other than the global lifetimes.

```
pixfirewall(config)# crypto map map-name seq-num set security-association
        lifetime seconds seconds | kilobytes kilobytes
```

The SA lifetime in a crypto map entry overrides the global SA lifetime value.

Step 7   (Optional) Specify dynamic crypto maps.

```
pixfirewall(config)# crypto dynamic-map dynamic-map-name dynamic-seq-num
```

A dynamic crypto map entry is essentially a crypto map entry without all the parameters configured. It acts as a policy template, where the missing parameters are later dynamically configured (as the result of an IPSec negotiation) to match a peer's requirements. This allows peers to exchange IPSec traffic with the PIX Firewall even if the PIX Firewall does not have a crypto map entry specifically configured to meet all the peer's requirements.

Step 5: Apply Crypto Maps to an Interface

The next step in configuring IPSec is to apply the crypto map set to an interface using the following command:

```
pixfirewall(config)# crypto map map-name interface interface-name
```

The command applies the crypto map to an interface and activates the IPSec policy.

NOTE   PIX Firewall version 5.0 supports application of IPSec encryption on the outside interface only. PIX Firewall version 5.1 and later supports termination of IPSec encryption on any interface.

Consider the following example of applying a crypto map to an outside interface:

```
crypto map mymap interface outside
```

IPSec tunnels can be terminated on any interface. This does not mean you terminate traffic coming from the outside on the inside interface. Traffic terminated on the inside interface is traffic from the inside network. Traffic terminated on the outside is traffic from the outside. Traffic terminated on a Demilitarized Zone (DMZ) is traffic from the DMZ.

As soon as you apply the crypto map, the SAs should initialize. Only one crypto map set can be assigned to an interface. If multiple crypto map entries have the same *map-name* but a different *seq-num*, they are considered to be part of the same set and will all be applied to the interface. The crypto map entry with the lowest *seq-num* is considered the highest priority and is evaluated first.

Use the **show crypto map** command to verify crypto map configuration. Figure 6-4 shows a sample network. Example 6-4 contains the output of the **show crypto map** command for PIX1 of this sample network.

Figure 6-4   *Example Network*

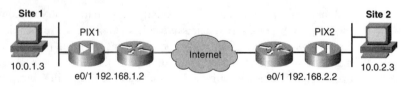

Example 6-4   *Crypto Map on PIX1*

```
pix1(config)# show crypto map

Crypto Map "peer2" 10 ipsec-isakmp
    Peer = 192.168.2.2
```

Example 6-4 *Crypto Map on PIX1 (Continued)*

```
access-list 101 permit ip host 192.168.1.10 host 192.168.2.10
  (hitcnt=0)
Current peer: 192.168.2.2
Security association lifetime: 4608000 kilobytes/28800 seconds
PFS (Y/N): N
Transform sets={ pix2, }
```

Example 6-5 shows an example of a crypto map for PIX2 from Figure 6-4.

Example 6-5 *Crypto Map on PIX2*

```
pix2(config)# show crypto map

Crypto Map "peer1" 10 ipsec-isakmp
  Peer = 192.168.1.2
  access-list 101 permit ip host 192.168.2.10 host 192.168.1.10 (hitcnt=0)
  Current peer: 192.168.1.2
  Security association lifetime: 4608000 kilobytes/28800 seconds
  PFS (Y/N): N
  Transform sets={ pix1, }
```

Step 6: Verify IPSec Configuration

The last step in configuring PIX Firewall IPSec is to verify the IPSec configuration accomplished in the previous steps. This section presents the methods and commands used to verify IPSec configuration.

View all configured access lists with the **show access-list** command. In the following example, the hitcnt=0 value shows that no traffic has been evaluated against this access list.

```
PIX2# show access-list
access-list 101 permit ip host 192.168.2.10 host
192.168.1.10 (hitcnt=0)
```

View the currently defined transform sets with the **show crypto ipsec transform-set** command. The command has the following syntax:

```
show crypto ipsec transform-set [tag transform-set-name]
```

tag *transform-set-name*	(Optional) Shows only the transform sets with the specified *transform-set-name*

If no keyword is used, all transform sets configured at the PIX Firewall are displayed.

In Example 6-6, the transform sets with the names mine and vrysecure are shown.

Example 6-6 show crypto ipsec transform-set

```
pixfirewall# show crypto ipsec transform-set
transform set mine: { esp-des  }
will negotiate = { Tunnel,  },
transform set vrysecure: { esp-3des ah-sha-hmac
esp-sha-hmac }
will negotiate = { Tunnel,  },
```

Use the **show crypto map** command to view the crypto map configuration. If no keywords are used, all crypto maps configured at the PIX Firewall are displayed. The command syntax is as follows:

```
show crypto map [interface interface | tag map-name]
```

interface *interface*	(Optional) Shows only the crypto map set applied to the specified *interface*
tag *map-name*	(Optional) Shows only the crypto map set with the specified *map-name*

In Example 6-7, the crypto map with the name mymap is shown. Note how the crypto map pulls the six IPSec-related values together.

Example 6-7 show crypto map

```
PIX1# show crypto map

Crypto Map: "mymap" pif: outside local address: 192.168.1.2

Crypto Map "mymap" 10 ipsec-isakmp
    Peer = 192.168.2.2
    access-list 101 permit ip host 192.168.1.10 host 192.168.2.10
    Current peer: 192.168.2.2
    Security-association lifetime: 4608000 kilobytes/3600 seconds
    PFS (Y/N): N
    Transform sets={ mine, }
```

Use the **show crypto ipsec security-association lifetime** command to view the current global IPSec SA lifetime.

In Example 6-8, the global IPSec SA lifetime is 2,305,000 kilobytes and 3600 seconds.

Example 6-8 show crypto ipsec security-association lifetime

```
PIX1# show crypto ipsec security-association lifetime
Security-association lifetime: 2305000 kilobytes/3600 seconds
```

Task 4: Test and Verify VPN Configuration

The last major task in configuring PIX Firewall IPSec is to test and verify the IKE and IPSec configuration accomplished in the previous tasks. This section summarizes the methods and commands used to test and verify VPN configuration.

Test and verify IKE configuration on the PIX Firewall with the commands listed in Table 6-1.

Table 6-1   **show** *Commands for Verifying IKE Configuration*

Command	Description
show access-list	Lists the **access-list** command statements in the configuration. Used to verify that general access lists permit IPSec traffic.
show isakmp	Displays configured ISAKMP policies in a format similar to a **write terminal** command.
show isakmp policy	Displays default and any configured ISAKMP policies.

Test and verify IPSec configuration on the PIX Firewall with the commands listed in Table 6-2.

Table 6-2   **show** *Commands for Verifying IPSec Configuration*

Command	Description
show access-list	Lists the **access-list** command statements in the configuration. Used to verify that crypto access lists select interesting traffic. Displays number of packets that matched the access list.
show crypto map	Displays crypto access lists assigned to a crypto map. Displays configured crypto map parameters.
show crypto ipsec transform-set	Displays configured IPSec transform sets.
show crypto ipsec security-association lifetime	Displays correct global IPSec SA lifetime values.

Monitor and manage IKE and IPSec communications between the PIX Firewall and IPSec peers with the commands in Table 6-3.

Table 6-3   *Commands to Manage IKE and IPSec Communications*

Command	Description
show isakmp sa	Displays the current status of ISAKMP SAs.
show crypto ipsec sa	Displays the current status of IPSec SAs. Useful for ensuring traffic is being encrypted.
clear isakmp	Clears ISAKMP SAs.

continues

Table 6-3 *Commands to Manage IKE and IPSec Communications (Continued)*

Command	Description
clear crypto ipsec sa	Clears IPSec SAs.
debug crypto isakmp	Displays ISAKMP (IKE) communications between the PIX Firewall and IPSec peers.
debug crypto ipsec	Displays IPSec communications between the PIX Firewall and IPSec peers.

Example 6-9 shows a sample **debug crypto isakmp** with annotations for you to consider as a successful IPSec SA setup. Note that the message **return status is IKMP_NO_ERROR** shown in Example 6-9 indicates that the IPSec SAs were set up properly.

Example 6-9 **debug crypto isakmp**

```
crypto_isakmp_process_block: src 10.0.2.3, dest 192.168.1.2
OAK_MM exchange
ISAKMP (0): processing SA payload. message ID = 0

ISAKMP (0): Checking ISAKMP transform 1 against priority 30 policy
ISAKMP:        encryption DES-CBC
ISAKMP:        hash MD5
ISAKMP:        default group 1
ISAKMP:        auth pre-share
ISAKMP (0): atts are acceptable. Next payload is 0
ISAKMP (0): SA is doing pre-shared key authentication using id type
 ID_IPV4_ADDR
return status is IKMP_NO_ERROR
! IKE has successfully negotiated a matching IKE policy
crypto_isakmp_process_block: src 10.0.2.3, dest 192.168.1.2
OAK_MM exchange
ISAKMP (0): processing KE payload. message ID = 0

ISAKMP (0): processing NONCE payload. message ID = 0

ISAKMP (0): processing vendor id payload

ISAKMP (0): processing vendor id payload
return status is IKMP_NO_ERROR
! IKE has authenticated the IPSec peer.
crypto_isakmp_process_block: src 10.0.2.3, dest 192.168.1.2
OAK_MM exchange
ISAKMP (0): processing ID payload. message ID = 0
ISAKMP (0): processing HASH payload. message ID = 0
ISAKMP (0): processing NOTIFY payload 608 protocol 1
        spi 0, message ID = 0
ISAKMP (0): SA has been authenticated

ISAKMP (0): ID payload
```

Example 6-9   **debug crypto isakmp** *(Continued)*

```
            next-payload : 8
            type        : 1
            protocol    : 17
            port        : 500
            length      : 8
ISAKMP (0): Total payload length: 12
return status is IKMP_NO_ERROR
! IKE main mode is complete, quick mode is starting
crypto_isakmp_process_block: src 10.0.2.3, dest 192.168.1.2
OAK_QM exchange
oakley_process_quick_mode:
OAK_QM_IDLE
ISAKMP (0): processing SA payload. message ID = -1121843667

ISAKMP : Checking IPSec proposal 1
! IPSec quick mode is negotiating IPSec proposals

ISAKMP: transform 1, ESP_DES
ISAKMP:    attributes in transform:
ISAKMP:        authenticator is HMAC-SHA
ISAKMP:        encaps is 1
ISAKMP (0): atts are acceptable.IPSEC(validate_proposal_request): proposal part
#1,
   (key eng. msg.) dest= 192.168.1.2, src= 10.0.2.3,
     dest_proxy= 192.168.1.10/255.255.255.255/0/0 (type=1),
     src_proxy= 10.0.2.3/255.255.255.255/0/0 (type=1),
     protocol= ESP, transform= esp-des esp-sha-hmac ,
     lifedur= 0s and 0kb,
     spi= 0x0(0), conn_id= 0, keysize= 0, flags= 0x4

ISAKMP (0): processing NONCE payload. message ID = -1121843667

ISAKMP (0): processing ID payload. message ID = -1121843667
ISAKMP (0): ID_IPV4_ADDR src 10.0.2.3 prot 0 port 0
ISAKMP (0): processing ID payload. message ID = -1121843667
ISAKMP (0): ID_IPV4_ADDR dst 192.168.1.10 prot 0 port 0IPSEC(key_engine): got a
queue event...
IPSEC(spi_response): getting spi 0x934e180e(2471368718) for SA
        from        10.0.2.3 to       192.168.1.2 for prot 3

return status is IKMP_NO_ERROR
! IPSec proposals negotiated and authenticated. Setting up SPIs.
crypto_isakmp_process_block: src 10.0.2.3, dest 192.168.1.2
OAK_QM exchange
oakley_process_quick_mode:
OAK_QM_AUTH_AWAITIPSEC(map_alloc_entry): allocating entry 2

IPSEC(map_alloc_entry): allocating entry 1
! Setting up IPSec SA database in memory

ISAKMP (0): Creating IPSec SAs
        inbound SA from       10.0.2.3 to       192.168.1.2
```

continues

Example 6-9 *debug crypto isakmp (Continued)*

```
          (proxy 10.0.2.3 to     192.168.1.10)
          has spi -1823598578 and conn_id 2 and flags 4
          outbound SA from     192.168.1.2 to        10.0.2.3
          (proxy 192.168.1.10 to        10.0.2.3)
          has spi -505941059 and conn_id 1 and flags 4IPSEC(key_engine):
          got a queue event...
IPSEC(initialize_sas): ,
  (key eng. msg.) dest= 192.168.1.2, src= 10.0.2.3,
    dest_proxy= 192.168.1.10/0.0.0.0/0/0 (type=1),
    src_proxy= 10.0.2.3/0.0.0.0/0/0 (type=1),
    protocol= ESP, transform= esp-des esp-sha-hmac ,
    lifedur= 0s and 0kb,
    spi= 0x934e180e(2471368718), conn_id= 2, keysize= 0, flags= 0x4
IPSEC(initialize_sas): ,
  (key eng. msg.) src= 192.168.1.2, dest= 10.0.2.3,
    src_proxy= 192.168.1.10/0.0.0.0/0/0 (type=1),
    dest_proxy= 10.0.2.3/0.0.0.0/0/0 (type=1),
    protocol= ESP, transform= esp-des esp-sha-hmac ,
    lifedur= 0s and 0kb,
    spi= 0xe1d7f3bd(3789026237), conn_id= 1, keysize= 0, flags= 0x4
! IPSec SAs set up, ready for IPSec traffic!

return status is IKMP_NO_ERROR
! This is the message you want to see!
```

Summary

This chapter focused on the configuration of an IPSec VPN on Cisco Secure PIX Firewall using preshared keys. It identified the four tasks that are required to configure IPSec:

1 Prepare for IKE and IPSec

2 Configure IKE

3 Configure IPSec

4 Test and verify IPSec

The chapter covered each individual task and identified the steps that are required to perform each task. Each task was explained in great detail, along with configuration examples that will empower you to implement these technologies in your place of work.

Now that you have learned how to configure the PIX for preshared keys, the next chapter looks at configuring the PIX for CA support.

Review Questions

1 What command enables you to view the default IPSec policy parameters?

2 With PIX v5.0, can you terminate an IPSec VPN on the inside interface?

3 When typing in the **isakmp policy** commands, what keyword enables preshared authentication?

4 What global command configures the PIX firewall so that IPSec VPN traffic will flow through the firewall, bypassing any conduits and access lists?

5 When creating a crypto access list, what do you do to ensure that specific traffic is encrypted?

6 What command enables ISAKMP on the outside interface?

7 What is the default value for the **isakmp identity** command?

8 What is the default Diffie-Hellman key size?

9 What commands displays the transform sets that are configured on the PIX Firewall?

10 What two modes of identity for ISAKMP are supported by the PIX firewall?

CHAPTER 7

Configuring the Cisco PIX Firewall for CA Site-to-Site

This chapter covers how to configure a Cisco Secure PIX Firewall certificate authority (CA) support for Internet Protocol Security (IPSec). After presenting an overview of the configuration process, the chapter shows you each major step of the configuration.

This chapter covers the following topics:

- Configure CA support tasks
- Task 1: Prepare for IPSec
- PIX CA support overview
- Task 2: Configure CA support
- Task 3: Configure IKE
- Task 4: Configure IPSec
- Task 5: Test and verify VPN configuration

Configure CA Support Tasks

This chapter covers how to configure the PIX Firewall to work with a CA. It does not cover the configuration of the CA server, only how the Cisco products interact with one. The lab provides you with the opportunity to configure components in a way that mimics a real network. This section presents an overview of the major tasks you will have to perform to configure a PIX Firewall for CA support.

The IPSec configuration process can be summarized in five major tasks, outlined as follows. To provide more detail, the general tasks used to configure IPSec encryption on the PIX Firewall are summarized here. Subsequent sections of this chapter discuss the CA configuration tasks and steps in detail. Tasks and steps that are identical to those of preshared keys are not covered in detail. Please refer to Chapter 6, "Configuring the Cisco PIX Firewall for Preshared Keys Site-to-Site," for the detailed explanation of these steps.

- **Task 1: Prepare for IPSec**—This task consists of several steps to identify CA server details, determine IPSec policies, ensure that the network works, and ensure that the PIX Firewall can support IPSec.

- **Task 2: Configure CA support**—This task consists of several configuration steps that are required to enable the PIX Firewall to use a CA server.

- **Task 3: Configure Internet Key Exchange (IKE) parameters**—This task consists of several configuration steps that ensure that IKE can set up secure channels to desired IPSec peers. Then IKE can set up IPSec SAs, enabling IPSec sessions.

- **Task 4: Configure IPSec parameters**—This task consists of several configuration steps that specify IPSec SA parameters between peers and set global IPSec values.

- **Task 5: Test and verify VPN configuration**—After you configure IPSec, you need to verify that you have configured it correctly and ensure that it works.

Task 1: Prepare for IPSec

Successful implementation of an IPSec network requires advance preparation before beginning configuration of individual PIX Firewalls. This section outlines how to determine network design details to configure a PIX Firewall for CA support.

You must plan in advance if you want to configure IPSec encryption correctly the first time and minimize misconfiguration. You should begin this task by defining the IPSec security policy based on the overall company security policy. Some planning steps follow:

Step 1 **Determine CA server details**—This includes variables such as the type of CA server to be used, the IP address, and the CA administrator contact information.

Step 2 **Determine IKE (IKE phase one) policy**—Determine the IKE policies between peers based on the number and location of IPSec peers.

Step 3 **Determine IPSec (IKE phase two) policy**—Identify IPSec peer details such as IP addresses and IPSec modes. You then configure crypto maps to gather all IPSec policy details together.

Step 4 **Check the current configuration**—Use the **write terminal, show isakmp [policy], show crypto map,** and many other **show** commands, which are covered later in this chapter in the "Test and Verify VPN Configuration" section.

Step 5 **Ensure that the network operates without encryption**—Ensure that basic connectivity has been achieved between IPSec peers using the desired IP services before configuring IPSec. You can use the **ping** command to check basic connectivity.

Step 6   **Ensure that access lists are compatible with IPSec**—Ensure that perimeter routers and the PIX outside interfaces permit IPSec traffic. Implicitly permit IPSec packets to bypass PIX access lists and conduits. In this step, you will need to enter the **sysopt connection permit-ipsec** command.

NOTE   Step 1 and Step 2 are covered in detail in this chapter. The other steps are presented for review purposes. Refer to Chapter 6 for a detailed explanation of Steps 3 through 6.

Step 1: Determine CA Server Details

Successful implementation of an IPSec network requires advanced planning before beginning configuration of individual routers. This section outlines how to prepare for IKE and CA support.

Configuring CA is complicated. Having a detailed plan lessens the chances of improper configuration. Some planning steps include the following:

- **Determine the type of CA server to use**—CA servers come in a multitude of configurations and capabilities. You must determine which one fits your needs before configuration. Requirements include, but are not limited to, Rivest, Shamir, and Adelman (RSA) key type; certificate revocation list (CRL) capabilities; and support for Registration Authority (RA) mode.

- **Identify the CA server IP address, host name, and URL**—This information is necessary if you will be using Cisco Encryption Technology (CET) and Lightweight Directory Access Protocol (LDAP).

- **Identify the CA server administrator contact information**—Arrange for your certificates to be validated if the process is not automatic.

The goal of these planning steps is to be ready for CA support configuration.

You need to have a CA available to your network before you configure CA. The CA must support Cisco's Public Key Infrastructure (PKI) protocol and the Simple Certificate Enrollment Protocol (SCEP).

Figure 7-1 shows an example of CA server details that you should gather before beginning the configuration. The diagram and table in Figure 7-1 illustrate the network topology and CA server details used in this chapter.

Figure 7-1   *Determine CA Server Details*

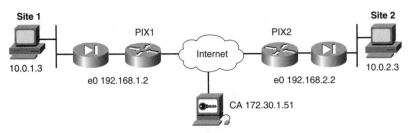

Parameter	CA Server
Type of CA server	Entrust
Host name	entrust-ca
IP address	172.30.1.51
URL	www.ca.com
Administrator contact	1-800-555-1212

Step 2: Determine IKE (IKE Phase One) Policy

You should determine the IKE policy details to enable the selected authentication method, then configure that method. Having a detailed plan lessens the chances of improper configuration. Some planning steps include the following:

- **Determine the key distribution method**—Determine the key distribution method based on the numbers and locations of IPSec peers. For small networks, you might wish to manually distribute keys. For larger networks, you might wish to use a CA server to support scalability of IPSec peers. You must then configure Internet Security Association Key Management Protocol (ISAKMP) to support the selected key distribution method.

- **Determine the authentication method**—Choose the authentication method based on the key distribution method. The PIX Firewall supports either preshared keys, RSA encrypted nonces, or RSA signatures to authenticate IPSec peers. This chapter focuses on using RSA signatures.

- **Identify IPSec peer's IP addresses and host names**—Determine the details of all the IPSec peers that will use ISAKMP and RSA signatures for establishing SAs. You will use this information to configure IKE.

- **Determine ISAKMP policies for peers**—An ISAKMP policy defines a combination, or *suite*, of security parameters to be used during the ISAKMP negotiation. Each ISAKMP negotiation begins by each peer agreeing on a common (shared) ISAKMP policy. The ISAKMP policy suites must be determined in advance of configuration. You must then configure IKE to support the policy details you determined. Some ISAKMP policy details include the following:

— Encryption algorithm

— Hash algorithm

— IKE SA lifetime

An IKE policy defines a combination of security parameters used during the IKE negotiation. A group of policies makes up a *protection suite* of multiple policies that enable IPSec peers to establish IKE sessions and establish SAs with minimal configuration.

Creating IKE Policies for a Purpose

IKE negotiations must be protected, so each IKE negotiation begins by each peer agreeing on a common (shared) IKE policy. This policy states which security parameters will be used to protect subsequent IKE negotiations.

After the two peers agree upon a policy, the security parameters of the policy are identified by an SA established at each peer. These SAs apply to all subsequent IKE traffic during the negotiation.

You can create multiple prioritized policies at each peer to ensure that at least one policy will match a remote peer's policy.

Defining IKE Policy Parameters

You can select specific values for each IKE parameter per the IKE standard. You choose one value over another, based on the security level you desire and the type of IPSec peer to which you will connect. There are five parameters to define in each IKE policy, as outlined in Table 7-1 and Figure 7-2. Table 7-1 shows the default values of each parameter, and Figure 7-2 shows the relative strengths.

Table 7-1   *IKE Policy Parameters*

Parameter	Accepted Values	Keyword	Default
Message encryption algorithm	DES	**des**	DES
	3DES	**3des**	
Message integrity (hash) algorithm	SHA-1 (HMAC variant)	**sha**	SHA-1
	MD5 (HMAC variant)	**md5**	
Peer authentication method	Preshared keys		RSA signatures
	RSA signatures	**preshare**	
		rsa-sig	

continues

Table 7-1   *IKE Policy Parameters (Continued)*

Parameter	Accepted Values	Keyword	Default
Key exchange parameters (Diffie-Hellman group identifier)	768-bit Diffie-Hellman or	1	768-bit Diffie-Hellman
	1024-bit Diffie-Hellman	2	
ISAKMP-established SA's lifetime	Can specify any number of seconds	—	86,400 seconds (one day)

Figure 7-2   *IKE Policy Example*

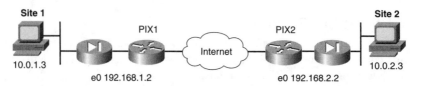

Parameter	Site 1	Site 2
Encryption algorithm	DES	DES
Hash algorithm	SHA	SHA
Authentication method	RSA signatures	RSA signatures
Key exchange	768-bit D-H	768-bit D-H
IKE SA lifetime	86400 seconds	86400 seconds

You can select specific values for each ISAKMP parameter using the ISAKMP standard. You choose one value over another based on the security level you desire and the type of IPSec peer to which you will connect. There are five parameters to define in each IKE policy, as presented in Table 7-2. Table 7-2 shows the relative strength of each parameter. You can select specific values for each ISAKMP parameter using the ISAKMP standard.

Table 7-2   *ISAKMP Parameters*

Parameter	Strong	Stronger
Message encryption algorithm	DES	3DES
Message integrity (hash) algorithm	MD5	SHA-1
Peer authentication method	Preshare	RSA Encryption RSA Signature
Key exchange parameters (Diffie-Hellman group identifier)	D-H Group 1	D-H Group 2
ISAKMP-established SA's lifetime	86,400 seconds	Less than 86,400 seconds

You should determine IKE policy details for each IPSec peer before configuring IKE. Figure 7-2 shows a summary of some IKE policy details that will be configured in examples in this chapter. The authentication method of RSA signatures is used for CA support.

NOTE	Refer to Chapter 6 for a detailed explanation of Steps 3 through 6.

PIX CA Support Overview

The PIX Firewall supports the following open CA standards:

- **IKE**—A hybrid protocol that implements Oakley and Skeme key exchanges inside the ISAKMP framework. Although IKE can be used with other protocols, its initial implementation is with the IPSec protocol. IKE provides authentication of the IPSec peers, negotiates IPSec keys, and negotiates IPSec SAs.

- **Public-Key Cryptography Standard #7 (PKCS #7)**—A standard from RSA Security Inc. used to encrypt and sign certificate enrollment messages.

- **Public-Key Cryptography Standard #10 (PKCS #10)**—A standard syntax from RSA Security Inc. for certificate requests. The PIX Firewall automatically creates the certificate requests as part of the SCEP process.

- **RSA keys**—RSA is the public key cryptographic system developed by Ronald Rivest, Adi Shamir, and Leonard Adelman. RSA keys come in pairs: one public key and one private key.

- **X.509v3 certificates**—Certificate support that allows the IPSec-protected network to scale by providing the equivalent of a digital ID card to each device. When two devices wish to communicate, they exchange digital certificates to prove their identity (thus removing the need to manually exchange public keys with each peer or to manually specify a shared key at each peer). These certificates are obtained from a CA. X.509 is part of the X.500 standard.

- **CA interoperability**—CA interoperability permits CAs to communicate with your PIX Firewall so that it can obtain and use digital certificates from the CA. Although IPSec can be implemented in your network without the use of a CA, using a CA with SCEP provides manageability and scalability for IPSec.

SCEP

The PIX Firewall supports the SCEP to automate the exchange of certificates with a CA server.

The SCEP is an Internet Engineering Task Force (IETF) draft sponsored by Cisco that provides a standard way of managing the certificate lifecycle. This initiative is important for driving open development for certificate handling protocols that can be interoperable with many vendors' devices.

PKCS #7 and #10 are acronyms for the Public-Key Cryptography Standards #7 and #10. These are standards from RSA Security Inc. used to encrypt and sign certificate enrollment messages.

The Manual Enrollment Process

SCEP provides two authentication methods: manual authentication and authentication based on a preshared secret. In the manual mode, the end entity submitting the request is required to wait until the CA operator, using any reliable out-of-band method, can verify its identity. An MD5 fingerprint generated on the PKCS # must be compared out-of-band between the server and the end entity. SCEP clients and CAs (or RAs, if appropriate) must display this fingerprint to a user to enable this verification, if manual mode is used. When using a preshared secret scheme, the server should distribute a shared secret to the end entity that can uniquely associate the enrollment request with the given end entity. The distribution of the secret must be private: only the end entity should know this secret. When creating the enrollment request, the end entity is asked to provide a challenge password. When using the preshared secret scheme, the end entity must type in the redistributed secret as the password. In the manual authentication case, the challenge password is also required because the server might challenge an end entity with the password before any certificate can be revoked. Later on, this challenge password will be included as a PKCS #10 attribute and will be sent to the server as encrypted data. The PKCS #7 envelope protects the privacy of the challenge password with Data Encryption Standard (DES) encryption.

CA Servers Interoperable with PIX Firewall

There several other CA vendors that interoperate with PIX Firewalls, as follows:

- **Entrust Technologies, Inc.**—Entrust/PKI 4.0
- **VeriSign**—OnSite 4.5
- **Baltimore Technologies**—UniCERT v3.05
- **Microsoft Corporation**—Windows 2000 Certificate Services 5.0

Each of the CA vendors supports the SCEP for enrolling PIX Firewalls. Cisco is using the Cisco Security Associate Program to test new CA and PKI solutions with the Cisco Secure family of products. More information on the Security Associate Program can be found at the following URL:

www.cisco.com/warp/public/cc/so/neso/sqso/csap/index.shtml

Entrust Technologies

The Entrust CA server is one of the servers interoperable with Cisco. One of the major differences among CA servers is the question of who administers it.

Entrust is software that is installed and administered by the user. The Cisco IOS interoperates with the Entrust/PKI 4.0 CA server. Entrust/PKI delivers the ability to issue digital IDs to any device or application supporting the X.509 certificate standard, meeting the need for security, flexibility, and low cost by supporting all devices and applications from one PKI. Entrust/PKI offers the following features:

- **Requirements**—Entrust runs on the Windows NT 4.0 (required for Cisco interoperability), Solaris 2.6, HP-UX 10.20, and AIX 4.3 operating systems. Entrust requires RSA usage keys on the routers. You must use PIX Firewall release 5.1 and later.

- **Standards supported**—Entrust supports CA services and the RA capability, SCEP, and PKCS #10.

Refer to the Entrust Web site at www.entrust.com for more information.

VeriSign OnSite 4.5

The VeriSign OnSite CA server is interoperable with PIX Firewalls. VeriSign administrates the CA, providing the certificates as a service.

VeriSign's OnSite 4.5 solution delivers a fully integrated enterprise PKI to control, issue, and manage IPSec certificates for PIX Firewalls and Cisco routers. VeriSign OnSite is a service administered by VeriSign. VeriSign OnSite offers the following features:

- **Requirements**—There are no local server requirements. Configure the router for CA mode with a high (greater than 60 second) retry count. You must use PIX Firewall release 5.1 and later.

- **Standards supported**—It supports SCEP, x509 certificate format, and PKCS #7, #10, #11, #12.

Refer to the VeriSign Web site at www.verisign.com for more information.

Baltimore Technologies

Baltimore Technologies has implemented support for SCEP in UniCERT (Baltimore's CA server) as well as the PKI Plus toolkit; these make it easy for customers to enable certificates within their environments.

- **Requirements**—The current release of the UniCERT CA module is available for Windows NT. You must use PIX Firewall release 5.2 and later.

- **Standards supported**—The following standards are supported with this CA server: X509 v3, X.9.62, X.9.92, X9.21-2; CRl v2; RFC 2459; PKCS #1, #7, #10, #11, #12; RFC 2510, RFC 2511; SCEP; LDAP v2, LDAP v3; DAP; SQL; TCP/IP; POP3; SMTP; HTTP; OCSP; FIPS 186-1, FIPS 180-1, FIPS 46-3, and FIPS 81 CBC.

Refer to the Baltimore Web site at www.baltimore.com for more information.

Microsoft Windows 2000 Certificate Services 5.0

Microsoft has integrated SCEP support into the Windows 2000 CA server through the Security Resource Kit for Windows 2000. This support lets customers use SCEP to obtain certificates and certificate revocation information from Microsoft Certificate Services for all of Cisco's VPN security solutions.

- **Requirements**—You need a compatible PC capable of running Windows 2000 Server. You must use PIX Firewall release 5.2 and later.

- **Standards supported**—The following standards are supported with this CA server: X.509 version 3, CRL version 2, PKCS family (PKCS #7, #10, #12), PKIX, SSL version 3, Kerberos v5 RFC 1510, 1964 tokens, SGC, IPSec, PKINIT, PC/SC, and IETF 2459.

See Chapter 3, "Configuring Cisco IOS Routers for Preshared Keys Site-to-Site," for more information about configuring the Microsoft Windows 2000 CA for SCEP support.

Refer to the Microsoft Web site at www.microsoft.com for more information.

Enroll a Device with a CA

The typical process for enrolling in a CA follows:

Step 1   Configure the PIX Firewall for CA support.

Step 2   The public and private keys are generated on the PIX Firewall.

Step 3   The PIX Firewall authenticates the CA server.

Step 4   The PIX Firewall sends a certificate request to the CA.

Step 5   The CA signs the certificate.

Step 6   The CA returns the certificate to the PIX Firewall and posts the certificate in the public repository (directory).

Most of these steps have been automated by Cisco and the SCEP protocol that is supported by many CA server vendors. Each vendor determines how long certificates are valid. Contact the relevant vendor to determine how long the certificates will be valid in your particular case.

Task 2: Configure CA Support

Configuring PIX Firewall CA support requires careful attention for successful implementation. Having a detailed plan will lessen the chances of improper configuration. Some planning steps and their associated commands follow:

Step 1   **Manage Flash memory usage (optional)**—CA certificates, CRLs, and RSA key pairs might use up a significant amount of Flash memory space and might need to be monitored.

Step 2   **Configure the PIX Firewall's time and date**— The PIX Firewall must have an accurate time and date to enroll with a CA server.

Step 3   **Configure the PIX Firewall's host name and domain name**—The host name and domain name are required to associate the fully qualified domain name (FQDN) with the keys and certificates used by IPSec.

Step 4   **Generate RSA signature key pairs**—The RSA signature key pairs are used to sign and encrypt IKE key management messages used to obtain a certificate.

Step 5   **Declare a CA**—Specify the nickname and IP address of the CA.

Step 6   **Configure CA communication parameters**—Specify CA, RA, and retry parameters.

Step 7   **Authenticate the CA**—Obtain the CA's public key and certificate.

Step 8   **Request signed certificates**—Request signed certificates from your CA for all of your PIX Firewall's RSA key pairs.

Step 9   **Save the configuration**—Save the configuration to Flash memory.

Step 10 **Verify CA support configuration**—Verify CA support configuration with various **show** commands.

Step 11 **Monitor and maintain CA interoperability (optional)**—Delete certificates and update CRLs.

Step 1: Manage Flash Memory Usage (Optional)

In some cases, storing certificates and CRLs locally will not present a problem. However, in other cases, memory might become an issue—particularly if your CA supports an RA and a large number of CRLs are stored on your PIX Firewall. A PIX Firewall stores the following types of certificates:

- RSA signature key pairs
- Its own certificate

- The CA's certificate
- Two RA certificates (only if the CA supports RA)

The PIX Firewall stores the following numbers of CRLs:

- One, if the CA does not support an RA
- Multiple, if the CA supports an RA

Step 2: Set the PIX Firewall's Date and Time

Ensure that the PIX Firewall's time and date have been accurately set with the **show clock** command. The clock must be accurately set before generating RSA key pairs and enrolling with the CA server because the keys and certificates are time-sensitive.

To set the PIX Firewall's time and date, use the **clock set** configuration command. The command syntax is as follows:

```
clock set hh:mm:ss day month year
clock set hh:mm:ss month day year
```

hh:mm:ss	Current time in hours (military format), minutes, and seconds
day	The current day of the month, for example, 1
month	The current month expressed as the first three characters of the month, for example, apr for April
year	The current year expressed as four digits, for example, 2001

The following example sets the time to one second before midnight, December 31, 2000:

```
PIX1(config)# clock set 23:59:59 31 dec 2000
```

Cisco's PKI protocol uses the clock to make sure that a CRL is not expired. Otherwise, the CA might reject or allow certificates based on an incorrect time stamp.

NOTE   The lifetime of a certificate and the CRL is checked in GMT time. If you are using IPSec with certificates, set the PIX Firewall clock to GMT time to ensure that CRL checking works correctly.

Step 3: Configure the PIX Firewall's Host Name and Domain Name

You must configure the PIX Firewall's host name and IP domain name if this has not already been done. This is required because the PIX Firewall assigns a FQDN to the keys and certificates used by IPSec, and the FQDN is based on the host name and IP domain name you assign to the PIX Firewall. For example, a certificate is named "pix1.xyz.com" based on a PIX Firewall host name of "pix1" and a PIX Firewall IP domain name of "xyz.com."

To configure the PIX Firewall's host name and IP domain name, there are two commands to use. To configure the PIX Firewall's host name, use the following command:

```
hostname newname
```

To configure the PIX Firewall's IP domain name, use the following command:

```
domain-name name
```

Step 4: Generate RSA Key Pairs

RSA key pairs are used to sign and encrypt IKE key management messages and are required before you can obtain a certificate for your PIX Firewall.

To generate an RSA key pair, enter the following command in configuration mode:

```
ca generate rsa {key | specialkey} key_modulus_size
```

key	This specifies that one general purpose RSA key pair will be generated.
specialkey	This specifies that two special purpose RSA key pairs will be generated instead of one general purpose key.
key_modulus_size	The size of the key modulus, which is between 512 and 2048 bits. Choosing a size greater than 1024 bits might cause key generation to take a few minutes, but it increases key entropy or life.

The **ca generate rsa** command is not saved in the PIX Firewall configuration. However, the keys generated by this command are saved in the persistent data file in Flash memory, which is never displayed to the user or backed up to another device.

In the following example, one general purpose RSA key pair is to be generated. The selected size of the key modulus is 512.

```
pixfirewall(config)#ca generate rsa key 512
```

Step 5: Declare a CA

Declare one CA to be used by your PIX Firewall with the **ca identity** command in configuration mode. You can also specify the location of the CA server's CGI script and the LDAP IP address, if used. The command syntax is as follows:

```
ca identity ca_nickname ca_ipaddress [:ca_script_location] [ldap_ip address]
```

ca_nickname	The CA's name. Enter any string that you desire. (If you previously declared the CA and just want to update its characteristics, specify the name you previously created.) The CA might require a particular name, such as its domain name.
ca_ipaddress	The CA's IP address.
:ca_script_location	The default location and script on the CA server is /cgi-bin/pkiclient.exe. If the CA administrator has not put the CGI script in this location, provide the location and the name of the script in the **ca identity** command.
ldap_ip address	(Optional) Specify the IP address of the LDAP server. By default, querying a certificate or a CRL is done with Cisco's PKI protocol. If the CA supports LDAP, query functions can also use LDAP.

An example of entering a **ca identity** command is as follows:

```
pixfirewall(config)#ca identity labca 172.30.1.51
```

Step 6: Configure CA Communication Parameters

Configure CA communication parameters with the **ca configure** command in configuration mode. You can use the command to indicate whether to contact the CA or an RA to obtain a certificate. Use different parameters for each type of supported CA. The command syntax is as follows:

```
ca configure ca_nickname {ca | ra} retry_period retry_count [crloptional]
```

ca_nickname	The CA's name. Use the nickname entered with the **ca identity** command.
**ca	ra**	Indicates whether to contact the CA or RA when using the **ca configure** command. Some CA systems provide an RA, which the PIX Firewall contacts instead of the CA.
retry_period	Specifies the number of minutes the PIX Firewall waits before resending a certificate request to the CA when it does not receive a response from the CA to its previous request. Specify from 1 to 60 minutes. By default, the firewall retries every minute.

retry_count	Specifies how many times the PIX Firewall will resend a certificate request when it does not receive a certificate from the CA for the previous request. Specify from 1 to 100. The default is 0, which indicates that there is no limit to the number of times the PIX Firewall should contact the CA to obtain a pending certificate.
crloptional	Allows other peers' certificates to be accepted by your PIX Firewall even if the appropriate CRL is not accessible to your PIX Firewall. The default is without **crloptional**.

An example of defining VeriSign CA server-related commands is as follows. The IP address of onsiteipsec.verisign.com server is 172.31.1.50.

```
pixfirewall(config)#ca identity vsec.cisco.com 172.31.1.50
pixfirewall(config)#ca configure vsec.cisco.com ca 1 20 crloptional
```

Note that the CA mode is specified.

An example of defining a Baltimore or an Entrust CA server is as follows. The IP address of the CA server is 172.30.1.51.

```
pixfirewall(config)#ca identity labca 172.30.1.51 172.30.1.51
pixfirewall(config)#ca configure labca ra 1 20 crloptional
```

The second IP address is for an LDAP query server running on the same host. Note that the RA mode is specified.

An example of defining a Microsoft Windows 2000 CA is as follows:

```
pixfirewall(config)#ca identity labca 172.30.1.51:/certsrv/mscep/mscep.dll
pixfirewall(config)#ca configure labca ra 1 20 crloptional
```

Step 7: Authenticate the CA

Authenticate the CA to verify that it is legitimate by obtaining its public key and its certificate with the **ca authenticate** command in configuration mode. After entering the command, manually authenticate the CA's public key by contacting the CA administrator to compare the CA certificate's fingerprint. An RA, if used (as in the Entrust CA), acts as a proxy for a CA. The command syntax is as follows:

```
ca authenticate ca_nickname [fingerprint]
```

ca_nickname	The CA's name. Use the nickname entered with the **ca identity** command.

fingerprint	A key consisting of alphanumeric characters the PIX Firewall uses to authenticate the CA's certificate. The fingerprint is optional and is used to authenticate the CA's public key within its certificate. The PIX Firewall discards the CA certificate if the fingerprint that you included in the command statement is not equal to the fingerprint within the CA's certificate. Depending on the CA you are using, you might need to ask your local CA administrator for this fingerprint. You also have the option to authenticate the public key manually by comparing the two fingerprints after you receive the CA's certificate, rather than entering it within the command statement.

An example of authenticating a CA is as follows:

```
pixfirewall(config)#ca authenticate labca
```

The certificate has the following attributes:

Fingerprint: 93700c31 4853ec4a ded81400 43d3c82c

Step 8: Request Signed Certificates

Request signed certificates from your CA for all your PIX Firewall's RSA key pairs using the **ca enroll** command. Before entering this command, have your CA administrator authenticate your PIX Firewall manually before granting its certificates. The command syntax is as follows:

```
ca enroll ca_nickname challenge_password [serial] [ipaddress]
```

ca_nickname	The CA's name. Use the nickname entered with the **ca identity** command.
challenge_password	A required password that gives the CA administrator some authentication when a user calls to ask for a certificate to be revoked. It can be up to 80 characters in length.
serial	Specifies the PIX Firewall's serial number (optional).
ipaddress	The PIX Firewall's IP address (optional).

The **ca enroll** command requests certificates from the CA for all your PIX Firewall's RSA key pairs. This task is also known as *enrolling* with the CA.

During the enrollment process, you are prompted for a challenge password that can be used by the CA administrator to validate your identity. Do not forget the password you use. (Technically, enrolling and obtaining certificates are two separate events, but they both occur when the **ca enroll** command is issued.)

Your PIX Firewall needs a signed certificate from the CA for each of your PIX Firewall's RSA key pairs. If you already have a certificate for your keys, you will not be able to complete this command; instead, you will be prompted to remove the existing certificate first.

If you want to cancel the current enrollment request, use the **no ca enroll** command.

An example of authenticating a CA is as follows:

```
pixfirewall(config)#ca enroll labca mypassword1234567
```

The argument **mypassword1234567** in the example is a password, which is not saved with the configuration.

NOTE   The password is required if your certificate needs to be revoked, so it is crucial that you remember this password. Note it and store it in a safe place.

The **ca enroll** command requests as many certificates as there are RSA key pairs. You need to perform this command only once, even if you have special usage RSA key pairs.

NOTE   If your PIX Firewall reboots after you issued the **ca enroll** command but before you received the certificates, you must reissue the command and notify the CA administrator.

Step 9: Save the Configuration

Save your configuration with the **ca save all** and **write memory** commands.

- The **ca save all** command allows you to save the PIX Firewall's RSA key pairs; the CA, the RA, and the PIX Firewall's certificates; and the CA's CRLs in the persistent data file in Flash memory between reloads. The **no ca save** command removes the saved data from PIX Firewall's Flash memory. The **ca save** command itself is not saved with the PIX Firewall configuration between reloads.
- The **write memory** command stores current CA configuration in Flash memory.

Step 10: Verify CA Support Configuration

Use the **show ca identity** command to view the current CA identity settings stored in RAM.

Use the **show ca configure** command to view CA communication parameter settings.

Use the **show ca certificate** command to verify that the enrollment process was successful and to view PIX Firewall, CA, and RA certificates.

Use the **show ca mypubkey rsa** command to view your RSA key pairs. Example 7-1 displays sample output from the **show ca mypubkey rsa** command.

Example 7-1 **show ca mypubkey rsa** *Command Output*

```
% Key pair was generated at: 15:34:55 Jan 01 2000

Key name: labca.cisco.com
Usage: General Purpose Key
Key Data:
305c300d 06092a86 4886f70d 01010105 00034b00 30480241 00c31f4a ad32f60d
6e7ed9a2 32883ca9 319a4b30 e7470888 87732e83 c909fb17 fb5cae70 3de738cf
6e2fd12c 5b3ffa98 8c5adc59 1ec84d78 90bdb53f 2218cfe7 3f020301 0001.
```

Step 11: Monitor and Maintain CA Support

The following steps are optional, depending on your particular requirements:

- Request a CRL
- Delete PIX Firewall's RSA keys and certificates
- Delete CA data from Flash memory

Request a CRL

Request a CRL at any time with the **ca crl request** command. The PIX Firewall automatically requests a CRL from the CA at various times, depending on whether the CA is in the RA mode or not. If the CA is not in the RA mode, a CRL is requested whenever the system reboots and finds that it does not already contain a valid (unexpired) CRL. If the CA is in the RA mode, no CRL can be obtained until a peer's certificate is sent by an IKE exchange. When a CRL expires, the PIX Firewall automatically requests an updated one. Until a new valid CRL is obtained, the PIX Firewall will not accept peers' certificates.

Delete PIX Firewall's RSA Keys and Certificates

Delete all your PIX Firewall's RSA keys with the **ca zeroize rsa** command. The command deletes all RSA keys that were previously generated by your PIX Firewall. If you issue this command, you must also perform two additional tasks. Perform these tasks in the following order:

Use the **no ca identity** command to manually remove the PIX Firewall's certificates from the configuration. This deletes all the certificates issued by the CA.

Ask the CA administrator to revoke your PIX Firewall's certificates at the CA. Supply the challenge password you created when you originally obtained the PIX Firewall's certificates using the **crypto ca enroll** command.

Delete CA Data from Flash Memory

The **no ca save** command removes the PIX Firewall's RSA key pairs; the CA, the RA, and the PIX Firewall's certificates; and the CA's CRLs from the persistent data file in Flash memory.

Example of a CA Server Configuration

Example 7-2 shows a sample of CA commands for an Entrust CA server.

Example 7-2   *CA Commands for an Entrust CA Server*

```
pix1# write terminal
!
hostname Pix1
domain-name labca.cisco.com
!
ca identity labca 172.30.1.51:cgi-bin/pkiclient.exe 172.30.1.51
ca configure labca ra 1 100 crloptional
```

NOTE   You must use the **show ca mypubkey rsa** command to view your RSA key pairs. You must use the **show ca certificate** command to view PIX Firewall, CA, and RA certificates.

Task 3: Configure IKE

NOTE   The following steps are identical to those for configuring preshared keys except for Step 2, which is the only step covered here. Refer to Chapter 6 for the detailed explanation of each step not covered here.

Configuring IKE consists of three essential steps.

Step 1   **Enable or disable IKE**—Enable or disable IKE (ISAKMP) negotiation for authentication and key exchange. Set the ISAKMP identity.

Step 2   **Create IKE policies**—Define a suite of IKE policies to establish ISAKMP peering between two IPSec endpoints.

Step 3   **Verify IKE configuration**—The **write terminal** and **show isakmp policy** commands display configured policies.

Step 2: Create IKE Policies

The next major step in configuring the Pix Firewall ISAKMP support is to define a suite of ISAKMP policies. The goal of defining a suite of IKE policies is to establish ISAKMP peering between two IPSec endpoints. Use the IKE policy details gathered during the planning task. Configure an IKE phase one policy with the **isakmp policy** command to match expected IPSec peers:

Step 1   Identify the policy with a unique priority number.

```
pixfirewall(config)# isakmp policy priority
```

Step 2   Specify the encryption algorithm. The default is **des**.

```
pixfirewall(config)# isakmp policy priority encryption {des | 3des}
```

Step 3   Specify the hash algorithm. The default is **sha**.

```
pixfirewall(config)# isakmp policy priority hash {md5 | sha}
```

Step 4   Specify the authentication method.

```
pixfirewall(config)# isakmp policy priority authentication {pre-share |
rsa-sig}
```

NOTE   If you specify the authentication method using a CA server, you must use the rsa-sig authentication method.

Step 5   Specify the Diffie-Hellman group identifier. The default is **group 1**.

```
pixfirewall(config)# isakmp policy priority group {1 | 2}
```

Step 6   Specify the IKE SA's lifetime. The default is **86400**.

```
pixfirewall(config)# isakmp policy priority lifetime seconds
```

NOTE	PIX Firewall software has preset default values. If you enter a default value for a given policy parameter, it will not be written in the configuration. If you do not specify a value for a given policy parameter, the default value is assigned. You can observe configured and default values with the **show isakmp policy** command.

When configuring ISAKMP (IKE) for certificate-based authentication, it is important to match the IKE identity type with the certificate type. The **ca enroll** command used to acquire certificates will, by default, get a certificate with the identity based on host name. The default identity type for the **isakmp identity** command is based on the address instead of the host name. You can reconcile this disparity of identity types by using the **isakmp identity hostname** command when configuring CA support.

If you are using RSA signatures as your authentication method in your IKE policies, Cisco recommends you set each participating peer's identity to the host name. Otherwise, the ISAKMP security association to be established during phase one of IKE might fail.

Use the **no isakmp identity hostname** command to reset the IKE identity to the default value of IP address.

Task 4: Configure IPSec

The next major task in configuring PIX Firewall IPSec is to configure IPSec parameters that you previously determined. This section presents the steps used to configure IPSec parameters for IKE RSA signatures.

NOTE	The following steps are identical to those for configuring preshared keys. Refer to Chapter 6 for the detailed explanation of each step.

The general tasks and commands used to configure IPSec encryption on the PIX Firewall are summarized as follows. Along with this chapter, they are covered in detail in Chapter 6.

Step 1   Configure crypto access lists with the **access-list** command.

Step 2   Configure transform set suites with the **crypto ipsec transform-set** command.

Step 3   Configure crypto maps with the **crypto map** command.

Step 4   Configure global IPSec SA lifetimes with the **crypto ipsec security-association lifetime** command.

Step 5 Apply crypto maps to the terminating/originating interface with the **crypto map** *map-name* **interface** command.

Step 6 Verify IPSec configuration using the variety of available **show** commands.

Task 5: Test and Verify VPN Configuration

The last major task in configuring PIX Firewall IPSec is to test and verify the IKE and IPSec configuration accomplished in the previous tasks. This section summarizes the methods and commands used to test and verify the VPN configuration including CA, IKE, and IPSec configuration.

NOTE   Although many of the test and verify commands are used the same as when configuring preshared keys, there are some commands unique to RSA signatures.

Test and verify CA configuration with the commands in Table 7-3.

Table 7-3   *Commands to Test and Verify CA Configuration*

Command	Description
show ca identity	Displays the CA your PIX Firewall uses
show ca configure	Displays the parameters for communication between the PIX Firewall and the CA
show ca mypubkey rsa	Displays the PIX Firewall's public RSA keys
show ca certificate	Displays the current status of requested certificates and relevant information of received certificates, such as CA and RA certificates

Debug CA messages with the **debug crypto ca** command. This command displays communications between the PIX Firewall and the CA server.

Delete RSA keys and CA certificates with the commands in Table 7-4.

Table 7-4   *Commands to Delete RSA Keys and CA Certificates*

Command	Description
ca zeroize rsa	Deletes all RSA keys that were previously generated by your PIX Firewall. If you issue this command, you must also enter the **no ca identity** command to delete CA certificates and ask the CA administrator to revoke your PIX Firewall's certificates at the CA.
no ca identity	Manually removes the PIX Firewall's certificates from the configuration; this command deletes all the certificates issued by the CA.

Test and Verify IKE Configuration

Test and verify IKE configuration on the PIX Firewall with the commands in Table 7-5.

Table 7-5   *Commands to Test and Verify IKE Configuration*

Command	Description
show access-list	Lists the **access-list** command statements in the configuration. Used to verify general access lists to permit IPSec traffic.
show isakmp	Displays configured ISAKMP policies in a format similar to a **write terminal** command.
show isakmp policy	Displays default and any configured ISAKMP policies.

Test and Verify IPSec Configuration

Test and verify IPSec configuration on the PIX Firewall with the commands in Table 7-6.

Table 7-6   *Commands to Test and Verify IPSec Configuration*

Command	Description
show access-list	Lists the **access-list** command statements in the configuration. Used to verify that the crypto access lists select interesting traffic. Displays number of packets that matched the access list.
show crypto map	Displays the configured crypto map parameters.
show crypto ipsec transform-set	Displays the configured IPSec transform sets.
show crypto ipsec security-association lifetime	Displays the correct global IPSec SA lifetime values.

Monitor and Manage IKE and IPSec Communications

Monitor and manage IKE and IPSec communications between the PIX Firewall and IPSec peers with the commands in Table 7-7.

Table 7-7   *Commands to Monitor and Manage IKE and IPSec Communications*

Command	Description
show isakmp sa	Displays the current status of ISAKMP SAs
show crypto ipsec sa	Displays the current status of IPSec SAs—useful for ensuring traffic is being encrypted
clear crypto isakmp sa	Clears ISAKMP SAs
clear crypto ipsec sa	Clears IPSec SAs
debug crypto isakmp	Displays ISAKMP (IKE) communications between the PIX Firewall and IPSec peers
debug crypto ipsec	Displays IPSec communications between the PIX Firewall and IPSec peers

Summary

This chapter provided detailed information on how to configure a Cisco Secure PIX Firewall to use a CA for IPSec VPNs. It started by looking at the tasks involved in configuring CA support for IPSec encryption. Many of these tasks were the same as in Chapter 6, which covers preshared key support for Cisco PIX-based VPNs. This chapter also provided an overview of CAs and their related technologies. Following this overview, the chapter looked at the configuration steps involved in configuring CA support for a Cisco IOS router. After the CA was configured, the chapter continued with the rest of the IPSec configuration tasks until the VPN was established.

Now that you have configured both preshared keys and CA support on Cisco PIX Firewalls, Chapter 8, "Troubleshooting Cisco PIX Firewall VPNs," looks at the troubleshooting tools that are available for Cisco PIX-based IPSec VPNs.

Review Questions

1 SCEP stands for what?

2 What is the maximum RSA key modulus size?

3 In its default state, which PIX-compatible CA does not support SCEP?

4 Why must you set the time and date on a PIX Firewall before enabling CA support?

5 What is the minimum RSA key modulus size?

6 What are the RSA key pairs used for?

7 What command allows you to save the PIX Firewall's RSA key pairs; the CA, the RA, and PIX Firewall's certificates; and the CA's CRLs in the persistent data file in Flash memory between reloads?

8 Which peer authentication method is considered to be the stronger, preshared or RSA encryption?

9 What command removes the PIX Firewall's RSA key pairs; the CA, the RA, and PIX Firewall's certificates; and the CA's CRLs from the persistent data file in Flash memory?

10 What command deletes all RSA keys that were previously generated by your PIX Firewall?

CHAPTER 8

Troubleshooting Cisco PIX Firewall VPNs

The previous chapters cover the configuration of Internet Protocol Security (IPSec) virtual private networks (VPNs) on Cisco Secure PIX Firewalls. Basic troubleshooting scenarios are presented within these previous chapters. This chapter presents a sample network and explains some basic troubleshooting that can be done to alleviate common problems when configuring a PIX-based IPSec VPN. You will see the sample IPSec configurations for the PIX Firewalls. The chapter then displays the various **show** and **debug** outputs related to the common problems that will be introduced into this example network. This will help you to diagnose and troubleshoot common problems you might come across in a real-world deployment.

This chapter covers the following topics:

- **Sample IPSec network configuration**—A basic PIX configuration is presented.
- **Configuring IPSec**—The basic configuration is changed to configure the IPSec VPN.
- **Troubleshooting the IPSec configuration**—Once the VPN is established, errors are introduced to simulate typical problems. This section explains the methods that can be used to identify these errors.

Sample IPSec Network Configuration

Figure 8-1 shows the sample network referred to in this troubleshooting chapter. The diagram presents two hosts (Host A and Host B) that are connected over the public Internet. The requirement of the network configuration is for a VPN to be established between PIX A and PIX B to facilitate the protected connection from Host A to Host B. PIX A and PIX B are connected to the Internet by two routers. These routers are not filtering any traffic or adding any firewalling functionality.

Figure 8-1 *Sample IPSec Network*

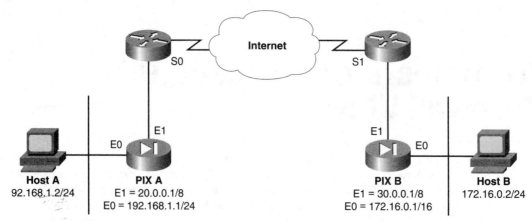

Host A and Host B are both using RFC 1918-compliant private addresses that are not routable on the Internet.

The initial configurations are shown in Example 8-1 and Example 8-2.

Example 8-1 *PIX A Initial Configuration*

```
Building configuration...
: Saved
:
PIX Version 6.0(1)
nameif ethernet0 outside security0
nameif ethernet1 inside security100
nameif ethernet2 intf2 security10
nameif ethernet3 intf3 security15
nameif ethernet4 intf4 security20
nameif ethernet5 intf5 security25
enable password 8Ry2YjIyt7RRXU24 encrypted
passwd 2KFQnbNIdI.2KYOU encrypted
hostname PIXA
fixup protocol ftp 21
fixup protocol http 80
fixup protocol h323 1720
fixup protocol rsh 514
fixup protocol smtp 25
fixup protocol sqlnet 1521
fixup protocol sip 5060
fixup protocol skinny 2000
names
pager lines 24
logging on
logging console debugging
interface ethernet0 auto
interface ethernet1 auto
interface ethernet2 auto shutdown
```

Example 8-1 *PIX A Initial Configuration (Continued)*

```
interface ethernet3 auto shutdown
interface ethernet4 auto shutdown
interface ethernet5 auto shutdown
mtu outside 1500
mtu inside 1500
mtu intf2 1500
mtu intf3 1500
mtu intf4 1500
mtu intf5 1500
ip address outside 20.0.0.1 255.0.0.0
ip address inside 192.168.1.1 255.255.255.0
ip address intf2 127.0.0.1 255.255.255.255
ip address intf3 127.0.0.1 255.255.255.255
ip address intf4 127.0.0.1 255.255.255.255
ip address intf5 127.0.0.1 255.255.255.255
ip audit info action alarm
ip audit attack action alarm
no failover
failover timeout 0:00:00
failover poll 15
failover ip address outside 0.0.0.0
failover ip address inside 0.0.0.0
failover ip address intf2 0.0.0.0
failover ip address intf3 0.0.0.0
failover ip address intf4 0.0.0.0
failover ip address intf5 0.0.0.0
pdm history enable
arp timeout 14400
global (outside) 1 20.0.0.10
nat (inside) 0 access-list 100
nat (inside) 1 0.0.0.0 0.0.0.0 0 0
route outside 0.0.0.0 0.0.0.0 20.0.0.2 1
timeout xlate 3:00:00
timeout conn 1:00:00 half-closed 0:10:00 udp 0:02:00 rpc 0:10:00 h323
    0:05:00 sip 0:30:00 sip_media 0:02:00
timeout uauth 0:05:00 absolute
aaa-server TACACS+ protocol tacacs+
aaa-server RADIUS protocol radius
no snmp-server location
no snmp-server contact
snmp-server community public
no snmp-server enable traps
floodguard enable
sysopt connection permit-ipsec
no sysopt route dnat
telnet timeout 5
ssh timeout 5
terminal width 80
Cryptochecksum:363f79b5e872a02f30191bca7cec86ea
: end
[OK]
PIXA#
```

Example 8-2 shows the PIX B initial configuration from Figure 8-1.

Example 8-2 *PIX B Initial Configuration*

```
Building configuration...
: Saved
:
PIX Version 6.0(1)
nameif ethernet0 outside security0
nameif ethernet1 inside security100
nameif ethernet2 intf2 security10
enable password 8Ry2YjIyt7RRXU24 encrypted
passwd 2KFQnbNIdI.2KYOU encrypted
hostname PIXB
fixup protocol ftp 21
fixup protocol http 80
fixup protocol h323 1720
fixup protocol rsh 514
fixup protocol smtp 25
fixup protocol sqlnet 1521
fixup protocol sip 5060
fixup protocol skinny 2000
names
pager lines 24
logging on
logging console debugging
interface ethernet0 auto
interface ethernet1 auto
interface ethernet2 auto shutdown
mtu outside 1500
mtu inside 1500
mtu intf2 1500
ip address outside 30.0.0.1 255.0.0.0
ip address inside 172.16.0.1 255.255.0.0
ip address intf2 127.0.0.1 255.255.255.255
ip audit info action alarm
ip audit attack action alarm
pdm history enable
arp timeout 14400
global (outside) 1 30.0.0.10
nat (inside) 0 access-list 100
nat (inside) 1 0.0.0.0 0.0.0.0 0 0
route outside 0.0.0.0 0.0.0.0 30.0.0.2 1
timeout xlate 3:00:00
timeout conn 1:00:00 half-closed 0:10:00 udp 0:02:00 rpc 0:10:00 h323 0:05:00 sip
0:30:00 sip_media 0:02:00
timeout uauth 0:05:00 absolute
aaa-server TACACS+ protocol tacacs+
aaa-server RADIUS protocol radius
no snmp-server location
no snmp-server contact
snmp-server community public
no snmp-server enable traps
floodguard enable
```

Example 8-2 *PIX B Initial Configuration (Continued)*

```
sysopt connection permit-ipsec
no sysopt route dnat
telnet timeout 5
ssh timeout 5
terminal width 80
Cryptochecksum:2cefdbd73aee6bc4ae93e850d0950bb7
: end
[OK]
PIXB#
```

Because both of these PIXs also provide access to the public Internet and act as the single egress point from the network, they both have static default routes pointing to local next hop routers.

Both of the next hop routers' Serial interfaces are publicly addressed and connected. Before you start the IPSec configuration, you have to ensure that the PIX Firewalls can communicate with each other. For the IPSec peer relationship to be formed, Layer 3 communication must be established between both peers. The best way to check this is to ping the remote IPSec peer from the local IPSec peer at each end, as shown in Example 8-3.

Example 8-3 **ping** *Output*

```
PIXA# ping 30.0.0.1
        30.0.0.1 response received -- 0ms
        30.0.0.1 response received -- 0ms
        30.0.0.1 response received -- 0ms

PIXB# ping 20.0.0.1
        20.0.0.1 response received -- 0ms
        20.0.0.1 response received -- 0ms
        20.0.0.1 response received -- 0ms
```

You can see from the results in Example 8-3 that PIX A can ping the outside interface of PIX B and vice versa. This confirms that communication between these peers exists.

Configuring IPSec

Now that you have a working routing configuration, you can add the IPSec components to get to a stage where you have a fully working IPSec configuration. Once you have reached this point, this chapter will then introduce errors to the configuration and compare the results as a troubleshooting exercise.

The IPSec configurations are displayed in Example 8-4 and Example 8-5.

Example 8-4 *PIX A IPSec Configuration*

```
access-list 100 permit ip 192.168.1.0 255.255.255.0 172.16.0.0 255.255.0.0
crypto ipsec transform-set myset esp-des esp-sha-hmac
crypto map newmap 10 ipsec-isakmp
crypto map newmap 10 match address 100
crypto map newmap 10 set peer 30.0.0.1
crypto map newmap 10 set transform-set myset
crypto map newmap interface outside
isakmp enable outside
isakmp key thisisthekey address 30.0.0.1 netmask 255.255.255.255
isakmp identity address
isakmp policy 10 authentication pre-share
isakmp policy 10 encryption des
isakmp policy 10 hash md5
isakmp policy 10 group 1
isakmp policy 10 lifetime 86400
```

Example 8-5 shows the PIX B IPSec configuration.

Example 8-5 *PIX B IPSec Configuration*

```
access-list 100 permit ip 172.16.0.0 255.255.0.0 192.168.1.0 255.255.255.0
crypto ipsec transform-set myset esp-des esp-sha-hmac
crypto map newmap 10 ipsec-isakmp
crypto map newmap 10 match address 100
crypto map newmap 10 set peer 20.0.0.1
crypto map newmap 10 set transform-set myset
crypto map newmap interface outside
isakmp enable outside
isakmp key thisisthekey address 20.0.0.1 netmask 255.255.255.255
isakmp identity address
isakmp policy 10 authentication pre-share
isakmp policy 10 encryption des
isakmp policy 10 hash md5
isakmp policy 10 group 1
isakmp policy 10 lifetime 86400
```

Refer to Chapter 6, "Configuring the Cisco PIX Firewall for Preshared Keys Site-to-Site," and Chapter 7, "Configuring the Cisco PIX Firewall for CA Site-to-Site," on how to configure IPSec on Cisco PIX Firewalls if you require an explanation of any of the configuration lines.

With this configuration in the PIX Firewalls, you can now verify that Host A can successfully ping Host B using the VPN over the public Internet.

By default, all IPSec traffic is disallowed through the firewall. A Network Address Translation (NAT) and conduit/access list must exist for IPSec traffic to flow through the firewall, as in any other traffic flow. However, if a crypto map is assigned to an interface,

IPSec traffic for that crypto map is allowed to bypass the adaptive security algorithm (ASA) with the default **sysopt connection permit-ipsec** command.

show Commands

In this working state, look at the output of a few **show** commands to ascertain what a normal configuration will show.

There are numerous **show** commands that can be used to verify IPSec operation. These **show** commands can be split into two sections.

- **Display show commands**—Display information about the IPSec configuration
- **Information show commands**—Display information about the state of the IPSec connections on the PIX Firewall

Display **show** Commands

This section covers the output of three display **show** commands: **show crypto ipsec transform-set**, **show crypto map**, and **show crypto isakmp policy**. The output shown is from PIX A. The output from PIX B is identical for the **show crypto ipsec transform-set** and **show crypto isakmp policy** commands; it must be in order for an IPSec peer to be established. The **show crypto map** output for PIX B will reflect PIX A as its peer.

The **show** command in Example 8-6 displays the configured IPSec transform set. Note that it is using esp-des and esp-sha-hmac within the transform set. The default mode for IPSec is tunnel.

Example 8-6 **show crypto ipsec transform-set** *Output*

```
PIXA# show crypto ipsec transform-set

Transform set myset: { esp-des esp-sha-hmac  }
   will negotiate = { Tunnel,  },
```

The output in Example 8-7 shows the configured crypto map that is called newmap. The information here appertains to the remote IPSec peer and also to the access list that controls the encryption of the IPSec traffic.

Example 8-7 **show crypto map** *Output*

```
PIXA# show crypto map

Crypto Map: "newmap" interfaces: { outside }

Crypto Map "newmap" 10 ipsec-isakmp
        Peer = 30.0.0.1
        access-list 100 permit ip 192.168.1.0 255.255.255.0 172.16.0.0 255.255.0.0
(hitcnt=0)
```

continues

Example 8-7 show crypto map *Output (Continued)*

```
                Current peer: 30.0.0.1
                Security association lifetime: 4608000 kilobytes/28800 seconds
                PFS (Y/N): N
                Transform sets={ myset, }
```

In Example 8-8 you can see the default policy (priority 65535) and the configured ISAKMP policy of 10. You can see that it is using preshared and Diffie-Hellman group 1.

Example 8-8 show crypto isakmp policy *Output*

```
PIXA# show crypto isakmp policy

Protection suite of priority 10
        encryption algorithm:   DES - Data Encryption Standard (56 bit keys).
        hash algorithm:         Message Digest 5
        authentication method:  Pre-Shared Key
        Diffie-Hellman group:   #1 (768 bit)
        lifetime:               86400 seconds, no volume limit
Default protection suite
        encryption algorithm:   DES - Data Encryption Standard (56 bit keys).
        hash algorithm:         Secure Hash Standard
        authentication method:  Rivest-Shamir-Adleman Signature
        Diffie-Hellman group:   #1 (768 bit)
        lifetime:               86400 seconds, no volume limit
```

Information **show** Commands

Once data that matches the IPSec access list has passed the interface with the crypto map applied to it, the VPN will be established. At this point, some additional commands can be entered that show various states of the IPSec components. The commands that this section covers are **show crypto engine** and **show crypto ipsec sa**. For this test, you will initiate a ping from Host A to Host B and look at the commands on PIX B.

The output in Example 8-9 shows the two IPSec connection maps for the firewall. You can see that there are two used connections (one inbound and one outbound), and both of these are active. This confirms that the VPN is established.

Example 8-9 show crypto engine *Output*

```
PIXB#show crypto engine
Crypto Engine Connection Map:
    size = 8, free = 6, used = 2, active = 2
```

The output of the **show crypto ipsec sa** command is displayed in Example 8-10. Quite a lot of information is presented by this command. The start of the command shows the interface and crypto map name that is associated with the interface. Then the inbound and outbound SAs are shown. These are either Authentication Header (AH) or Encapsulating

Security Payload (ESP) security associations (SAs). In this case, because the example only uses ESP, there is no AH inbound or outbound SA.

Example 8-10 show crypto ipsec sa *Output*

```
PIXB# show crypto ipsec sa

interface: outside
    Crypto map tag: newmap, local addr. 20.0.0.1

    local  ident (addr/mask/prot/port): (192.168.1.0/255.255.255.0/0/0)
    remote ident (addr/mask/prot/port): (172.16.0.0/255.255.0.0/0/0)
    current_peer: 30.0.0.1
      PERMIT, flags={origin_is_acl,}
     #pkts encaps: 0, #pkts encrypt: 0, #pkts digest 0
     #pkts decaps: 3, #pkts decrypt: 3, #pkts verify 3
     #pkts compressed: 0, #pkts decompressed: 0
     #pkts not compressed: 0, #pkts compr. failed: 0, #pkts decompress failed: 0
     #send errors 0, #recv errors 0

      local crypto endpt.: 20.0.0.1, remote crypto endpt.: 30.0.0.1
      path mtu 1500, ipsec overhead 56, media mtu 1500
      current outbound spi: 963bff3d

     inbound esp sas:
      spi: 0xcbba6d8e(3417992590)
        transform: esp-des esp-sha-hmac ,
        in use settings ={Tunnel, }
        slot: 0, conn id: 1, crypto map: newmap
        sa timing: remaining key lifetime (k/sec): (4607999/28034)
        IV size: 8 bytes
        replay detection support: Y

     inbound ah sas:

     outbound esp sas:
      spi: 0x963bff3d(2520514365)
        transform: esp-des esp-sha-hmac ,
        in use settings ={Tunnel, }
        slot: 0, conn id: 2, crypto map: newmap
        sa timing: remaining key lifetime (k/sec): (4608000/28025)
        IV size: 8 bytes
        replay detection support: Y

     outbound ah sas:
```

In Example 8-10, you can also see next to the PERMIT statement that it was a condition met by an access control list (ACL) that initiated the IPSec connection.

Troubleshooting the IPSec Configuration

In the previous section, you successfully configured an IPSec VPN between PIX A and PIX B. This was to provide a connection between Host A and Host B over the public Internet. You then ran various **show** commands and outlined what to look for in a working configuration. This working configuration gives you a platform to introduce planned errors and watch the results.

This section covers the most common errors associated with the configuration of IPSec on Cisco PIX Firewalls.

- Incompatible Internet Security Association Key Management Protocol (ISAKMP) policies
- Differing preshared keys between the IPSec peers
- Incorrect IPSec access lists
- Wrong crypto map placement
- Routing issues

Incompatible ISAKMP Policies

The ISAKMP policy on each of the IPSec peers must match in order for the IPSec VPN to be established.

Look at the ISAKMP policies for PIX A and PIX B. The command to display the ISAKMP policy is **show crypto isakmp policy,** as shown in Example 8-11 and Example 8-12.

Example 8-11 *ISAKMP Policy on PIX A*

```
PIXA# show crypto isakmp policy

Protection suite of priority 10
        encryption algorithm:   DES - Data Encryption Standard (56 bit keys).
        hash algorithm:         Message Digest 5
        authentication method:  Pre-Shared Key
        Diffie-Hellman group:   #1 (768 bit)
        lifetime:               86400 seconds, no volume limit
Default protection suite
        encryption algorithm:   DES - Data Encryption Standard (56 bit keys).
        hash algorithm:         Secure Hash Standard
        authentication method:  Rivest-Shamir-Adleman Signature
        Diffie-Hellman group:   #1 (768 bit)
        lifetime:               86400 seconds, no volume limit
```

Example 8-12 displays the **show crypto isakmp policy** output for PIX B.

Example 8-12 *ISAKMP Policy on PIX B*

```
PIXB# show crypto isakmp policy

Protection suite of priority 10
        encryption algorithm:   DES - Data Encryption Standard (56 bit keys).
        hash algorithm:         Message Digest 5
        authentication method:  Pre-Shared Key
        Diffie-Hellman group:   #1 (768 bit)
        lifetime:               86400 seconds, no volume limit
Default protection suite
        encryption algorithm:   DES - Data Encryption Standard (56 bit keys).
        hash algorithm:         Secure Hash Standard
        authentication method:  Rivest-Shamir-Adleman Signature
        Diffie-Hellman group:   #1 (768 bit)
        lifetime:               86400 seconds, no volume limit
```

You can see from the output in Example 8-11 and Example 8-12 that both of these PIXs have two ISAKMP policies, or protection suites. The first has a priority of 10, and the default has a priority of 65535, although this value is not shown. You can also see that the values for the priority 10 suite all match between PIX A and B. This is essential for ISAKMP negotiation.

The values controlled by the ISAKMP policy are

- Encryption algorithm
- Hash algorithm
- Authentication method
- Diffie-Hellman group
- SA lifetime

On the Cisco PIX Firewall, these values are all set from global configuration mode with the **isakmp** command. The output in Example 8-13 shows the available options with the **isakmp** command.

Example 8-13 isakmp *Command Options*

```
PIXA(config)# isakmp ?
usage: isakmp policy <priority> authen <pre-share|rsa-sig>
        isakmp policy <priority> encrypt <des|3des>
        isakmp policy <priority> hash <md5|sha>
        isakmp policy <priority> group <1|2>
        isakmp policy <priority> lifetime <seconds>
        isakmp key <key-string> address <ip> [netmask <mask>] [no-xauth]
  [no-config-mode]
        isakmp enable <if_name>
        isakmp identity <address|hostname>
```

continues

Example 8-13 isakmp *Command Options (Continued)*

```
            isakmp keepalive <seconds> [<retry seconds>]
            isakmp client configuration address-pool local <poolname> [<pif_name>]
            isakmp peer fqdn|ip <fqdn|ip> [no-xauth] [no-config-mode]
```

In addition to the **show** commands, the command **debug crypto isakmp** is also of great use when troubleshooting ISAKMP issues. This command actually displays the full ISAKMP exchange as it occurs in the PIX Firewall. The full debug output for a ping from Host B to the inside interface of PIX A is shown in Example 8-14.

Example 8-14 *Output from* **debug crypto isakmp**

```
crypto_isakmp_process_block: src 30.0.0.1, dest 20.0.0.1
OAK_MM exchange
ISAKMP (0): processing SA payload. message ID = 0

ISAKMP (0): Checking ISAKMP transform 1 against priority 10 policy
ISAKMP:       encryption DES-CBC
ISAKMP:       hash MD5
ISAKMP:       default group 1
ISAKMP:       auth pre-share
ISAKMP (0): atts are acceptable. Next payload is 0
ISAKMP (0): SA is doing pre-shared key authentication using id type ID_IPV4_ADDR
return status is IKMP_NO_ERROR
crypto_isakmp_process_block: src 30.0.0.1, dest 20.0.0.1
OAK_MM exchange
ISAKMP (0): processing KE payload. message ID = 0

ISAKMP (0): processing NONCE payload. message ID = 0

ISAKMP (0): processing vendor id payload

ISAKMP (0): processing vendor id payload

ISAKMP (0): remote peer supports dead peer detection

ISAKMP (0): processing vendor id payload

ISAKMP (0): speaking to another IOS box!

return status is IKMP_NO_ERROR
crypto_isakmp_process_block: src 30.0.0.1, dest 20.0.0.1
OAK_MM exchange
ISAKMP (0): processing ID payload. message ID = 0
ISAKMP (0): processing HASH payload. message ID = 0
ISAKMP (0): SA has been authenticated

ISAKMP (0): ID payload
        next-payload : 8
        type         : 1
        protocol     : 17
        port         : 500
        length       : 8
```

Example 8-14 *Output from* **debug crypto isakmp** *(Continued)*

```
ISAKMP (0): Total payload length: 12
return status is IKMP_NO_ERROR
crypto_isakmp_process_block: src 30.0.0.1, dest 20.0.0.1
OAK_QM exchange
oakley_process_quick_mode:
OAK_QM_IDLE
ISAKMP (0): processing SA payload. message ID = 2342393309

ISAKMP : Checking IPSec proposal 1

ISAKMP: transform 1, ESP_DES
ISAKMP:    attributes in transform:
ISAKMP:       encaps is 1
ISAKMP:       SA life type in seconds
ISAKMP:       SA life duration (basic) of 28800
ISAKMP:       SA life type in kilobytes
ISAKMP:       SA life duration (VPI) of  0x0 0x46 0x50 0x0
ISAKMP:       authenticator is HMAC-SHA
ISAKMP (0): atts are acceptable.
ISAKMP (0): processing NONCE payload. message ID = 2342393309

ISAKMP (0): processing ID payload. message ID = 2342393309
ISAKMP (0): ID_IPV4_ADDR_SUBNET src 172.16.0.0/255.255.0.0 prot 0 port 0
ISAKMP (0): processing ID payload. message ID = 2342393309
ISAKMP (0): ID_IPV4_ADDR_SUBNET dst 192.168.1.0/255.255.255.0 prot 0 port 0
ISAKMP (0): processing NOTIFY payload 24578 protocol 1
        spi 0, message ID = 2342393309
ISAKMP (0): processing notify INITIAL_CONTACT
return status is IKMP_NO_ERROR60
ISAKMP (0): sending NOTIFY message 11 protocol 3
crypto_isakmp_process_block: src 30.0.0.1, dest 20.0.0.1
OAK_QM exchange
oakley_process_quick_mode:
OAK_QM_AUTH_AWAIT
ISAKMP (0): Creating IPSec SAs
        inbound SA from       30.0.0.1 to       20.0.0.1 (proxy
     172.16.0.0 to    192.168.1.0)
        has spi 2018067353 and conn_id 2 and flags 4
        lifetime of 28800 seconds
        lifetime of 4608000 kilobytes
        outbound SA from      20.0.0.1 to       30.0.0.1 (proxy
     192.168.1.0 to      172.16.0.0)
        has spi 2776158804 and conn_id 1 and flags 4
        lifetime of 28800 seconds
        lifetime of 4608000 kilobytes
return status is IKMP_NO_ERROR2302: deleting SA, (sa) sa_dest= 20.0.0.1,
 sa_prot= 50, sa_spi= 0xcbba6d8e(3417992590), sa_trans= esp-des esp-sha-hmac
 , sa_conn_id= 1
```

From the output in Example 8-14, notice the shaded portion. This shaded portion shows that the ISAKMP values are acceptable, and the PIX Firewall continues with the ISAKMP negotiation process.

So this is what the debug output looks like in a working configuration. But what if you change a value in the ISAKMP policy?

In this example, the hash value is changed from MD5 to the default SHA on PIX A. After that, you will observe the output from the **debug crypto isakmp** command.

First, look at the newly configured ISAKMP policy on PIX A, as shown in Example 8-15.

Example 8-15 *Newly Configured ISAKMP Policy on PIX A*

```
PIXA# show crypto isakmp policy

Protection suite of priority 10
        encryption algorithm:   DES - Data Encryption Standard (56 bit keys).
        hash algorithm:         Secure Hash Standard
        authentication method:  Pre-Shared Key
        Diffie-Hellman group:   #1 (768 bit)
        lifetime:               86400 seconds, no volume limit
Default protection suite
        encryption algorithm:   DES - Data Encryption Standard (56 bit keys).
        hash algorithm:         Secure Hash Standard
        authentication method:  Rivest-Shamir-Adleman Signature
        Diffie-Hellman group:   #1 (768 bit)
        lifetime:               86400 seconds, no volume limit
```

The shaded portion of Example 8-15 shows that the hash algorithm has been changed from MD5 to SHA. Now if you carry out the same ping, Host B to PIX A, as before and look at the debug output, you will see a different result, as shown in Example 8-16.

Example 8-16 *Output from* **debug crypto isakmp**

```
OAK_MM exchange
ISAKMP (0): processing SA payload. message ID = 0
ISAKMP (0): Checking ISAKMP transform 1 against priority 10 policy
ISAKMP:      encryption DES-CBC
ISAKMP:      hash MD5
ISAKMP:      default group 1
ISAKMP:      auth pre-share
ISAKMP (0): atts are not acceptable. Next payload is 0
ISAKMP (0): Checking ISAKMP transform 1 against priority 65535 policy
ISAKMP:      encryption DES-CBC
ISAKMP:      hash MD5
ISAKMP:      default group 1
ISAKMP:      auth pre-share
ISAKMP (0): atts are not acceptable. Next payload is 0
ISAKMP (0): no offers accepted!
ISAKMP (0): SA not acceptable!
return status is IKMP_ERR_TRANS
```

You can clearly see from this debug output that there was a failure in the ISAKMP negotiation. This is because the ISAKMP values are unacceptable. They are classed as unacceptable because they do not match.

Differing Preshared Keys Between the IPSec Peers

The preshared secret keys must be *exactly* the same on both of the IPSec peers. These keys are compared during the ISAKMP Phase One authentication. There are two steps to check for here. The first step is to ensure that both PIX Firewalls are using preshared authentication in their ISAKMP policies. This can be identified with the **show crypto isakmp** command. The output in Example 8-17 and Example 8-18 is the result of the aforementioned command on both PIX A and B.

Example 8-17 *ISAKMP Policy on PIX A*

```
PIXA# show crypto isakmp
isakmp enable outside
isakmp key ******** address 30.0.0.1 netmask 255.255.255.255
isakmp identity address
isakmp policy 10 authentication pre-share
isakmp policy 10 encryption des
isakmp policy 10 hash md5
isakmp policy 10 group 1
isakmp policy 10 lifetime 86400
```

Example 8-18 displays the **show crypto isakmp** output for PIX B.

Example 8-18 *ISAKMP Policy on PIX B*

```
PIXB# show crypto isakmp
isakmp enable outside
isakmp key ******** address 20.0.0.1 netmask 255.255.255.255
isakmp identity address
isakmp policy 10 authentication pre-share
isakmp policy 10 encryption des
isakmp policy 10 hash md5
isakmp policy 10 group 1
isakmp policy 10 lifetime 86400
```

Check that the authentication method on both of the firewalls is set to preshared key; you can see from the Example 8-17 and Example 8-18 that it is. If the authentication methods do not match between the firewalls, then the ISAKMP negotiation will fail, as outlined in the previous section.

You know that the PIX Firewalls are both using preshared keys as their authentication method. On a Cisco IOS router, you can view the preshared secret key with the **show crypto isakmp key** command. On the Cisco PIX Firewall, once the preshared key is entered, there is no way to display it. When you look at the configuration either onscreen or printed, the preshared key will always be replaced with eight asterisks (*). To generate a fault here, this example changes one of the preshared key values to differ from its IPSec peer.

After this configuration change, when you try to ping from Host A to Host B, the VPN will not be established because of the failure of the preshared key in the ISAKMP negotiation.

Incorrect IPSec Access Lists

The IPSec access list triggers the VPN to be set up between the IPSec peers. This access list operates in a very similar manner to an access list that is used for dial-on-demand routing (DDR). With DDR, interesting traffic (as defined by the access list) causes the BRI interface to be raised and the ISDN call to be placed. The same is true for the IPSec access list. In the initial state, traffic that meets the access list initiates the IPSec process. Once the IPSec connection is established, only traffic that meets the IPSec access list will be encrypted and delivered through the IPSec tunnel. This is a very important point to remember, and it is where the IPSec access list differs from the DDR access list.

This chapter's example has been using an access list on both PIX A and PIX B. These access lists are mirrors of each other. The source in the PIX A access list is the destination in the PIX B access list, and vice versa. These access lists encrypt anything from the local Ethernet network to the remote Ethernet network.

NOTE   It is important to note the slight change in the way access lists are configured on a Cisco PIX Firewall compared with a Cisco IOS router. On a router, the format for an extended access list contains the source and destination networks along with what is called a *wildcard mask*. The wildcard mask is the reverse of a subnet mask. The Cisco PIX Firewalls' implementation of access lists uses subnet masks instead.

For example, an access list to permit anything from 192.168.1.0/24 to 172.16.0.0/16 would be configured as follows:

Cisco IOS:

```
Router(config)#access-lists 101 permit ip 192.168.1.0
   0.0.0.255 172.16.0.0 0.0.255.255
```

Cisco PIX:

```
PIX(config)#access-list 101 permit ip 192.168.1.0
   255.255.255.0 172.16.0.0 255.255.0.0
```

Note that the Cisco IOS router uses wildcard masks and the PIX uses subnet masks.

To introduce an error that provides a troubleshooting example, you can change the IPSec access list on PIX A to have an incorrect source address. You will then ping from Host A to

Host B, and the traffic will not kick off the IPSec process and will not be routable to the destination.

The current IPSec access list on PIX A is as follows:

```
PIXA# show access-list
access-list 100 permit ip 192.168.1.0 255.255.255.0 172.16.0.0
    255.255.0.0 (hitcnt=11)
```

This access list encrypts traffic from the 192.168.1.0/24 network that is destined for the 172.16.0.0/16 network. You are going to make a subtle change to this access list that will break the IPSec process. Remove the existing access list and add the following line of configuration:

```
PIXA# show access-list
access-list 100 permit ip 192.168.2.0 255.255.255.0 172.16.0.0
    255.255.0.0 (hitcnt=11)
```

Note that this will encrypt traffic from the 192.168.2.0/24 network and not the original 192.168.1.0/24 network. After making this change, Host A attempts to ping Host B. Obviously, this fails.

If you are ever faced with a real-world problem similar to this, the first step should always be to ascertain whether the VPN is established between the IPSec peers. There are various ways to accomplish this on a Cisco IOS router, but the easiest way is to use the **show crypto engine** command. This command displays the current state of the IPSec connections, if any. Running this command on PIX A has the following result:

```
PIXA#show crypto engine
Crypto Engine Connection Map:
    size = 8, free = 8, used = 0, active = 0
```

You can see from the output that there are no active IPSec connections. If you can ascertain that relevant traffic has passed the connection that should start the IPSec process, the problem points to the IPSec access list. A simple sanity check of the IPSec access list should be enough to remedy the problem.

Wrong Crypto Map Placement

On the VPN terminating interface, you have to apply the crypto map. For example, to apply the crypto map newmap to the outside interface, the command would be:

```
PIXA(config)# crypto map newmap interface outside
```

This command will make the interface a VPN termination point. Any traffic leaving this interface will be checked against the IPSec access list. If the traffic matches the IPSec access list, it will be encrypted to the standard defined in the related transform set and delivered to the IPSec peer as defined in the crypto map. A useful command for looking at the crypto map applied to an interface is **show crypto map**. The output in Example 8-19 shows this command run on PIX A.

Example 8-19 show crypto map *Output on PIX A*

```
PIXA# show crypto map

Crypto Map: "newmap" interfaces: { outside }

Crypto Map "newmap" 10 ipsec-isakmp
        Peer = 30.0.0.1
        access-list 100 permit ip 192.168.1.0 255.255.255.0 172.16.0.0 255.255.0.0
(hitcnt=11)
        Current peer: 30.0.0.1
        Security association lifetime: 4608000 kilobytes/28800 seconds
        PFS (Y/N): N
        Transform sets={ myset, }
```

You can see from the output in Example 8-19 that crypto map newmap is applied to the outside interface. The output of this command also shows you the IPSec access list, the IPSec peer, the SA settings, the perfect forward secrecy (PFS) status, and the related transform set.

If there is a problem with IPSec traffic, and you have confirmed that the IPSec access list is correct, the crypto map placement might be a good next step to check. If the crypto map is not applied to the outbound interface, traffic will never get encrypted for IPSec to forward it to its peer.

Routing Issues

There are two routing issues that have to be addressed. Both of these issues can cause problems that result in the failure of the IPSec process. The first routing issue concerns routing to the IPSec peer. The second routing issue concerns routing the required packets to the interface with the crypto map applied.

Layer 3 communications have to be established between the IPSec peers. This was covered earlier in this chapter, where you saw that a simple ping between the IPSec peers is adequate to confirm it. If the IPSec peers cannot establish Layer 3 communications, the IPSec process will never be complete and the peers will never be adjacent to each other. In the sample network in Figure 8-1, there are two firewalls that are publicly addressed and connected over the public Internet. In this instance, both peers should be able to ping each other on the outside (Internet-connected) interface.

The other routing issue is related to the delivery of the packets from the local firewall to the remote network over the IPSec tunnel. Take Figure 8-1 as an example. You can see that Host A is on network 192.168.1.0/24 and Host B is on the 172.16.0.0/16 network. For Host A to communicate with Host B, a valid route has to exist in the IP routing table of PIX A to the

Host B network address. This follows basic IP routing principles. Looking at the IP routing table in Example 8-20, you can see that a default route exists out of the outside interface to 20.0.0.2.

Example 8-20 *Routing Table on PIX A*

```
PIXA# show route
        outside 0.0.0.0 0.0.0.0 20.0.0.2 1 OTHER static
        outside 20.0.0.0 255.0.0.0 20.0.0.1 1 CONNECT static
        intf2 127.0.0.1 255.255.255.255 127.0.0.1 1 CONNECT static
        inside 192.168.1.0 255.255.255.0 192.168.1.1 1 CONNECT static

C    20.0.0.0/8 is directly connected, Serial0
C    192.168.1.0/24 is directly connected, Ethernet0
S*   0.0.0.0/0 is directly connected, Serial0
```

Because this example uses a static default route, a problem will not be caused with the routing of the packets. Host A will send a packet with source address of 192.168.1.2 and the destination address of 172.16.0.2. PIX A does not have a specific route for the 172.16.0.0/16 network, but the default route will direct this at the outside interface. The crypto map is applied to the outside interface and the traffic matches the IPSec access list, so it gets encrypted and tunneled to the destination.

The important part to remember is that you have to ensure that the firewall will forward the packet to the interface where the crypto map exists. A default route or a specific route for the remote network will normally suffice in this situation.

Summary

This chapter looked at a basic implementation of IPSec on Cisco Secure PIX Firewalls between two sites over the Internet. You saw a working VPN and then introduced example errors into the configuration. You looked at the relevant commands that can be used on the PIX Firewall to troubleshoot the sample problems that were introduced. These troubleshooting commands and techniques can be used in real-world troubleshooting scenarios.

Review Questions

1 On a Cisco IOS router, the command **show crypto isakmp key** will display the configured preshared keys. What command will do this on the Cisco Secure PIX Firewall?

2 What command on the PIX Firewall would place crypto map newmap to the outside interface?

3 What is the purpose of the **sysopt connection permit-ipsec** command?

4 On the Cisco PIX Firewall, what command shows you the number of free, used, and active crypto connection maps?

5 What is the default SA lifetime?

6 What configuration mode on the Cisco PIX Firewall do you enter the ISAKMP information from?

7 What would be the access list on a PIX Firewall to encrypt all traffic from the network 10.1.0.0/16 to 192.168.2.0/25?

8 By default, is all IPSec traffic allowed or disallowed through the firewall?

9 When you view the IPSec configuration of a PIX Firewall, what character is used to mask the preshared key?

10 Does the Cisco PIX use a wildcard or subnet mask for IPSec access lists?

Cisco VPN Concentrator VPNs

CHAPTER 9

Configuring the Cisco VPN 3000 for Remote Access Using Preshared Keys

This chapter explains how to configure the Cisco VPN 3000 concentrator for Internet Protocol Security (IPSec) using preshared keys for authentication. After presenting an overview of the process, the chapter shows you each major step of the configuration.

This chapter covers the following topics:

- Initial configuration of the Cisco VPN 3000 Concentrator series
- Browser configuration of the Cisco VPN 3000 Concentrator series
- Configuration of the IPSec VPN Client

This chapter follows an example based on the requirements to provide a VPN solution for the I.B. Widget Corporation. The I.B. Widget Corporation has the following characteristics, which can be seen in Figure 9-1.

- Client
    - **Network interface card (NIC) IP address**—172.31.1.1
    - **Virtual IP address**—10.0.1.20
- Cisco VPN 3000 Concentrator
    - Internal authentication server
    - **Private IP address**—10.0.1.5
    - **Public (Internet) IP address**—192.168.1.5
- Corporate servers
    - **Windows NT domain and Dynamic Host Configuration Protocol (DHCP) server**—10.0.1.10

Figure 9-1 *I.B. Widget Corporation*

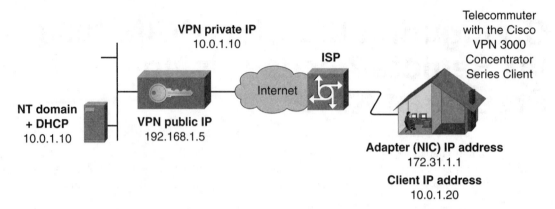

The VPN Concentrator has the following physical connections. These can be seen in Figure 9-2.

- Power cables
  - 100-240 VAC with universal power factor correction.
- Console port
  - Need to configure the Concentrator so operator can access the Concentrator through the browser
  - At a minimum, operator needs to use command-line interface (CLI) to configure the private LAN port.
  - Serial port needs to be configured for 9600 bps 8N1.

The IPSec server has the following LAN ports:

- **Private**—Connected to corporate LAN.
- **Public**—Connected to Internet.
- LAN ports can be 10/100M Ethernet.

Figure 9-2   *VPN Concentrator Physical Connections*

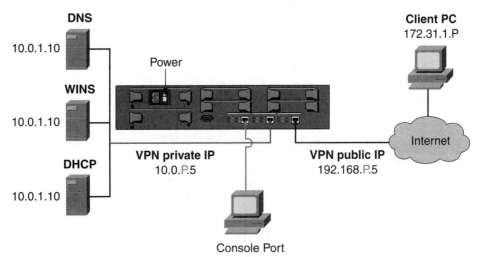

Initial Configuration of the Cisco VPN 3000 Concentrator Series

This section explains configuring the Cisco VPN 3000 Concentrator series with the CLI. When you first install the VPN 3000 Concentrator, you have to configure the basic parameters with a CLI before you can gain access to the browser management interface.

Configure a Private LAN with the CLI

The private LAN on the Cisco VPN 3000 Concentrator series initially must be configured with the CLI. Once the private interface is configured, you can use the browser management interface. You can see from the I.B. Widget scenario outlined previously that the internal interface IP address is 10.1.0.5/24.

Connect to the CLI using a straight Ethernet cable with a RJ45-to-DB9 converter attached or the supplied straight through RS-232 DB9 cable. Connect the other end of the straight Ethernet cable to another RJ45-to-DB9 converter and attach this to a PC running a terminal client. Connect in the usual way.

NOTE   Be sure to use a straight Ethernet cable, as a standard Cisco console cable will not work.

Once connected, from the main CLI menu, select Option 1 to go to configuration mode, then select Option 2 to go to interface configuration mode.

The following output will be displayed.

```
This table shows current IP addresses.
    Interface              Address/Subnet Mask           MAC Address
--------------------------------------------------------------------------
Ethernet 1 - Private  ¦      0.0.0.0/0.0.0.0            ¦
Ethernet 2 - Public   ¦      0.0.0.0/0.0.0.0            ¦
Ethernet 3 - External ¦      0.0.0.0/0.0.0.0            ¦
--------------------------------------------------------------------------
1) Configure Ethernet #1 (Private)

Interfaces -> 1

1) Enable/Disable
2) Set IP Address
3) Set Subnet Mask
4) Select IP Filter
5) Select Ethernet Speed
6) Select Duplex
7) Set Ports Routing Config
8) Back
```

Select Option 2 and add 10.1.0.5/24 as the IP address of the private (inside) interface.

This configures the private (inside) interface so that you are in a position to use the browser-based VPN Manager.

NOTE   Remember to save your changes before you exit the CLI.

NOTE   A Concentrator received from the factory presents the CLI Quick Configuration mode, where you are prompted for basic system parameters, such as date and time, and private and public IP addresses.

Browser Login

The browser-based Manager can be used to further configure the Cisco VPN 3000 Concentrator series.

To connect to the browser Manager, perform the following steps:

Step 1 To access the Concentrator from a browser, point the browser to the IP address of the private interface of the Concentrator that you have just configured in the CLI mode. In our example, this address is 10.1.0.5.

Step 2 Enter **admin** for the Login.

Step 3 Enter **admin** for the Password.

Step 4 Click **Login** to continue.

Figure 9-3 shows the initial login screen of the browser-based Manager.

Figure 9-3 *Initial Login Screen*

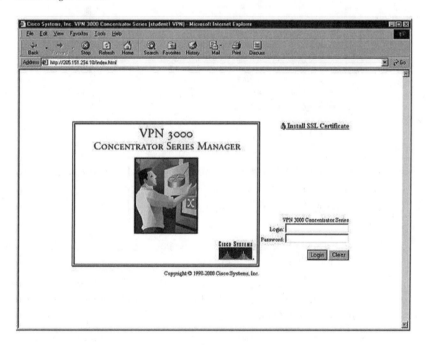

NOTE It is a good idea to change the Admin user account and password. Refer to Chapter 11, "Monitoring and Administration of Cisco VPN 3000 Remote Access Networks," for details on how to do this.

Graphical User Interface

Figure 9-4 shows the main screen of the Concentrator after logging in to the device.

Figure 9-4   *Concentrator Graphical User Interface*

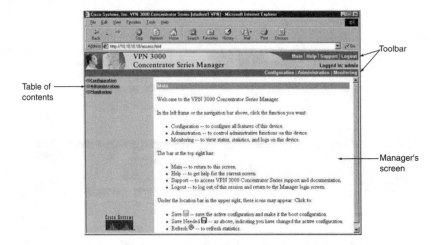

The following is an explanation of Figure 9-4:

- The top frame (VPN 3000 Concentrator Series Manager toolbar) provides quick access to manager functions.

- The left frame (table of contents) provides the table of contents to the Manager's screens.

- The main frame (Manager's screen) displays the current Cisco VPN 3000 Concentrator Manager's screen.

  — From here, you can navigate the Manager using either the table of contents in the left frame or the VPN 3000 Concentrator Series Manager toolbar at the top of the frame.

  — Select a title on the left frame of the screen, and the Concentrator brings up the Manager screen for that section in the main frame.

- Configuration

  — When finished with the configuration screen, click **Apply**.

  — **Apply** allows the configuration to take effect immediately.

  — To save the changes to memory, click the **Save Needed** icon. If you reboot without saving, your configuration changes are lost.

Quick Configuration

Quick Configuration allows you to configure the minimal parameters for operation. It automatically allows single-user IPSec tunnels and permits remote Client connection through an ISP. The Main Menu is used to configure all features.

Perform the following steps to compile the Quick Configuration:

Step 1 Install and power up the hardware.

Step 2 Configure the private or public LAN with the CLI.

Step 3 Use Quick Configuration to get IPSec up and running.

NOTE   You can only run Quick Configuration once. You must reboot to the factory default configuration to run it again.

Browser Configuration of the Cisco VPN 3000 Concentrator Series

After configuring the Cisco VPN 3000 Concentrator series with the CLI, you can use the browser interface to configure the remaining items. This section explains using the browser interface to configure the Cisco VPN 3000 Concentrator series.

You will be configuring the VPN Concentrator for the I.B. Widget client with the VPN 3000 Client to access the private network using the VPN.

This configuration can be broken down into a series of steps. Each step is covered in upcoming sections, with screenshots of the actual configuration from within the browser-based VPN Manager. The ease of configuration, a major strength of the VPN Concentrator series, will become apparent.

The configuration steps are as follows:

Step 1 Configure the system properties.

Step 2 Assign addresses.

Step 3 Configure the IPSec group.

Step 4 Add a user to the group.

Step 1: Configure the System Properties

You have already configured the private interface of the Concentrator with the CLI to establish a browser-based VPN connection to the Concentrator. You can also configure the public interface with the CLI, but in this case, you will configure it through the browser-based VPN Manager.

Clicking **Configuration** and then **Interfaces** in the left pane of the VPN Manager enables you to add the IP address to the public interface. This is shown in Figure 9-5.

The IP Interfaces screen has the following characteristics:

- It displays the current configuration of the IP interfaces.
  - **Private**—Interface toward the internal network
  - **Public**—Interface toward the public network (Internet)
  - **External**—Interface toward the external network
- The private LAN interface was configured with the CLI.

You need to configure the public (Internet-facing or outside) interface. To do this, click the actual interface or the "Public" underlined text in the main window.

Figure 9-5   *IP Interfaces*

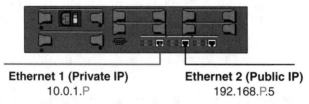

Ethernet 1 (Private IP)   **Ethernet 2 (Public IP)**
10.0.1.P   192.168.P.5

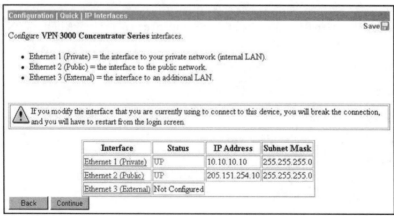

The public IP interface has the following characteristics:

- **Enabled**—Make sure this box is checked to enable the interface.
- **IP Address**—Address on the public network to access the Internet.

  Enter the IP address for this interface, using dotted decimal notation (for example, 192.168.1.5). Note that 0.0.0.0 is not allowed.

- **Subnet Mask**—Enter the subnet mask for this interface using dotted decimal notation (for example, 255.255.255.0). The Manager automatically supplies a standard subnet mask appropriate for the IP address you just entered. For example, the IP address 192.168.1.5 is a Class C address, and the standard subnet mask is 255.255.255.0. You can accept this entry or change it. Note that 0.0.0.0 is not allowed.

- **Filter**—Click the drop-down menu button and select the Public (Default) filter, which allows non-source-routed inbound and outbound tunneling protocols plus ICMP and drops everything else. This is the default filter for Ethernet 2.

- **Speed**—Keep the default value.

This configuration can be seen in Figure 9-6.

Figure 9-6 *Public IP Interface*

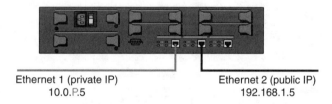

Ethernet 1 (private IP)   Ethernet 2 (public IP)
10.0.P.5   192.168.1.5

Configuration | Quick | IP Interfaces | Ethernet 2

You are modifying the interface you are using to connect to this device. If you make any changes, you will break the connection and you will have to restart from the login screen.

Configuring Ethernet Interface 2 (Public).

Enabled ☑

IP Address ⎢192.168.1.5

Subnet Mask ⎢255.255.255.0

MAC Address 00.90.A4.00.03.51

Filter ⎢2. Public (Default) ▼

Speed ⎢10/100 auto ▼

Duplex ⎢Auto ▼

[Apply] [Cancel]

Now that the public and private interfaces and routing are configured, you can configure the other values required to initiate the VPN. Before you do this, it is a good idea to configure a few more items relating to the VPN Concentrator itself.

One of these items is the routing behavior of the Concentrator. The concentrator is classed as a device running an IP stack. Therefore, it is required to have an internal routing table to communicate in an internetwork. The easiest way to do this is to use a static default route, although you can configure the Concentrator to use dynamic routing protocols such as Open Shortest Path First (OSPF). You are going to use the address 192.168.1.1 as the static default route. This is the IP address of the Ethernet interface of the router that separates the VPN Concentrator from the public Internet.

To configure this, click **Configuration** > **IP Routing** > **Default Gateways** in the left pane of the VPN Manager. Then add the IP address into the Default Gateway text box, as shown in Figure 9-7.

Figure 9-7   *Default Gateway*

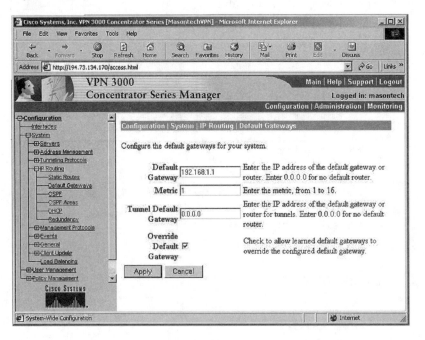

Clicking **Configuration** in the left pane and then **System** and **General** allows you to configure the Concentrator Identification, Time and Date, Sessions, and Authentication parameters. It is a good idea to configure at least the Identification and Time and Date values. This facilitates a unique host name for the Concentrator, and setting the correct date and time is very important to ensure that logging, accounting, and security access information is correct.

Step 2: Assign Addresses

At this stage, the public and private interfaces are configured, along with the default gateway to allow communication across the Internetwork. You now have to assign addresses. Addresses are assigned by clicking **Configuration** and **Address Assignment** in the left pane of the VPN browser window.

In Cisco VPN 3000 Concentrator address management, you deal with the second set of IP addresses. These are the private IP addresses that get assigned to Clients.

You must select at least one method from the following:

- **Use Client Address**—Check this box to let the Client specify its own IP address. For maximum security, it is recommended that you control IP address assignment and not use Client-specified IP addresses.

- **Per User**—Check this box to assign IP addresses retrieved from an authentication server on a per-user basis. If you are using an authentication server (external or internal) that has IP addresses configured, using this method is recommended.

- **Use DHCP**—Check this box to use a Dynamic Host Configuration Protocol (DHCP) server to assign IP addresses.

- **Configured Pool**—Check this box to use the Cisco VPN 3000 Concentrator to assign IP addresses from an internal configured pool.

For this example with the I.B. Widget solution, you are going to check the DHCP option and enter the address **10.0.1.10** as the IP address of the DHCP server. This DHCP server exists on the private network. Figure 9-8 shows this configuration.

Figure 9-8   *Address Assignment*

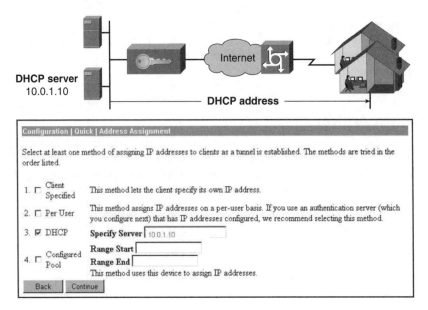

Step 3: Configure the IPSec Group

Identify groups and users based on the following:

- **Corporate remote access strategy**—Different users, departments, companies (extranet).

- **The need to accommodate different access and usage requirements**—Define hours, duration, protocols, idle timeouts, simultaneous logins, and so on.

- **How you can cater to different needs**—Develop the concept of users and groups.

  Different requirements can be defined according to users and groups.

- **Default group**—Base template.

- **Groups**—Inherit from the base group or change specific parameters based on the requirements of the group, such as the following:

  — **Corporate 7/24**—Default group

  — **Telesales 8-5 Monday–Friday**—Telesales group

By configuring the base group first, the specific groups second, and users as members of groups third, you can quickly manage access and usage rights for large numbers of users.

The following points for groups and users are important:

- Groups and users have attributes that determine their access to and use of the Concentrator.

- Users are members of groups, and groups are members of the base group.

- Users inherit attributes from groups, and groups inherit attributes from the base group.

- The following are attribute points to note:

  — Base group attributes are the default, or system-wide, attributes.

  — You can configure a maximum of 100 groups and users (combined) in the Cisco VPN 3000 Concentrator internal server.

  — Both users and groups have names and passwords.

  — A user can be a member of only one group.

- Users who are not members of a specific group are, by default, members of the base group. Therefore, to ensure maximum security and control, you should assign all users to appropriate specific groups and configure base group attributes carefully.

- You can change group attributes, thereby changing attributes for all its members at the same time.

- You can delete a group, but when you do so, all its members revert to the base group. Deleting a group, however, does not delete its members' user profiles.

You have to configure an IPSec group with specific settings before you can create the users. To do this, click **Configuration> User Management> Groups** in the left pane of the VPN Manager.

Clicking the **Add Group** button displays the screen shown in Figure 9-9.

Figure 9-9   *Group Configuration—Identity*

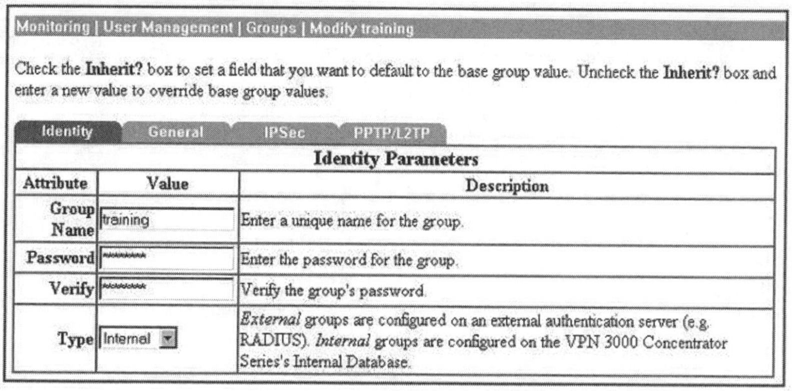

There are four tabs on this screen: **Identity**, **General**, **IPSec**, and **PPTP/L2TP**. Start by looking at the **Identity** Tab.

The **General** tab contains the following parameters:

- **Group Name**—Enter a unique name for this specific group. The maximum is 32 characters. Our example uses "training" as the group name.

- **Password**—Enter a unique password for this specific group. The minimum is 4 characters, and the maximum is 32 characters. The field displays only asterisks.

- **Verify**—Reenter the group password to verify it. The field displays only asterisks.

- **Type**—Click the drop-down menu button and choose the type of group:

  — **Internal**—Use the internal Cisco VPN 3000 Concentrator authentication server to authenticate groups for IPSec tunneling. The internal server is the default selection.

After configuring the settings on the **Identity** tab, clicking the **General** tab shows the screen in Figure 9-10.

Figure 9-10 *Group Configuration—General*

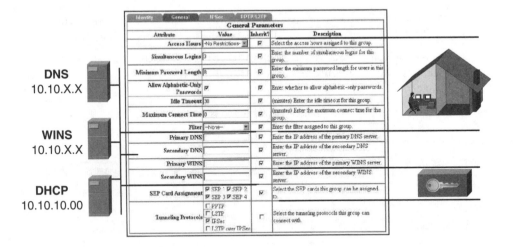

The following settings are available on the General configuration page:

- **Access Hours**—Click the drop-down menu button and select the named hours when group users can access the Cisco VPN 3000 Concentrator.

    — **No Restrictions**—No restrictions on access hours

    — **Never**—No access at any time

    — **Business hours**—Access 9 a.m. to 5 p.m., Monday through Friday

- **Simultaneous Logins**—Enter the number of simultaneous logins that group users are permitted. The minimum is 1; default is 3. Although there is no maximum limit, allowing several could compromise security and affect performance.

- **Minimum Password Length**—Enter the minimum number of characters for group user passwords. The minimum is 1, the default is 8, and the maximum is 32.

- **Allow Alphabetic-Only Passwords**—Check the box to allow base group user passwords with alphabetic characters only (the default). To protect security, it is strongly recommended that you do not allow such passwords.

- **Idle Timeout**—Enter the base group idle timeout period in minutes. If there is no communication activity on the connection in this period, the system terminates the connection.

- **Maximum Connect Time**—Enter the group maximum connection time in minutes. At the end of this time, the system terminates the connection.

You can also add the IP addresses of the DNS and WINS servers. Ensure that only IPSec is selected for the group as the tunneling protocol.

After configuring the **General** tab, clicking the **IPSec** tab displays the following, as shown in Figure 9-11.

Figure 9-11 *Group Configuration—IPSec*

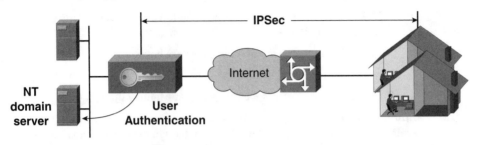

Click the drop-down menu and choose the IPSec security association (SA) assigned to group IPSec Clients. During tunnel establishment, the Client and server negotiate an SA that governs authentication, encryption, encapsulation, key management, and so on.

Select the following:

- **Tunnel Type**—Can be either remote access or LAN to LAN. In this case, it is remote access.

- **Authentication**—Relates to how users within the group are authenticated (i.e., Internal, NT, SDI, RADIUS)

- **Mode Configuration**—Allows the Concentrator to push information down to the Client.

Further down this screen, the Mode Configuration parameters are presented. The Mode Configuration allows the VPN Concentrator to push the IPSec settings down to the VPN Client.

To perform mode configuration, select the following:

- **Option**—This is enabled for IPSec Client-to-LAN applications. Mode Configuration enables the Concentrator to push information down to the Client. Mode configuration is based on the Internet Engineering Task Force (IETF) IPSec Working Group Internet Draft.

- **Banner**—Enter a banner or text string that this group's IPSec Client will see on the username/password screen when they log in, up to 128 characters.

- **Split Tunneling Network List**—Allows the Concentrator to push down specific IP addresses to the Client. If the traffic is bound for one of these addresses, it is encrypted and sent to the Concentrator. If the IP address is different from the pushed addresses, the message is sent in the clear and therefore is routable by the ISP.

- **WINS and DNS**—These values are pushed to the Client. Registry files are overwritten while tunnel is in use. Tunnel is disconnected and original registry values are restored.

- **IP address from the Concentrator, DHCP, or RADIUS server.**

- **Allow Password Storage on the Client**—Allows user to store password on Client.

- **IPSec through NAT**—IPSec packets are wrapped in UDP so firewalls and routers can perform NAT. To be enabled, the feature must be enabled at both ends, IPSec Client and Concentrator.

These settings can be seen in Figure 9-12.

This completes the necessary steps to configure the IPSec group. This information is required by the VPN Client when configuring the VPN session on the Client.

Figure 9-12 *Group Configuration—IPSec Mode*

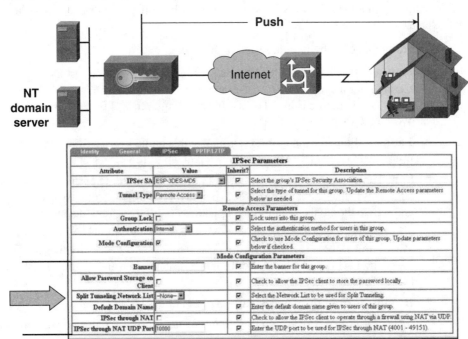

Step 4: Add a User to the Group

The last step in configuring the VPN is to configure a user. When the VPN Client is configured, you manually enter the group information into the configuration. This authenticates the VPN session against the Concentrator and initiates the IPSec process. Once the group is successfully authenticated, you then have to authenticate against a user. This user account can exist either on the local VPN Concentrator as a user account or on an external authentication server. The external authentication servers supported by the VPN Concentrator are RADIUS, Windows NT Domain, or SDI.

If using an internal user account, you must tie this user account to the IPSec group that you previously configured.

For the I.B. Widget Corporation example that you have been working through, you are going to use external authentication against a Windows NT Domain Controller that has the IP address 10.10.10.100.

Authentication for IPSec is assigned by group. Each group could conceivably be authenticated by a different server type: Windows NT, SDI, RADIUS, and so on. When the group needs to be authenticated, the Concentrator goes down the list until it finds the first instance of the assigned authentication server.

The Concentrator then tests whether it can communicate with that server. If communication is good, the user is or is not authenticated. If the Concentrator cannot communicate with the first server, it goes down the list to the next instance of that server type.

Figure 9-13 shows the settings for the I.B. Widget example.

Figure 9-13 *External Authentication*

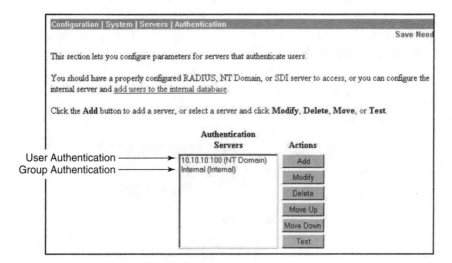

You can see from Figure 9-13 that you are using the Windows NT Domain Controller at 10.10.10.100 for user authentication.

Once external authentication is configured, a very useful authentication test can be carried out from the VPN Manager. The authentication test can help eliminate the section of the network between the Concentrator and the authentication server. You type in the username and password for the authentication server. The Concentrator then attempts to log in to the authentication server. The Concentrator returns either a success or a failure pop-up window.

This completes the required configuration of the VPN Concentrator. You now have to configure the VPN Client to work with the VPN Concentrator.

Configuration of the IPSec VPN Client

This section explains how to configure and use the IPSec Client on the Cisco VPN 3000 Concentrator series, using the settings on the VPN Concentrator that were covered earlier in this chapter.

Cisco Systems VPN 3000 Client is a software program that runs on Win 95/98/NT4.0/2000. The VPN Client on a remote PC, communicating with VPN Concentrator at an enterprise or service provider, creates a secure connection over the Internet that lets you access a private network as if you were an onsite user. The following commands are available on the initial screen, which can be seen in Figure 9-14:

- **New button**—This launches the New Connection Entry Wizard. It walks you through the creation of a new connection entry.

- **Options drop-down menu**—After a connection is created, the Options drop-down menu lets you change or set optional parameters.

- **Connect button**—Enables you to launch the VPN Client connection.

- **Connection Entry window**—Unique name for this VPN connection.

- **Host name or IP address of remote server window**—Address of the VPN Concentrator's public interface.

Figure 9-14 *Cisco IPSec Client*

IPSec Client Options

The Options drop-down menu allows you to configure or change the following optional parameters:

- **Clone**—This feature enables you to copy a connection entry with all its properties.

- **Delete**—This feature enables you to delete a connection entry.

- **Rename**—You can rename a connection entry (not case-sensitive).

- **Create shortcut**—You can create a shortcut for your desktop.

- **Properties**—Enables you to configure and change the properties of the connection. (See the the next section for more information.)

- **Import**—Used to import the IPSecdlr.ini file. (This is explained later.)

Properties

Under Properties are three tabs: **General**, **Authentication**, and **Connections**.

- **General tab**—There are two versions of the **General** tab, depending on which operating system you are using, Windows 95/98 or Windows NT4.0. The Win 95/98 version provides more parameters. The two versions are as follows:

  — **Allowing IPSec through NAT mode (Microsoft Windows 95/98/NT)**— IPSec through NAT lets you use the Cisco Systems VPN Client to connect to the VPN Concentrator with UDP through a firewall or router that is running NAT. Both the Concentrator and the Client need IPSec over UDP enabled for this connection.

  — **Logging on to Microsoft networks (Microsoft Windows 95/98 only): Use default system logon credentials**—Use the logon username and password resident on your PC to log on to the Microsoft network, for example, student4. Prompt for network logon credentials—If your logon username and password differ from the private network, the private network prompts you for the username and password.

- **Authentication tab**—The Concentrator and Client connection can be authenticated with either group name and password or digital certificates. The **Authentication** tab allows you to set your authentication information. You need to choose one method, group or certificates, with the radio buttons.

  — **Group access information**—Group name and password must match what is configured for this group under **Configuration > User Management > Groups > Identity**. Entries are case-sensitive.

  — **Certificates**—For certificates to be exchanged, the radial button must be selected. In the drop-down menu, any personal certificates loaded on your PC are listed. Select the certificate to be exchanged with the Concentrator during connection establishment. If no personal certificates are loaded in your PC, the box is blank.

- **Connections tab**—The private network might include one or more backup VPN Concentrators to use if the primary VPN Concentrator is not available. Your system administrator tells you whether to enable a backup VPN Concentrator and gives you its address. Do the following:

— Check **Enable Backup server(s)** to enable this feature. Once selected, click **Add** to enter the IP address of the backup Concentrator. Your Client attempts to connect to your primary Concentrator first. If that Concentrator cannot be reached, the Client accesses the backup list for the addresses of available backup Concentrators.

— Connect to the Internet with Dial Up Networking (DUN). Connecting to a private network using a dialup connection is typically a two-step process. Use a dialup connection to your Internet service provider. Use the VPN Client to connect to the private network. Connecting to the Internet with DUN automatically launches the DUN connection before making the VPN connection. This entry opens the DUN properties dialog box.

Configuring the Client for Remote Users

You can preconfigure VPN Clients for remote users by creating a Client configuration file, IPSecdlr.ini, and distributing it with the VPN Client software. This configuration file can include all, or only some, of the parameter settings. Users must configure those settings not preconfigured. After you have successfully imported the IPSecdlr.ini file, the VPN Client software automatically deletes the file.

VPN Client Program Menu

When you install the VPN Client, you are provided with the following **Program** menu, as shown in Figure 9-15.

Figure 9-15 *Cisco VPN Client Program Menu*

The following options are available on the Cisco Systems VPN Client **Program** menu:

- **Help**—On the **Program** menu, choose **Start > Programs > Altiga Networks VPN Client > Help**. Press **F1** at any window while using the VPN Client. Choose the **Help** button (on windows that display it). Choose **Help** from the menu that appears when you click the logo in the title bar.

- **Log Viewer**—Displays the Client event log. Examining the event log can often help a network administrator diagnose problems with an IPSec connection between a VPN Client and a VPN Concentrator. The Log View application collects event messages from all processes that contribute to the Client-Concentrator connection. From the toolbar, you can do the following:

  — Save the log file.

  — Print the log file.

  — Capture event messages to the log.

  — Filter the events.

  — Clear the event log.

  — Search the event log.

- **Set MTU**—The maximum transmission unit (MTU) parameter determines the largest packet size in bytes that the Client application can transmit through the network.

  With IPSec over UDP, the IPSec packets are wrapped in UDP so that firewalls and routers performing NAT can handle the IPSec packets. With large UDP packets, devices can fragment the packet. Unfortunately, many firewalls and routers doing NAT do not let fragments through. Fragments are dropped. It might be necessary to restrict the MTU size of the IPSec over UDP packets. The MTU parameter determines the largest packet size in bytes that the Client application can transmit through the network. A large size (for example, over 1400) can increase fragmentation. Using 1400 or smaller usually prevents fragmentation. Select the network adapter and MTU option size. 1400 is the recommended choice for IPSec over UDP. You must reboot for changes to take effect.

- **Uninstall VPN 3000 Client**—Only one Client can be loaded at a time. When upgrading, the old Client must be uninstalled before the new Client is installed.

- **VPN Dialer**—Used to launch the VPN Client.

Summary

This chapter covered the initial configuration of the Cisco VPN 3000 Concentrator. It started by presenting a very simple scenario where the I.B. Widget Corporation had a VPN Concentrator and a client using the VPN Concentrator Client. The chapter covered the initial configuration of the Concentrator from the CLI. Once an interface had been configured through the CLI with an IP address, the chapter moved on to the browser-based VPN Manager.

The chapter then covered the steps required on the VPN Concentrator and the VPN Client to facilitate communication over the VPN. You saw the ease of configuration and the ease of use of the VPN 3000 Concentrator series.

Now that you have configured a preshared key example, the next chapter covers certificate authority (CA) support and the VPN 3000 Concentrator.

Review Questions

1   What is the minimum configuration on the CLI to use the browser-based VPN Manager?

2   When connecting a console to use the CLI, what cable should you use?

3   When using the browser-based VPN Manager for the first time, what is the default username and password pair?

4   Looking at the left pane of the VPN Manager, what are the three selectable options?

5   You configure the private IP address with the CLI and then reboot the Concentrator and try to access the VPN Manager using Internet Explorer. You cannot access the VPN Manager. What is the probable cause of this?

6   From a networking point of view, along with the IP addresses for the private and public interfaces, what else is required in order for the Concentrator to work in an internetwork?

7   What are the four options for IP address assignment on the VPN Concentrator?

8   Which program menu item launches the VPN Client and initiates the VPN communication?

9   What is the recommended MTU size for IPSec over UDP?

10   The VPN Concentrator can act in a way similar to a DHCP server or a DHCP relay agent. If it is acting similar to a DHCP server, what else must you configure on the VPN Concentrator?

CHAPTER 10

Configuring the Cisco VPN 3000 for Remote Access Using Digital Certificates

This chapter teaches you how to configure the Cisco VPN 3000 for remote access using digital certificates for authentication. After presenting an overview of the process, the chapter shows you each major step of the configuration.

This chapter covers the following topics:

- Certificate generation on the VPN 3000 Concentrator
- Validating certificates
- Configuring the Cisco VPN 3000 Concentrator series for CA support
- Configuring the Cisco VPN Client to use the digital certificate

An overview of certificate authority (CA) principles is provided in Chapter 1, "VPNs and VPN Technologies."

Certificate Generation on the VPN 3000 Concentrator

To participate in a Public Key Infrastructure (PKI), an end user (or end entity) must obtain a digital certificate from the CA. This is known as the *enrollment process*. To obtain a certificate, the requestor generates a certificate request and sends it to the CA using a Public Key Cryptography Standards (PKCS) #10 certificate request. The CA will

- Transform the certificate request into a digital certificate (X.509 digital certificate)
- Sign the certificate with the CA private key
- Return the digital certificate to the requestor

The requestor installs the certificate into the Concentrator.

First, a public and private key pair is created on the local machine. The algorithm and the key length (512, 768, or 1024 bits) used to create the key pair is selected by the user. The Rivest, Shamir, and Adelman (RSA) signing is an algorithm designed by RSA Laboratories and defined by PKCS#1. Most PKI environments support RSA signing. The Directory System Agent (DSA) signing is a public algorithm backed by the United States government. DSA signing is supported by a limited number of PKI vendors (for example, NAI and Baltimore are two that support DSA signing).

User information (common name, organizational unit, organization, locality, state, and country) and the public key are included in the PKCS#10 request message. The requestor signs the PKCS#10 with its private key and forwards the request to the CA. The CA can use the requestor's public key to verify the authenticity of the PKCS#10.

Figure 10-1 shows an example of the certificate enrollment screen on the Concentrator that emulates the PKCS#10.

Figure 10-1 *Certificate Enrollment*

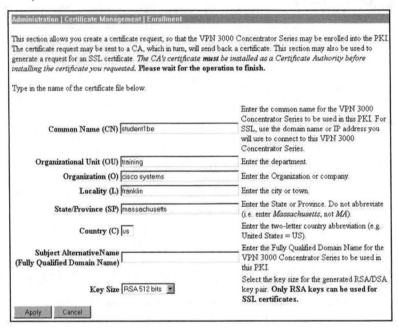

The certificate generation process is described in the following steps and is shown in Figure 10-2:

Step 1   The Concentrator or PC sends a PKCS#10 to the CA.

Step 2   The CA verifies the authenticity of the PKCS#10.

　　　　　　— CA decrypts the digital signature with the requestor's public key.

　　　　　　— The encrypted hash should match the CA's decrypted hash value.

Step 3   PKCS#10 is transformed into an identity certificate.

    — Some information is supplied from PKCS#10.

    — Some information is supplied by the CA.

    — The CA signature is created.

Step 4   A hash algorithm is performed on the combined attributes.

Step 5   A hash value is encrypted using the CA's private key.

Step 6   The identity certificate is sent to the Concentrator or PC.

Step 7   Information in the identity certificate is verified by the Concentrator.

    — It is verified with the CA's public key.

    — Only the CA's public key can decrypt certificates encrypted with the CA's private key.

Figure 10-2 *Generating Certificates*

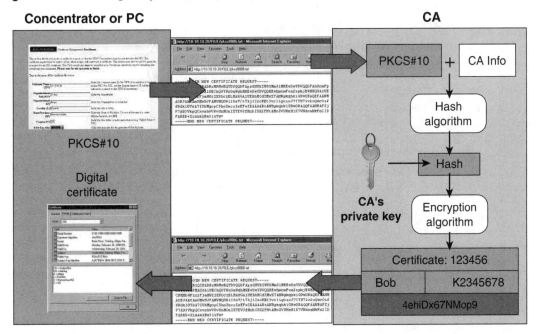

The X.509 certificate consists of specific fields and values. Figure 10-3 shows an example of a Microsoft Windows display of a certificate. The certificate has the following values:

- Certificate format version
  - Currently, X.509 version 1, 2, or 3.
- Certificate serial number
  - Unique certificate numerical identifier in the CA domain.
  - When a certificate is revoked, it is the certificate number that is listed on the CRL.
- Signature algorithm
  - Identifies the CA's public key and hashing algorithm.
- Issuer
  - Distinguished name of the CA.
- Validity period
  - Specifies the start and expiration dates for the certificate.
- Subject X.500 name
  - Distinguished name of the entity holding the private key.
- Subject public key information
  - Specifies the subject's public key and hashing algorithm.
- Extensions
  - Extends the certificate to allow additional information.
  - Subject alternative name.
  - CRL distribution points.
  - Additional information if configured in the CA.
- CA signature
  - The CA performs a hash function on the certificate contents and the hash is then signed with the CA's private key to ensure authenticity (reference: RFC 2459).

Figure 10-3 *Digital Certificates*

Validating Certificates

This section covers how digital certificates are validated and maintained.

Digital certificate validation is based on trust relationships within the PKI. If you trust A, and A says that B is valid, then you should trust B. This is the underlying premise with validation of certificates. When enrolling into a PKI, you must first obtain and install the CA certificates into the Concentrator. In doing so, you implicitly establish a trust relationship where any documents signed by those CAs are considered to be valid.

During Internet Key Exchange (IKE) negotiations, when an identity certificate is received from an IKE peer, the Concentrator validates the certificate by checking the following:

- **Signed by a CA that is trusted**—Checks the signature.
- **Not expired**—Valid from and to period is given.
- **Not revoked**—Certificate is not listed in the CRL.

Signature validation consists of the following steps:

Step 1   At the CA, the original identity certificate is put through a hash algorithm. The output hash is encrypted by the CA's private key, and the hash is appended to the end of the certificate.

Step 2   At the Concentrator, the identity certificate signature needs to be validated.

First path:

— The identification certificate is fed through the hash algorithm.

— Hash is calculated.

Second path:

— Identity certificate enclosed signature is decrypted using the CA's public key (found in the root certificate).

— The result is the original hash, as calculated by the CA.

Step 3   CA-generated hash and Concentrator-generated hash are compared.

— **Match**—Identity certificate is genuine.

— **No Match**—Invalid signature or identity certificate.

This process is shown in Figure 10-4.

In a hierarchical CA environment, there might be multiple certificates or one message with multiple certificates enclosed (PKCS #7). This is known as a *certificate chain* and consists of the following:

- **Root certificate**—According to the IETF-PKIX-Roadmap, this is "A certificate authority that is self signed; that is, the issuer of the certificate and the subject of the certificate are the same entity."

- **Subordinate CA certificates**

    — A chain of multiple certificates might be needed to extend from the identity certificate and end user back to the root certificate.

    — Each certificate is signed by the preceding certificate. This process goes up the chain to root certificate.

    — In Figure 10-5, the signature of a certificate from Jane is checked with the public key of the root certificate.

- **Identity certificate**—A certificate issued by a CA to an entity that binds the device's public key to a set of information that identifies the device.

Figure 10-4 *Signature Validation*

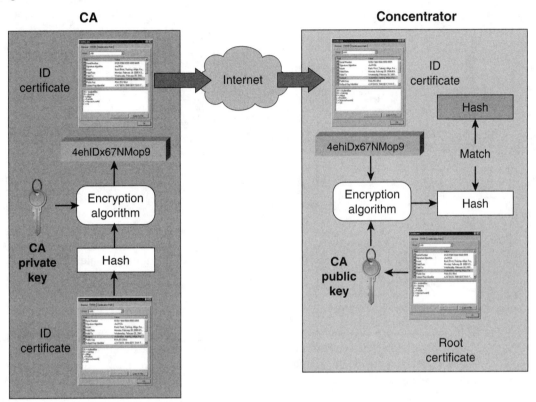

In a central CA flat environment, there are two certificates:

- Root certificate
- Identity certificate

In Figure 10-5, the signature of a certificate from Jane is checked with the public key of the root certificate.

Figure 10-5 *Certification Chain*

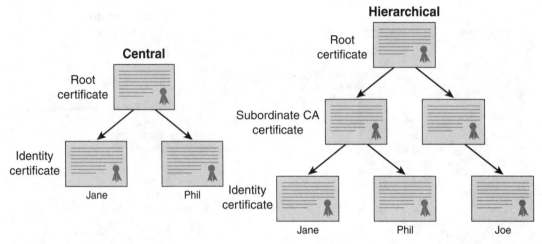

In a hierarchical environment, the ability to sign is delegated through a hierarchy.

The top is the root CA, which signs certificates for subordinate authorities.

Subordinate CAs, in turn, sign certificates for lower-level CAs.

To validate a user's certificate, the certificate must be validated up through the chain of authority. In Figure 10-5, Jane's certificate is validated with the public key of the subordinate CA certificate. The subordinate CA certificate is verified with the public key of the root certificate.

Validity Period

A certificate is valid for a specific period of time. The validity period (range) is set by the CA and consists of "Valid from" and "Valid to" fields. In the Concentrator, when you try to add a certificate, the validity range will be compared against the system clock. If the system clock is not within the validity range—either too early or too late—you will get an error message.

Figure 10-6 shows the validity period of a digital certificate.

Figure 10-6 *Validity Period*

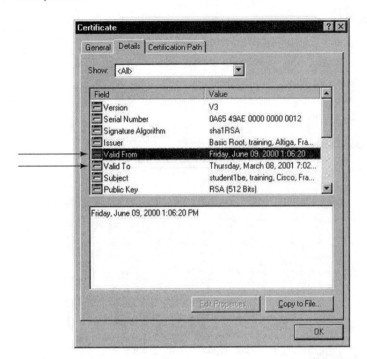

Certificate Revocation List

A certificate revocation list (CRL) is a list issued by the CA that contains certificates that are no longer valid. CRLs are signed by the CA and are released periodically or on demand. CRLs are valid for a specific amount of time, depending on the CA vendor used. Some reasons why a certificate might be invalidated are as follows:

- Change of user data (for example, the username)
- Key compromise
- Employee leaves organization

The CRL must be consulted by anyone using a certificate to make sure it is still valid. There is no requirement on devices to ensure the CRL is current.

A CRL, as viewed on a PC, has two tabs.

- **General**
  - **Issuer**—Name of the CA that issued the list
  - **Effective date**—Date the list was issued
  - **Next update**—Date of the next publication, which could be hourly, daily, weekly, and so on, as defined by the CA
- **Revocation List**

The **General** tab can be seen in Figure 10-7.

Figure 10-7 *CRL General Tab*

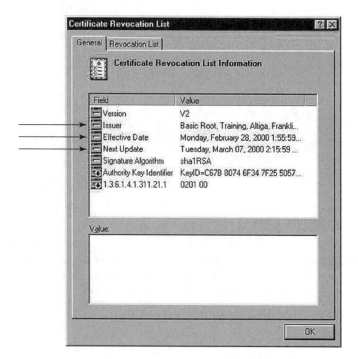

Within the **Revocation List** tab, a list of all revoked identity certificates, which are listed by certificate serial number, are displayed. Their revocation dates and times are included. An example of this is shown in Figure 10-8.

Figure 10-8 *CRL Revocation List Tab*

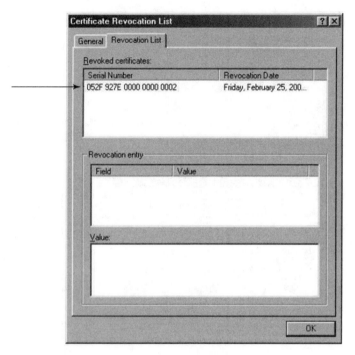

As part of the X.509 certificate, the CRL extensions include the CRL distribution point. The CRL distribution point information is included in the X.509 extension fields. If you double-click the CRL distribution point in the certificate, the URL of the CRL distribution point is included. This can be seen in Figure 10-9.

Figure 10-9 *CRL Distribution Point Location*

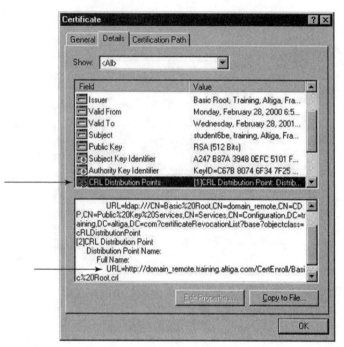

Certificate Authentication Process

The certificate authentication process consists of the following steps:

NOTE   Ensure that the date and time on the Concentrator is correct before attempting any of the following steps.

Step 1   The root certificate is loaded into the Concentrator.

Step 2   The identity certificate is loaded into and verified by the Concentrator.

The public signature on the root certificate is used to validate the identity certificate.

The result is pass or fail.

Step 3 **Certificate exchange**—Identity certificates are exchanged during IKE phase one negotiations to authenticate the peers.

Step 4 The received identity certificate from the peer is validated using the stored root certificate.

The root certificate holds the CA public key.

The public key is used to decode the hash (digital signature).

If the original and decoded hashes match, the certificate is valid.

Note the following important points about certificate validation:

- Validity period
  - The certificate must fall within the validity range.
  - The validity range can be found on certificates.
- CRL
  - This is optional.
  - If the serial number of the certificate is found on the CRL, the certificate is no longer valid.

Configuring the Cisco VPN 3000 Concentrator Series for CA Support

This section covers how to configure IPSec on the Cisco VPN 3000 Concentrator series using digital certificates.

You configure the Concentrator much the same as you would for preshared keys, substituting the digital certificates when necessary. Most of the other settings stay the same.

Concentrator Certificate Loading Process

The Concentrator certificate loading process consists of the following steps:

Step 1 Generate the certificate request and upload it to a CA.

Step 2 Root and identity certificates are transferred to the PC.

The CA generates the identity certificate.

The CA generates a root certificate.

Each is downloaded to a PC.

Step 3 Root and identity certificates are loaded into the Concentrator.

The root certificate is loaded first.

The identification certificate is loaded and validated against the root certificate.

This process can be seen in Figure 10-10.

Figure 10-10 *Concentrator Certificate Loading Process*

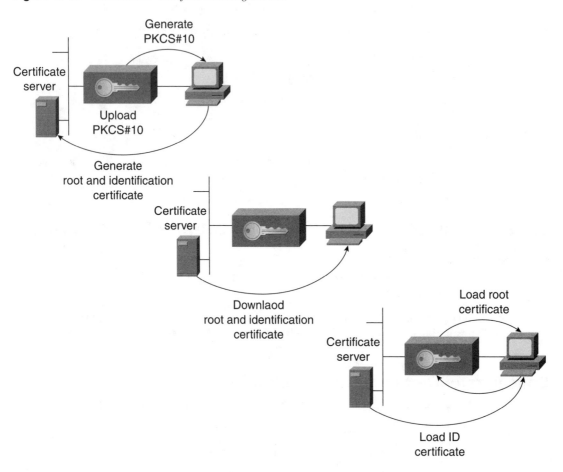

The Concentrator can generate the certificate request. The Concentrator enrollment request consists of the following:

- **Common name**—Unique name for the Concentrator.
- **Organizational unit**.
  — The Concentrator uses the organizational unit as the group name.
  — These must match end-to-end on the tunnel.
- **Organizational**—Company name.
- **The output is a new certificate request in the PEM format**—PKCS#10.

This process can be seen in Figure 10-11.

Figure 10-11 *Concentrator Generated PKCS#10*

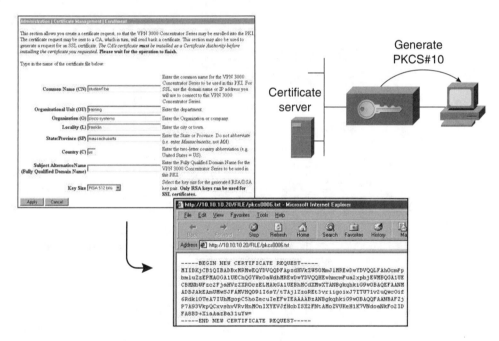

Once the certificate has been generated, it has to be uploaded to the CA.

Uploading the PKCS#10 to the CA involves the following steps:

Step 1 The PKCS#10 output of the Concentrator is copied and pasted into the CA.

Step 2 The CA processes the information.

Step 3 The CA produces an identity certificate.

Figure 10-12 shows this three-step process.

Figure 10-12   *Uploading the PKCS#10 to the CA*

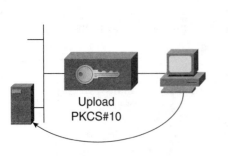

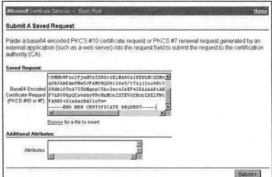

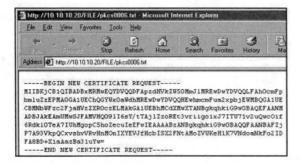

At this point, the certificate has to be downloaded and then installed into the Concentrator. Follow the instructions on the specific CA server to download the certificate to local storage. These files usually use the .cer extension.

Once the certificate file is stored locally, it can be installed to the Concentrator.

The following certificates need to be installed in the Concentrator:

- Root CA
- Issuing CA (subordinate or intermediate CA)
- Identity CA (VPN Concentrator)

Complete the following steps to install the certificates:

Step 1   Select the correct type of certificate. The root certificate must be installed first.

Step 2   Browse to the file's location.

Step 3   Click **Apply**.

When the identity certificate is loaded, it is validated using the root certificate. To be valid, the identity certificate needs to fall within the validity window, otherwise the identity certificate has expired.

NOTE   In the event that you receive an expiration error when loading your identity certificate, ensure that the Concentrator's date and time is correctly set.

Figure 10-13 shows the VPN Manager screens required to install the certificates.

Figure 10-13   *Certificate Installation*

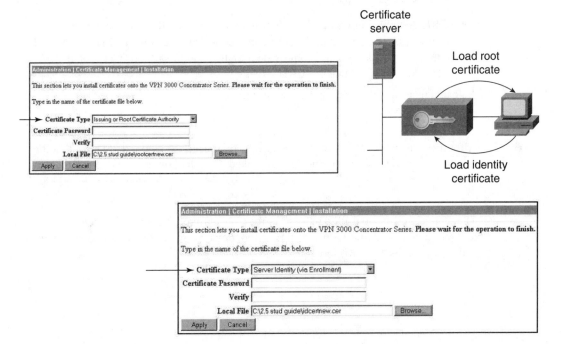

Two certificates are based in the Concentrator. These are the root certificate and the identity certificate.

The root certificate is used to verify the identity certificate. The identity certificate installed in this Concentrator is received from another Concentrator during IKE negotiations.

The root certificate contains the following information:

- **Subject**—The person or system that uses the certificate. For a CA root certificate, the Subject and Issuer are the same.

- **Issuer**—The CA or other entity (jurisdiction) that issued the certificate.

  Subject and Issuer consist of a specific-to-general identification hierarchy: CN, OU, O, L, SP, and C. These labels and acronyms conform to X.520 terminology, and they echo the fields on the Administration | Certificate Management | Enrollment screen.

- **Serial number**—Identifies the certificate. Each certificate issued by a CA or other entity must be unique. CRL checking uses this serial number.

- **Validity period**—The time period during which this certificate is valid.

  The format is MM/DD/YYYY at HH:MM:SS AM/PM to MM/DD/YYYY at HH:MM:SS AM/PM. Time uses 12-hour AM/PM notation and is local system time. The Manager checks the validity against the VPN Concentrator system clock, and it flags expired certificates.

- **CRL distribution point**—The distribution point for CRLs from this CA. If this information is included in the certificate in the proper format, and you enable CRL checking, you do not have to provide it on the Administration | Certificate Management | Certificates | CRL screen.

An example root certificate can be seen in Figure 10-14.

NOTE   After the Concentrator receives a new certificate, it needs to go out and verify that the certificate is still valid and has not been revoked. CRL lookup has to be enabled.

The identity certificate is used to identify the Concentrator. A copy of this certificate is sent to the remote Concentrator during IKE negotiations. You have the option to view, delete, and enable or disable CRL lookup.

Figure 10-14   *Root Certificate*

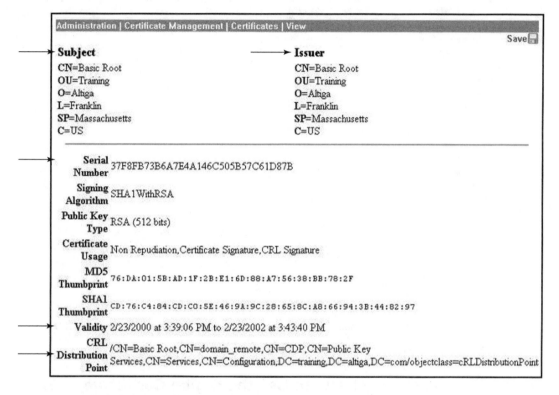

The identity certificate contains the following information:

- Subject
- Issuer
- Serial number
- Validity period
- CRL distribution point

An example identity certificate can be seen in Figure 10-15.

Figure 10-15   *Identity Certificate*

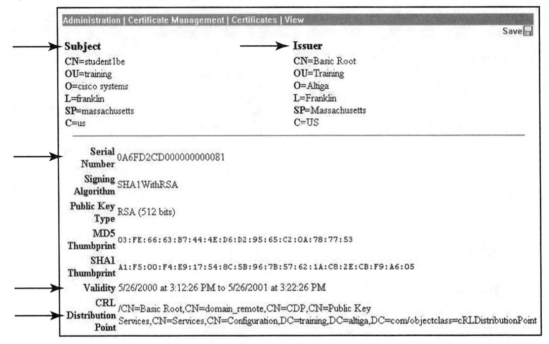

Configuring the Concentrator to Use the Digital Certificate

Now that the certificates are loaded on the Concentrator, a few configuration tasks differ from the default preshared key configuration covered in the previous chapter.

There are two places where you have to specify the use of a digital certificate instead of preshared keys. These are in the IKE proposal and the IPSec security association (SA).

The IKE proposal is a template that can be applied to IPSec SAs. The following can be configured:

- Authentication mode
- Authentication algorithm
- Encryption algorithm
- Key length and lifetime

NOTE   For the IPSec Client-to-LAN applications, the authentication mode is changed from preshared keys to digital certificates.

The IKE proposal screen is located under Configuration > System > Tunneling Protocols > IPSec, IKE Proposals > and Modify. An example of the screen can be seen in Figure 10-16, which shows the authentication mode set to use a digital certificate.

Figure 10-16   *IKE Proposal*

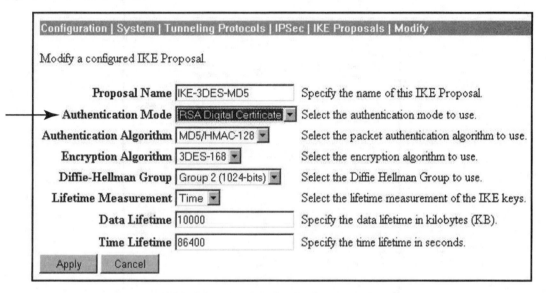

The IPSec SA screen is located under Configuration > Policy Management > Traffic Management > Security Associations. An example of this screen can be seen in Figure 10-17, with the relevant sections indicating the use of a digital certificate.

Note the following about IPSec SAs:

- The IPSec template is defined.
- At the bottom of the page, you need to choose which IKE template will be applied.
  - In this instance, the IKE proposal defined on the last page will be referenced.
  - The Student3LK certificate will be used during the certificate exchange.
- In the middle of the page, the IPSec parameters are defined.
  - 3DES
  - MD5
  - One day key lifetime is proposed

That completes the coverage of the required steps to request, download, install, and configure a digital certificate for a Cisco VPN 3000 Concentrator.

Figure 10-17 *IPSec SA*

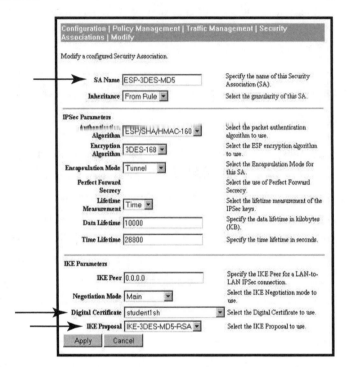

Configuring the Cisco VPN Client to Use the Digital Certificate

In addition to configuring a digital certificate on the Concentrator, you are required to install and configure a digital certificate on the VPN Client.

For the Client to participate in the certificate exchange, a certificate needs to be loaded on the PC. A certificate request form—PKCS#10—can be filled out at the CA. Some of the key fields of the Microsoft CA are as follows:

- The Department (OU) field must match the group defined on the Concentrator (case-sensitive).

- Key usage must be set for both.

- Keys must be marked as exportable.

You must download the certificate to the PC. Microsoft certificate services will load both an identity and root certificate in the Internet Explorer (IE) certificate store.

The PC needs to have both an identity certificate and a root certificate in IE. The Client references these certificates during certificate exchange with the Concentrator. Certificates can be viewed from IE by following these steps:

Step 1   Choose Toolbar Tools > Internet Options from the IE menu.

Step 2   Click the **Content** tab.

Step 3   Click **Certificates**.

Step 4   Click the **Personal** tab.

Step 5   Select **Trusted Root Certificate**.

Figure 10-18 displays the sample screens of the stored certificates you would expect to see.

Figure 10-18   *Stored Certificates*

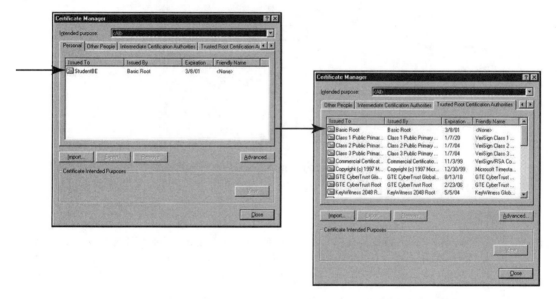

Once you have successfully downloaded and installed a digital certificate to a PC, you then have to configure the VPN Client to use this digital certificate.

The Client can use preshared keys or digital certificates for authentication.

Under the **Authentication** tab of the Client, select the following:

- **Group Access Information**—Preshared keys
- **Certificate**—Digital certificates (if certificates are to be used in this application, a certificate must already exist on the PC)

Figure 10-19 shows this screen with the certificate StudentBE configured.

Figure 10-19 *VPN Client with Digital Certificate*

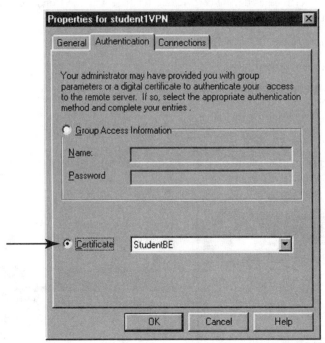

This completes the configuration of the VPN Client to use digital certificates.

Summary

The previous chapter looked at the initial configuration of a Cisco VPN 3000 Concentrator to establish a VPN with the VPN 3000 Client using a preshared secret key. This chapter introduced digital certificates to the Concentrator.

The chapter started by looking at the way the Concentrator handles the certificates, before going through a certificate request, download, and installation to the Concentrator. The chapter then looked at the configuration differences on the Concentrator to instruct it to use the digital certificates instead of the preshared keys. After the Concentrator configuration, the chapter also covered the remaining topic, which was to request, download, install, and configure a digital certificate on the VPN 3000 client.

Review Questions

1 What is the certificate request also known as?

2 The RSA signing is an algorithm designed by RSA Laboratories and defined by what?

3 What is an identity certificate?

4 What is a certificate validity period?

5 What is a certificate revocation list?

6 To use a digital certificate on the VPN 3000 Client, where must the certificate reside?

7 You receive an expiration error when loading your identity certificate; what is the first item to check?

8 In a hierarchical CA environment, what is the top of the hierarchy also known as?

9 How many certificates are based in the VPN Concentrator?

10 When using Microsoft certificate services, where are the certificates stored when downloaded?

CHAPTER 11

Monitoring and Administration of Cisco VPN 3000 Remote Access Networks

This chapter looks at how to monitor and administer Cisco VPN 3000 remote access networks. The VPN Concentrator browser-based VPN Manager application has three main sections. These are Configuration, Monitoring, and Administration. The previous two chapters provide detailed information on the configuration of Concentrator VPNs using preshared keys and digital certificates. This chapter focuses on the options available under the Monitoring and Administration options within VPN Manager.

This chapter covers the following topics:

- Monitoring the Cisco VPN 3000 Concentrator
- Administration of the Cisco VPN 3000 Concentrator

Monitoring the Cisco VPN 3000 Concentrator

This section presents an overview of monitoring activity and VPNs on the Cisco VPN 3000 Concentrator series.

The VPN Concentrator tracks many statistics and the status of many items essential to system administration and management. The monitoring section of the VPN Manager lets you view VPN Concentrator status, sessions, statistics, and event logs, including the following:

- **Routing Table**—Current valid routes, protocols, and metrics
- **Event Log**—Current event log in memory
- **System Status**—Current software revisions, uptime, system power supplies, Ethernet interfaces, front-panel LEDs, and hardware sensors
- **Sessions**—Currently active sessions sorted by protocol, SEP, and encryption, and top ten sessions sorted by data, duration, and throughput
- **General Statistics**—Point-to-Point Tunneling Protocol (PPTP), Layer 2 Tunneling Protocol (L2TP), IPSec, HTTP, events, Telnet, Domain Name System (DNS), authentication, accounting, filtering, and Virtual Router Redundancy Protocol

(VRRP), and Management Information Base II (MIB-II) objects for interfaces, TCP/UDP, IP, Internet Control Message Protocol (ICMP), and Address Resolution Protocol (ARP)

These Manager screens are read-only snapshots of data or status at the time the screen displays. Most screens have a **Refresh** button that you can click to get a fresh snapshot and update the screen. The Monitoring screen is selected by clicking the Monitoring option on the left pane of the VPN Manager httpHTTP-based application.

Figure 11-1 shows the main Monitoring index screen where you can see the previously covered selectable options.

Figure 11-1 *Monitoring Index*

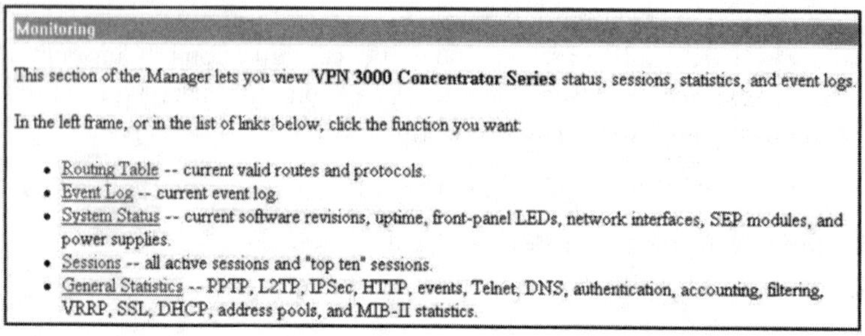

Monitoring

This section of the Manager lets you view **VPN 3000 Concentrator Series** status, sessions, statistics, and event logs.

In the left frame, or in the list of links below, click the function you want:

- Routing Table -- current valid routes and protocols.
- Event Log -- current event log.
- System Status -- current software revisions, uptime, front-panel LEDs, network interfaces, SEP modules, and power supplies.
- Sessions -- all active sessions and "top ten" sessions.
- General Statistics -- PPTP, L2TP, IPSec, HTTP, events, Telnet, DNS, authentication, accounting, filtering, VRRP, SSL, DHCP, address pools, and MIB-II statistics.

Monitoring the Routing Table

Selecting the Routing Table option from the main Monitoring index will take you to the Routing Table screen.

The Manager has the ability to view the VPN Concentrator's routing table. The IP routing subsystem examines the destination IP address of packets coming through the VPN Concentrator and forwards or drops them according to configured parameters.

The table includes all routes that the IP routing subsystem knows about, from whatever source: static routes, routing protocols, interface addresses, and so on. The Manager allows you to view

- Valid routes
- Addresses and mask
- Next hop
- Interface
- Protocol
- Age and metric

NOTE This information is also available through the command-line interface (CLI).

Figure 11-2 shows an example of the screen that is provided to monitor the routing table.

Figure 11-2 *Monitoring the Routing Table*

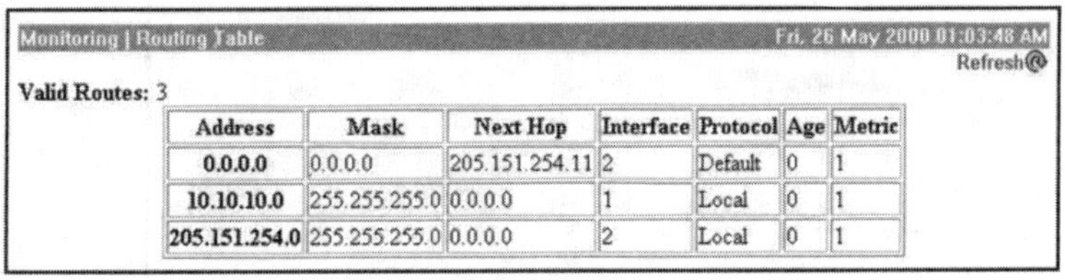

Address	Mask	Next Hop	Interface	Protocol	Age	Metric
0.0.0.0	0.0.0.0	205.151.254.11	2	Default	0	1
10.10.10.0	255.255.255.0	0.0.0.0	1	Local	0	1
205.151.254.0	255.255.255.0	0.0.0.0	2	Local	0	1

Monitoring the Event Log

Selecting the Event Log option from the main Monitoring index will take you to the Event Log screen.

The Monitoring | Event Log screen allows GUI access to see the events in the current event log. The ability to manage the event log file is also provided. Note the following:

- The events are stored in nonvolatile memory.
- The log holds 2048 events and wraps when it is full.
- The log file can be automatically saved on wrap.
- The severity can be managed based on importance.
- The events can be sent to a Trap Host or a Syslog Host.
- An e-mail can be sent to an administrator based on the severity of the event.
- The format can be multiline, comma delimited, or tab delimited.
- Administrator rights are required to view the event logs.

NOTE The event log can be retrieved from the Concentrator with Telnet, FTP, or HTTP.

Figure 11-3 shows an example of the screen that is provided to monitor the event log.

Figure 11-3 *Monitoring the Event Log*

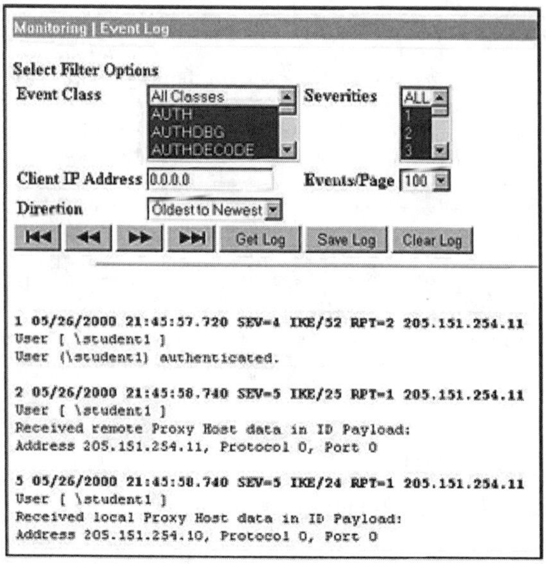

```
Monitoring | Event Log

Select Filter Options
Event Class      All Classes    ▲   Severities   ALL ▲
                 AUTH                             1
                 AUTHDBG                          2
                 AUTHDECODE ▼                     3  ▼

Client IP Address 0.0.0.0          Events/Page 100 ▼
Direction         Oldest to Newest ▼

 |◄◄ | ◄◄ | ►► | ►►| | Get Log | Save Log | Clear Log |


1 05/26/2000 21:45:57.720 SEV=4 IKE/52 RPT=2 205.151.254.11
User [ \student1 ]
User (\student1) authenticated.

2 05/26/2000 21:45:58.740 SEV=5 IKE/25 RPT=1 205.151.254.11
User [ \student1 ]
Received remote Proxy Host data in ID Payload:
Address 205.151.254.11, Protocol 0, Port 0

5 05/26/2000 21:45:58.740 SEV=5 IKE/24 RPT=1 205.151.254.11
User [ \student1 ]
Received local Proxy Host data in ID Payload:
Address 205.151.254.10, Protocol 0, Port 0
```

Monitoring the Status of the System

Selecting the System Status option from the main Monitoring index will take you to the System Status screen.

The Monitoring | System Status screen allows the administrator to view both hardware and software status. The System Status display allows you to view

- Bootcode rev and software rev
- Uptime
- Fan speed
- Temperature
- CPU utilization
- Active sessions
- Aggregate throughput
- LED status

The System Status display can be used for quick and easy checks of the basic systems operations.

Monitoring these statistics can also be accessed through the CLI or through Simple Network Management Protocol (SNMP).

Figure 11-4 shows an example of the screen that is provided to monitor the system status.

Figure 11-4 *Monitoring the System Status*

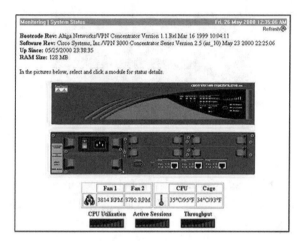

The screen in Figure 11-4 displays a graphical representation of the front and back of the VPN 3000 Concentrator.

From here, there are five further selectable areas that can be accessed by moving your mouse over the required area and clicking the left mouse button. These areas are as follows:

- **Front of the Concentrator**—This displays the Systems LED status.
- **Power supply**—This displays information on the Power Supply.
- **Private interface**—This displays information on the private interface.
- **Public interface**—This displays information on the public interface.
- **External interface**—This displays information on the external interface.

Monitoring the LED Status

Clicking anywhere on the front of the Concentrator from the main System Status screen will take you to the LED Status screen.

Here, a graphical representation of the actual LEDs on the Concentrator is shown. Figure 11-5 shows an example of the screen that is provided to monitor the LED status.

Figure 11-5 *Monitoring LED Status*

The LED indicator can be used to obtain the following information:

- **System**
  - **Green**—Power on.
  - **Amber**—System has crashed and halted: error.
  - **Off**—Power off. All other LEDs are off.

- **Ethernet Link Status**—1, 2, 3
  - **Green**—Connected to network and enabled.
  - **Blinking green**—Connected to the network and configured, but disabled.
  - **Off**—Not connected to network or not enabled.

- **Expansion Modules Insertion Status**—1, 2, 3, 4
  - **Green**—SEP module installed in the system.
  - **Off**—SEP module not installed in the system.

- **Expansion Modules Run Status**—1, 2, 3, 4
  - **Green**—SEP module operational.
  - **Off**—If installed, the SEP module failed diagnostics, or the encryption code is not running: error.

- **Fan Status**
  - **Green**—Operating normally.
  - **Amber**—Not running or the RPM is below normal range: error.

- **Power Supplies**—A, B
  - **Green**—Installed and operating normally.
  - **Amber**—Voltages are outside of normal ranges: error.
  - **Off**—Not installed.

Monitoring the Power Supply Status

Clicking anywhere on the power supply from the main System Status screen will take you to the Power status screen.

The Monitor System Status | Power screen enables the administrator to view all power supplies. Place the mouse cursor over the power supply and click it to view real-time statistics. You can also view the Concentrator's power supply status. The power supply status indicates the following:

- One or both power supplies, voltages, and status
- Main board voltages and status
- CPU voltages and status

NOTE   All of these items are available through SNMP monitoring.

Thresholds and alarms can be set for the power supplies by going to the Configuration | Interface. Highlight the power supply and click it. You can now set the thresholds and alarms.

Figure 11-6 shows an example of the screen that is provided to monitor the Power Supply status.

Figure 11-6   *Monitoring the Power Supply Status*

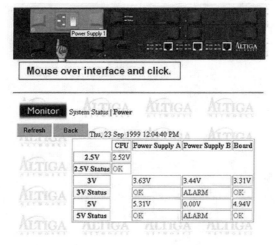

Monitoring the Concentrator Interfaces

Clicking any of the installed interfaces on the back of the Concentrator from the main System Status screen will take you to the Interface status screen for the selected interface.

The Monitor System Status | Interface screen allows the administrator to view all Ethernet interfaces. Place the mouse cursor over the Ethernet interface and click it to view real-time port statistics. The interface statistics allow you to view the following:

- IP address
- Status
- Rx/Tx unicast
- Rx/Tx multicast
- Rx/Tx broadcast

SNMP monitoring is available to monitor the interfaces and thresholds that can be configured to alarm the console when an event has occurred.

Figure 11-7 shows an example of the screen that is provided to monitor the interface status.

Figure 11-7 *Monitoring the Interface Status*

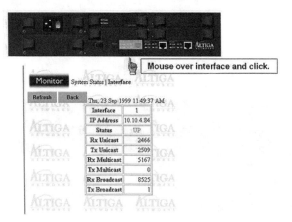

Monitoring Sessions

Selecting the Sessions option from the main Monitoring index will take you to the Sessions screen.

The Monitoring | Sessions screen shows comprehensive data for currently active user and administrator sessions on the VPN Concentrator. The following session information is available:

- **Refresh**—To update the screen and its data, click **Refresh**. The date and time indicate when the screen was last updated.

- **Active sessions**—The number of currently active sessions. Each session is a row in the session table.

- **Total sessions**—The total number of sessions since the VPN Concentrator was last booted or reset.

- **Username**—The login username for the active session.

- **IP address**—The IP address of the session user. For tunneled users, this is the private IP address assigned to or supplied by a remote user. Local identifies the console directly connected to the VPN Concentrator.

- **Protocol**—The protocol that the session is using.

Figure 11-8 shows an example of the screen that is provided to monitor the session status.

Figure 11-8 *Monitoring the Session Status*

Monitoring the General Statistics

Selecting the General Statistics option from the main Monitoring Index will take you to the General Statistics screen.

This section of the Manager shows statistics for traffic and activity on the VPN Concentrator since it was last booted or reset. The following can be monitored:

- **PPTP**—Total tunnels, sessions, received and transmitted control, and data packets and detailed current session data
- **L2TP**—Total tunnels, sessions, received and transmitted control, and data packets and detailed current session data
- **HTTP**—Total data traffic and connection statistics
- **Events**—Total events sorted by class, number, and count
- **Telnet**—Total sessions and current session inbound and outbound traffic
- **DNS**—Total requests, responses, timeouts, and so on
- **Authentication**—Total requests, accepts, rejects, challenges, timeouts, and so on
- **Accounting**—Total requests, responses, timeouts, and so on
- **Filtering**—Total inbound and outbound filtered traffic by the interface
- **VRRP**—Total advertisements, master router roles, errors, and so on
- **MIB-II Stats**—Interfaces, TCP/UDP, IP, ICMP, and ARP

Figure 11-9 shows an example of the screen that is provided, with the further options clearly visible.

Figure 11-9 *General Statistics*

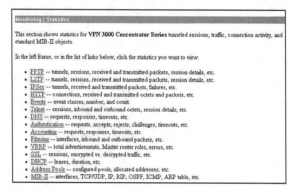

From the screen displayed in Figure 11-9, clicking an option will display a snapshot of the statistics for the chosen option. There is a **Refresh** button in the top right corner that can be used to refresh the statistics. Figure 11-10 shows an example of the PPTP statistics page.

Figure 11-10 *PPTP Statistics*

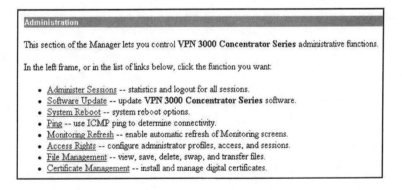

Administration of the Cisco VPN 3000 Concentrator

This section covers how to configure and perform basic administration on the Cisco VPN 3000 Concentrator series.

The VPN 3000 Concentrator series has three main options available from within the browser-based VPN Manager. These are Configuration, Administration, and Monitoring. Previous chapters covered Configuration. Monitoring is covered earlier in this chapter. This chapter now moves on to look at the remaining option, Administration.

Clicking Administration on the left pane of the VPN Manager will bring up the Administration index, as shown in Figure 11-11.

Figure 11-11 *Administration Index*

> **Administration**
>
> This section of the Manager lets you control **VPN 3000 Concentrator Series** administrative functions.
>
> In the left frame, or in the list of links below, click the function you want:
>
> - Administer Sessions -- statistics and logout for all sessions.
> - Software Update -- update **VPN 3000 Concentrator Series** software.
> - System Reboot -- system reboot options.
> - Ping -- use ICMP ping to determine connectivity.
> - Monitoring Refresh -- enable automatic refresh of Monitoring screens.
> - Access Rights -- configure administrator profiles, access, and sessions.
> - File Management -- view, save, delete, swap, and transfer files.
> - Certificate Management -- install and manage digital certificates.

The Administration section of the Manager lets you control administrative functions on the VPN Concentrator. The following functions are available:

- **Administer Sessions**—View statistics for and log out of sessions
- **Software Update**—Upload and update the VPN Concentrator software image
- **System Reboot**—Set options for VPN Concentrator shutdown and reboot
- **Ping**—Use ICMP ping to determine connectivity
- **Monitoring Refresh**—Enable automatic refresh of monitoring screens
- **Access Rights**—Configure administrator profiles, access, and sessions
- **File Management**—Copy, view, save, and delete system files
- **Certificate Management**—Install and manage digital certificates

Administer Sessions

The Administration | Sessions screen provides the following information:

- **Active sessions**—The number of sessions that are currently active.
- **Total sessions**—The total number of sessions since the VPN Concentrator was last booted or reset.
- **Username**—The username or login name for the session.
- **IP address**—The IP address from which the session is accessing the system. Local indicates a direct connection through the Console port on the system.
- **Duration**—The elapsed time (HH:MM:SS) between the session login time and the last screen refresh.
- **Actions/logout/ping**—To log out of a specific session, click **Logout**. The screen refreshes and shows the new session statistics.

Figure 11-12 shows an example of the Administration | Sessions screen.

Figure 11-12   *Administer Sessions*

Software Update

The Software Update screen lets you update the VPN Concentrator executable system software (the software image). The new image file must be accessible by the workstation you are using to manage the VPN Concentrator. This process uploads the file to the VPN Concentrator, which then verifies the integrity of the file. It takes a few minutes to upload and verify the software, and the system displays the progress. You will have to wait for the operation to finish.

To run the new software image, you must reboot the VPN Concentrator. The system prompts you to reboot when the update is finished.

WARNING   While the system is updating the image, do not perform any other operations that affect flash memory (listing, viewing, copying, deleting, or writing files). Doing so can corrupt memory.

System Reboot

The System Reboot screen lets you reboot or shut down (halt) the VPN Concentrator with various options. If you are logged in to the Manager when the system reboots or halts, it automatically logs you out and displays the main login screen. The options that the System Reboot screen lets you reboot or shut down (halt) with are as follows:

- **Reboot**—Rebooting terminates all sessions, resets the hardware, loads and verifies the software image, executes system diagnostics, and initializes the system. A reboot takes about 60 to 75 seconds.

- **Shutdown without automatic reboot**—Shut down the VPN Concentrator; that is, bring the system to a halt so you can turn off the power. Shutdown terminates all sessions and prevents new user sessions (but not administrator sessions).

- **Cancel a scheduled reboot/shutdown**—Cancel a reboot or shutdown that is waiting for a certain time or for sessions to terminate.

- **Save the active configuration at time of reboot**—Save the active configuration to the CONFIG file and reboot using that new file.

- **Reboot without saving the active configuration**—Reboot using the existing CONFIG file and without saving the active configuration.

- **Reboot with Factory/Default configuration**—Reboot using the factory defaults (that is, start the system as if it had no CONFIG file). This option does not destroy any existing CONFIG files, however.

Figure 11-13 shows an example of the System Reboot screen.

Figure 11-13 *System Reboot Screen*

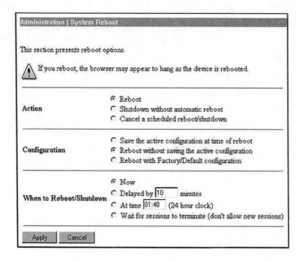

Ping

The Administration | Ping screen lets you use the ICMP ping (Packet Internet Groper) utility to test network connectivity. Specifically, the VPN Concentrator sends an ICMP Echo Request message to a designated host. If the host is reachable, it returns an Echo Reply message, and the Manager displays a Success screen. If the host is not reachable, the Manager displays an Error screen.

Monitoring Refresh

The Administration | Monitoring Refresh screen allows you to enable the automatic refreshing of the monitoring screen and also to set a refresh period.

Access Rights

The Administration | Access Rights screen presents you with three further options:

- **Administrators**—Allows you to add and modify administrators to the VPN Concentrator
- **Access Control List**—Allows you to add access lists for administration access
- **Access Settings**—Allows you to set the administrative session timeouts and limits

Administrators

Administrators are special users who can access and change the Configuration, Administration, and Monitoring functions on the VPN Concentrator. Only administrators can use the VPN Concentrator Manager. Cisco provides five predefined administrators:

- **admin**—System administrator with access to and rights to change all areas. This is the only administrator enabled by default (this is the only administrator who can log in to and use the VPN Concentrator Manager as supplied by Cisco).
- **config**—Configuration administrator with all rights except SNMP access.
- **isp**—Internet service provider administrator with limited general configuration rights.
- **mis**—Management information systems administrator with the same rights as config.
- **user**—User administrator with rights only to view system statistics.

Once an administrator has been configured, you then have to assign access rights to the administrator. Figure 11-14 shows the Administrator Access Rights screen.

Figure 11-14 *Administrator Access Rights*

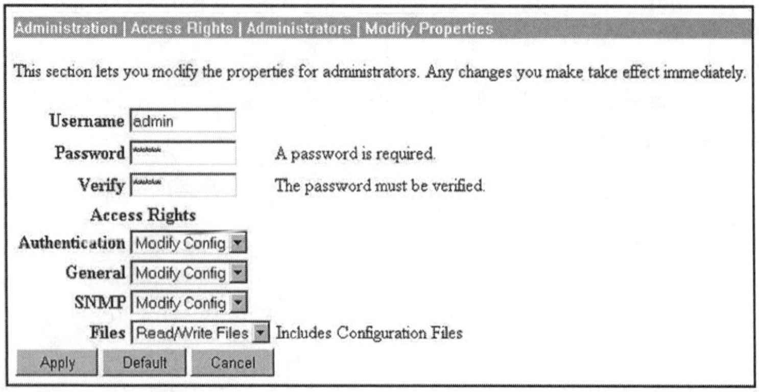

The access rights determine access to and rights in the VPN Concentrator Manager functional areas (Authentication or General) or by SNMP. Click the drop-down menu and choose from the following access rights:

- **None**—No access or rights.
- **Stats Only**—Access to only the Monitoring section of the VPN Concentrator Manager. No rights to change parameters.
- **View Config**—Access to permitted functional areas of the VPN Concentrator Manager, but no rights to change parameters.
- **Modify Config**—Access to permitted functional areas of the VPN Concentrator Manager, and rights to change parameters.

The following file access rights are available:

- **None**—No file access or management rights.
- **List Files**—See a list of files in the VPN Concentrator flash memory.
- **Read Files**—Read (view) files in flash memory.
- **Read/Write Files**—Read and write files in flash memory, clear or save the event log, and save the active configuration to a file.

Access Control List

The Access Control List section of the Manager lets you configure and prioritize the systems (workstations) that are allowed to access the VPN Concentrator Manager. For example, you might want to allow access only from one or two PCs that are in a locked room. If no systems are listed, anyone who knows the VPN Concentrator IP address and the administrator username and password combination can gain access.

To add an access control list, click the **Add** button on the Access Control List screen.

Figure 11-15 shows the Add screen to add an access control list.

Figure 11-15   *Add an Access Control List*

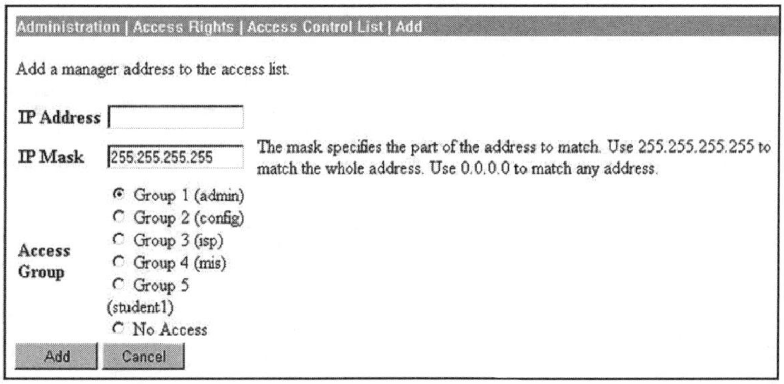

The Access Control List | Add screen allows you to modify the following:

- **IP address**—Enter the IP address of the workstation in dotted decimal notation (for example, 10.10.1.35).

- **IP mask**—Enter the mask for the IP address in dotted decimal notation. This mask lets you restrict access to a single IP address, a range of addresses, or all addresses. To restrict access to a single IP address, enter 255.255.255.255 (the default). To allow all IP addresses, enter 0.0.0.0. To allow a range of IP addresses, enter the appropriate mask.

- **Access group**—To assign rights of an administrator group to this IP address, click the appropriate radio button. Default is Group 1 (admin). You can assign only one group, or you can specify No Access.

Access Settings

The following access settings can be configured:

- **Session Idle Timeout**—Enter the timeout period in seconds for administrative sessions. If there is no activity for this period, the VPN Concentrator Manager session terminates. Default is 600 seconds, and there is no maximum.

- **Session Limit**—Enter the maximum number of simultaneous administrative sessions allowed. Default is 10, and there is no maximum.

- **Encrypt Config File**—To encrypt sensitive entries in the CONFIG file, check the box (default). The CONFIG file is in ASCII text format (.ini format). Check this box to encrypt entries such as passwords, keys, and user information.

The Access Settings screen can be seen in Figure 11-16.

Figure 11-16 *Access Settings Screen*

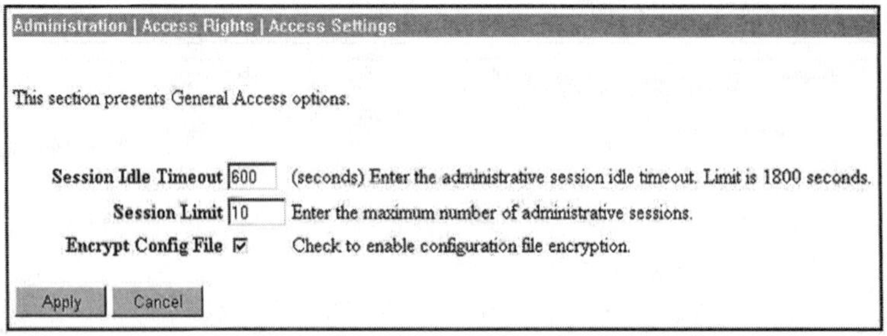

File Management

The File Management screen allows you to manage files on the VPN Concentrator. The following options are available:

- **Files**—View, save, and delete files.
- **Swap Config File**—Swap the backup and boot configuration files.
- **TFTP Transfer**—Transfer files with Trivial File Transfer Protocol (TFTP).

The following information and options are available from the File Management | Files screen:

- **Filename**—The name of the file in flash memory. The VPN Concentrator stores filenames as uppercase in the 8.3 naming convention.
- **Size (bytes)**—The size of the file in bytes.
- **Date/Time**—The date and time the file was created. The format is MM/DD/YY HH:MM:SS, with time in 24-hour notation.
- **Actions**—For a selected file, click the desired action link. The actions available to you depend on your access rights to files.
  - **View** (Save)—To view the selected file, click **View**. The Manager opens a new browser window to display the file.
  - **Delete**—To delete the selected file from flash memory, click **Delete**.
  - **Copy**—To copy a selected file within flash memory, click **Copy**.

The File Management | Files screen can be seen in Figure 11-17.

Figure 11-17   *File Management | Files*

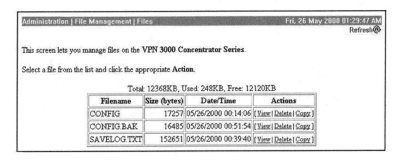

The Swap Configuration screen lets you swap the boot configuration file with the backup configuration file. Every time you save the active configuration, the system writes it to the CONFIG file, which is the boot configuration file. It also saves the previous CONFIG file as CONFIG.BAK—the backup configuration file. To reload the boot configuration file and make it the active configuration, you must reboot the system.

To reboot the system, click the highlighted link to go to the Administration | System Reboot screen.

The TFTP Transfer screen lets you use TFTP to transfer files to and from the VPN Concentrator flash memory. (Flash memory acts like a disk.) The VPN Concentrator acts as a TFTP client for these functions, accessing a TFTP server running on a remote system. All transfers are made in binary (octet) mode, and they copy—rather than move—files.

To use the following functions, you must have access rights to read/write files:

- **TFTP GET**—Get a file from the remote system (that is, copy a file from the remote system to the VPN Concentrator).

- **TFTP PUT**—Put a file on the remote system (that is, copy a file from the VPN Concentrator to the remote system).

- **Local File**—Enter the name of the file on the VPN Concentrator.

- **Remote File**—Enter the name of the file on the remote system. This filename must conform to naming conventions applicable to the remote system. Do not include a path.

The File Management | TFTP Transfer screen can be seen in Figure 11-18.

Figure 11-18   *File Management | TFTP Transfer*

```
Administration | File Management | TFTP Transfer

This screen lets you transfer files to/from the VPN 3000 Concentrator Series. Please wait for the operation to
finish.

    Concentrator File      Action        TFTP Server        TFTP Server File
[                    ]  [GET << ▼]  [                ]  [                   ]
[   OK   ]  [  Cancel  ]
```

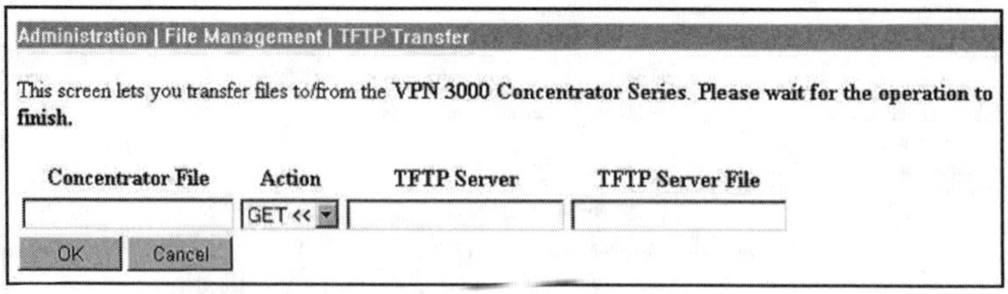

WARNING   If either filename is the same as an existing file, TFTP overwrites the existing file without asking for confirmation.

Certificate Management

The Certificate Management screen lets you manage digital certificates. Digital certificates are covered in Chapter 10, "Configuring the Cisco VPN 3000 for Remote Access Using Digital Certificates."

Summary

This chapter looked at the remaining two options available in the VPN Manager: Monitoring and Administration. It covered all of the available options under these two categories and showed examples of key screens to help familiarize you with the VPN Manager. Monitoring and Administration of the VPN Concentrator are key points that have to be mastered to get the full benefit of the VPN Concentrator and to protect the VPN Concentrator from external threats.

Review Questions

1 How can you get access to the event log on the VPN Concentrator, besides through the VPN Manager?

2 When manipulating images over TFTP, what happens if you name a file with the same name as an existing file?

3 How many events does the event log hold by default?

4 What rights are required to view event logs?

5 Looking at the System LED status, what does an amber LED signify?

6 From the Administration index screen, which option do you choose to delete a system file?

7 On average, how long does a full reboot take?

8 You want to limit the workstations that are allowed to access the VPN Manager of the Concentrator to only the ones where specific users will be working. What option is available to do this?

9 When performing a software update of the VPN Concentrator software, where must you locate the system software image in order for the VPN Manager to upload it to the Concentrator?

10 What are the default and maximum session timeout values?

Scaling Cisco VPN Solutions

CHAPTER 12

Scaling Cisco IPSec Virtual Private Networks

This chapter teaches you how to configure Internet Protocol Security (IPSec) features on combinations of Cisco routers, the PIX Firewall, the Cisco VPN 3000 Concentrator, and the Cisco VPN Clients for site-to-site and access topologies.

This chapter covers the following topics:

- Dynamic crypto maps
- Configure IPSec between Cisco routers and PIX Firewalls
- Configure VPN Concentrator to PIX Firewall site-to-site
- Extended authentication
- Wildcard preshared keys
- IKE mode configuration
- Tunnel endpoint discovery
- Perfect forward secrecy (PFS)
- IPSec with Network Address Translation (NAT)
- Configure PIX Firewall for Cisco VPN 3000 Client
- Configure PIX Firewall for Cisco Secure VPN 1.1 Client
- Configure Cisco IOS for Cisco Secure VPN 1.1 Client

Dynamic Crypto Maps

This section introduces dynamic crypto maps and then shows you how to configure them on Cisco routers and PIX Firewalls.

Dynamic crypto maps can ease IPSec configuration and are recommended for use with networks where the peers are not always predetermined. An example of this is mobile users (VPN Clients), as shown in Figure 12-1, which obtain dynamically assigned IP addresses. First, the mobile Clients need to authenticate themselves to the local PIX Firewall Internet Key Exchange (IKE) by something other than an IP address, such as a fully qualified domain name. Once authenticated, the security association (SA) request can be processed against a dynamic crypto map that is set up to accept requests (matching the specified local policy) from previously unknown peers.

Figure 12-1 *Mobile VPN Clients*

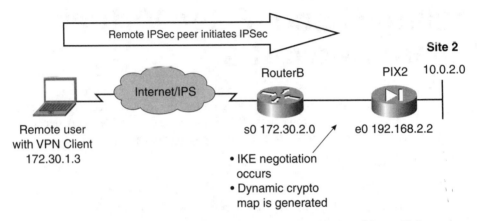

A dynamic crypto map entry is essentially a crypto map entry without all the parameters configured. It acts as a policy template where the missing parameters are later dynamically configured (as the result of an IPSec negotiation) to match a peer's requirements. This allows peers to exchange IPSec traffic with the PIX Firewall or Cisco IOS even if they do not have a crypto map entry specifically configured to meet all the peer's requirements.

Dynamic crypto maps are not used by the PIX Firewall or Cisco IOS to initiate new IPSec SAs with peers. Dynamic crypto maps are used when a peer tries to initiate an IPSec SA with the PIX Firewall or Cisco IOS. Dynamic crypto maps are also used in evaluating traffic.

A dynamic crypto map set is included by reference as part of a crypto map set. Any crypto map entries that reference dynamic crypto map sets should be the lowest priority crypto map entries in the crypto map set (that is, have the highest sequence numbers) so that the other crypto map entries are evaluated first. That way, the dynamic crypto map set is examined only when the other (static) map entries are not successfully matched.

PIX Firewall Dynamic Crypto Maps

This section details how to configure dynamic crypto maps on the PIX Firewall.

Dynamic crypto map entries, like static crypto map entries, are grouped into sets. A set is a group of dynamic crypto map entries all with the same *dynamic-map-name* but each with a different *dynamic-seq-num*.

If a set is configured, the data flow identity proposed by the IPSec peer must fall within a permit statement for this crypto access list. If a set is not configured, the PIX Firewall accepts any data flow identity proposed by the peer.

NOTE   Care must be taken if the **any** keyword is used in the access list, because the access list is used for packet filtering, as well as for negotiation.

Dynamic crypto map entries can optionally specify crypto access lists that limit traffic for which IPSec SAs can be established. A dynamic crypto map entry that does not specify an access list is ignored during traffic filtering. If there is only one dynamic crypto map entry in the static crypto map set, it must specify acceptable transform sets.

The **crypto dynamic-map** command has the following commands and syntax:

```
crypto dynamic-map dynamic-map-name dynamic-seq-num

crypto dynamic-map dynamic-map-name dynamic-seq-num match address acl_name

crypto dynamic-map dynamic-map-name dynamic-seq-num set peer
    hostname | ip-address

crypto dynamic-map dynamic-map-name dynamic-seq-num set pfs
    [group1 | group2]

crypto dynamic-map dynamic-map-name dynamic-seq-num set security-association
    lifetime seconds seconds | kilobytes kilobytes

crypto dynamic-map dynamic-map-name dynamic-seq-num set transform-set
    transform-set-name1 [transform-set-name9]
```

dynamic-map-name	Specifies the name of the dynamic crypto map set
dynamic-seq-num	Specifies the sequence number that corresponds to the dynamic crypto map entry
subcommand	Various subcommands (**match address**, **set transform-set**, and so on)

All the same parameters that are available in regular static crypto maps are available with dynamic crypto maps.

NOTE   Only the *transform-set* field is required to be configured within each dynamic crypto map entry. It is recommended to configure an access list for security.

Dynamic Crypto Map Example—PIX Firewall

Example 12-1 shows a dynamic crypto map on a PIX Firewall.

Example 12-1 *PIX—Dynamic Crypto Map*

```
Pixfirewall(confg)#crypto dynamic-map dynomap 210 set transform-set mine
Pixfirewall(confg)#crypto dynamic-map dynomap 210 match address 152

Pixfirewall(confg)#show crypto dynamic-map
Crypto Map Template "dynomap" 210
  access-list 152 permit ip host 192.168.1.10 any
  Current peer: 0.0.0.0
  Security association lifetime: 4608000 kilobytes/3600 seconds
  PFS (Y/N): N
  Transform sets={mine, }
```

Use care when using the **any** keyword in permit entries in dynamic crypto maps. If it is possible for the traffic covered by such a permit entry to include multicast or broadcast traffic, the access list should include **deny** entries for the appropriate address range. Access lists should also include **deny** entries for network and subnet broadcast traffic and for any other traffic that should not be IPSec protected.

You can add one or more dynamic crypto map sets into a static crypto map set with crypto map entries that reference the dynamic crypto map sets. You should set the crypto map entries referencing dynamic maps to be the lowest-priority entries in a crypto map set (that is, use the highest sequence numbers).

```
crypto map map-name seq-num ipsec-isakmp | ipsec-manual
    [dynamic dynamic-map-name]
```

map-name	The name of the crypto map set
seq-num	The number you assign to the crypto map entry
dynamic	Specifies that this crypto map entry is to reference a preexisting dynamic crypto map
dynamic-map-name	Specifies the name of the dynamic crypto map set to be used as the policy template

In Example 12-2, crypto map entry mymap 30 references the dynamic crypto map set dynomap, which can be used to process inbound SA negotiation requests. In this case, if the peer specifies a transform set that matches one of the transform sets specified in dynomap for a flow permitted by the access list 152, IPSec will accept the request and set up SAs with the peer without previously knowing about the peer. If accepted, the resulting

SAs (and temporary crypto map entry) are established according to the settings specified by the peer.

Example 12-2 *PIX—Dynamic Crypto Map Example*

```
pixfirewall(config)# write terminal


crypto dynamic-map dynomap 210 match address 152
crypto dynamic-map dynomap 210 set transform-set mine
crypto map mymap 30 ipsec-isakmp dynamic dynomap
crypto map mymap interface outside
crypto ipsec transform-set mine esp-3des esp-sha-hmac
access-list 152 permit ip host 192.168.1.10 any
```

The access list associated with *dynomap 210* is also used as a filter. Inbound packets that match a permit statement in this list (access-list 152) are dropped for not being IPSec protected. (The same is true for access lists associated with static crypto maps entries.) Outbound packets that match a permit statement without an existing corresponding IPSec SA are also dropped. The static crypto map is assigned to the interface.

Cisco IOS Dynamic Crypto Maps

This section details how to configure dynamic crypto maps on the Cisco IOS.

Dynamic crypto map entries, like static crypto map entries, are grouped into sets. A set is a group of dynamic crypto map entries all with the same *dynamic-map-name* but each with a different *dynamic-seq-num*.

To create a dynamic crypto map entry, use the commands in Table 12-1, starting in global configuration mode.

Table 12-1   *Creating a Dynamic Crypto Map Entry*

Step	Command	Purpose
1	**crypto dynamic-map** *dynamic-map-name dynamic-seq-num*	Create a dynamic crypto map entry.
2	**set transform-set** *transform-set-name1* [*transform-set-name2...transform-set-name6*]	Specify which transform sets are allowed for the crypto map entry. List multiple transform sets in order of priority (highest priority first). This is the only configuration statement required in dynamic crypto map entries.

NOTE	All other parameters are optional.

Dynamic crypto map entries can optionally specify crypto access lists that limit traffic for which IPSec SAs can be established. If there is only one dynamic crypto map entry in the crypto map set, it must specify acceptable transform sets.

Dynamic Crypto Map Example—Cisco IOS

The configuration shown in Example 12-3 creates a dynamic crypto map named mydynamicmap with a sequence number of 210. Note that all of the options available with a static crypto map are also available with dynamic crypto maps. Only the transform set is required with dynamic crypto maps.

Example 12-3 *Cisco IOS—Dynamic Crypto Map Example*

```
Router(config)# crypto dynamic-map mydynamicmap 210
router(config-dynamic-crypto-map)# ?


  set transform-set [set_name(s)]
  match address [access-list-id | name]
set peer [hostname | ip-address]
  set pfs [group1 | group2]
  set security-association lifetime {seconds seconds | kilobytes kilobytes}
```

You can add one or more dynamic crypto map sets into a crypto map set with crypto map entries that reference the dynamic crypto map sets. You should set the crypto map entries referencing dynamic maps to be the lowest-priority entries in a crypto map set (that is, use the highest sequence numbers).

```
crypto map map-name seq-num ipsec-isakmp | ipsec-manual
    [dynamic dynamic-map-name]
```

map-name	The name of the crypto map set
seq-num	The number you assign to the crypto map entry
dynamic	Specifies that this crypto map entry is to reference a preexisting dynamic crypto map
dynamic-map-name	Specifies the name of the dynamic crypto map set to be used as the policy template

Looking at Example 12-4, crypto map entry mymap 30 references the dynamic crypto map set mydynamicmap 210, which can be used to process inbound SA negotiation requests. In this case, if the peer specifies a transform set that matches one of the transform sets specified in mydynamicmap for a flow permitted by the access list 103, IPSec will accept the request and set up SAs with the peer without previously knowing about the peer. If accepted, the resulting SAs (and temporary crypto map entry) are established according to the settings specified by the peer.

Example 12-4 *Cisco IOS—Dynamic Crypto Map Example Configuration*

```
crypto ipsec transform-set mine esp-3des
!
crypto dynamic-map mydynamicmap 210
    set transform-set mine
    match address 103
!
crypto map mymap 30 ipsec-isakmp dynamic mydynamicmap
!
interface Serial0
    crypto map mymap
!
access-list 103 permit tcp 10.0.1.0 0.0.0.255 10.0.2.0 0.0.0.255
```

This concludes the configuration of dynamic crypto maps on Cisco PIX Firewalls and IOS routers. The next section looks at the configuration of an IPSec VPN between a PIX Firewall and an IOS router.

Configure IPSec Between Cisco Routers and PIX Firewalls

This section covers how to configure a Cisco router to connect to a PIX Firewall using IPSec. The section also covers how to configure a crypto map on a Cisco router to connect to multiple IPSec peers, and how to configure dynamic crypto maps on a PIX Firewall.

The network topology in Figure 12-2 shows that Router A can set up an IPSec tunnel to Router B, which was completed in Chapter 7, "Configuring the Cisco PIX Firewall for CA Site-to-Site." The goal is to enable Router A to also initiate IPSec to PIX 2, securing traffic of all Site 1 hosts to the Site 2 host 10.0.2.3 through the static on PIX 2. Static crypto maps are used in Router A, and dynamic crypto maps in PIX 2. The key to enabling a Cisco router with one interface to the Internet to connect to multiple peers is to create multiple crypto map groupings with different sequence numbers under one crypto map.

Figure 12-2 *Network Topology*

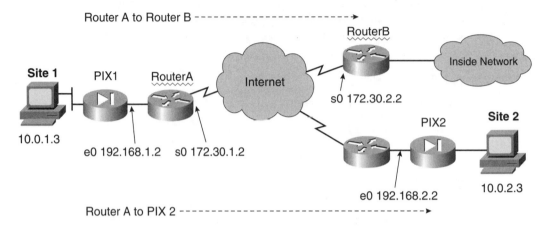

- Router A initiates IPSec to Router B
- Router A initiates IPSec to PIX 2
  — Secures traffic between all site 1 hosts to site 2 10.0.2.3 host
- Static crypto maps are used in Router A

IKE Policy

The IKE policy for connecting Router A and PIX 2 is shown in Table 12-2. Note that Rivest, Shamir, and Adelman (RSA) signatures are used for IKE authentication, SHA is used for the hash algorithm, and a shorter IKE SA lifetime is used.

Table 12-2 *IKE Policy*

Parameter	Router A	PIX 2
Encryption algorithm	DES	DES
Hash algorithm	SHA	SHA
Authentication method	RSA signatures	RSA signatures
Key exchange	768-bit Diffie-Hellman	768-bit Diffie-Hellman
IKE SA lifetime	43,200 seconds	43,200 seconds
Peer IP address	192.168.2.2	172.30.1.2

IPSec Policy

The IPSec policy uses **esp-des** and **esp-sha-hmac**, so a new transform set needs to be created. All hosts in the 10.0.1.0 network connect with IPSec to the Microsoft Windows NT server of address 10.0.2.3 at Site 2 (behind PIX 2). PIX 2 statically maps the host as IP address 10.0.2.3 to a global IP address of 192.168.2.10. The policy can be seen in Table 12-3.

Table 12-3 *IPSec Policy*

Policy	Router A	PIX 2
Transform set	ESP-DES	ESP-DES
	ESP-SHA-HMAC	ESP-SHA-HMAC
Peer host name	PIX 2	Router A
Peer IP address	192.168.2.2	172.30.1.2
Hosts to be encrypted	10.0.1.0	10.0.2.3
Traffic to be encrypted	IP	IP
SA establishment	Ipsec-isakmp	Ipsec-isakmp

Example Configurations

The partial configuration for Router A in Figure 12-2 is shown in Example 12-5.

Example 12-5 *Router A Configuration*

```
RouterA# show running-config

crypto isakmp policy 110
 hash md5
 authentication pre-share
!
crypto isakmp policy 120
 lifetime 43200
crypto isakmp identity hostname
!
crypto ipsec transform-set mine esp-des
crypto ipsec transform-set mine2 esp-des esp-sha-hmac
!
```

Example 12-5 shows how the IKE policy is implemented and that a transform set is set up using the IPSec policy.

A continuation of the partial configuration for Router A is shown in Example 12-6.

Example 12-6 **show running-config** *on Router A*

```
RouterA# show running-config
crypto map mymap 10 ipsec-isakmp
 set peer 172.30.2.2
 set transform-set mine
 match address 102
crypto map mymap 20 ipsec-isakmp
```

continues

Example 12-6 show running-config *on Router A (Continued)*

```
 set peer 192.168.2.2
 set transform-set mine2
 match address 104
!
interface Serial0/0
 ip address 172.30.1.2 255.255.255.0
 crypto map mymap
!
access-list 102 permit ip host 172.30.1.2 host 172.30.2.2
access-list 104 permit ip 192.168.1.0 0.0.0.255 host 192.168.2.10
```

The crypto map named mymap with a sequence number of 10 is from Chapter 6, "Configuring the Cisco PIX Firewall for Preshared Keys Site-To-Site" and enables connection to Router B.

The new crypto map with a sequence number of 20 enables connection to PIX 2.

The **show crypto map** command displays a summary of how the IPSec policy is configured, as shown in Example 12-7.

Example 12-7 show crypto map *on Router A*

```
RouterA# show crypto map
Crypto Map "mymap" 10 ipsec-isakmp
  Peer = 172.30.2.2
  Extended IP access list 102
   access-list 102 permit ip host 172.30.1.2 host 172.30.2.2
  Current peer: 172.30.2.2
  Security association lifetime: 4608000 kilobytes/3600 seconds
  PFS (Y/N): N
  Transform sets={ mine, }

Crypto Map "mymap" 20 ipsec-isakmp
  Peer = 192.168.2.2
  Extended IP access list 104
   access-list 104 permit ip 192.168.1.0 0.0.0.255 host 192.168.2.10
  Current peer: 192.168.2.2
  Security association lifetime: 4608000 kilobytes/3600 seconds
  PFS (Y/N): N
  Transform sets={ mine2, }
  Interfaces using crypto map mymap:Serial0/0
```

The crypto map mymap with a sequence number of 20 enables connection to PIX 2. Note that the access list points to the statics on both PIX 1 and PIX 2.

The partial configuration for PIX 2 is shown in Example 12-8.

Example 12-8 *The Configuration on PIX2*

```
pix2# write terminal

access-list 101 permit ip host 192.168.2.10 host 192.168.1.10
access-list 104 permit ip host 192.168.2.10 192.168.0.0 255.255.0.0
static (inside,outside) 192.168.2.10 10.0.2.3 netmask 255.255.255.255 0 0
crypto ipsec transform-set mine esp-des
crypto ipsec transform-set mine2 esp-des esp-sha-hmac
crypto dynamic-map mydyno 100 match address 104
crypto dynamic-map mydyno 100 set transform-set mine2 mine
crypto map peer1 10 ipsec-isakmp
crypto map peer1 10 match address 101
crypto map peer1 10 set peer 192.168.1.2
crypto map peer1 10 set transform-set mine
crypto map peer1 20 ipsec-isakmp dynamic mydyno
crypto map peer1 interface outside
```

Some points to note about the configuration are as follows:

- PIX 2 must be configured to allow Router A to connect to it.

- Access list 104 on PIX 2 is a mirror image of access list 104 on Router B.

- Access list 104 points to the statics on PIX 1 and PIX 2.

- PIX 2 is configured with a dynamic crypto map named mydyno.

- The previously configured crypto map peer1 with a sequence number of 10 enables PIX 1 to connect to PIX 2.

- A static crypto map with a different sequence number could be configured to permit connection to Router B.

A continuation of the partial configuration for PIX 2, showing how the IKE policy is configured, is shown in Example 12-9. Note that the new configuration commands enabling connection to Router A are shaded in Example 12-9.

Example 12-9 *IKE Policy*

```
isakmp enable outside
isakmp key cisco1234 address 192.168.1.2 netmask 255.255.255.255
isakmp identity hostname
isakmp policy 5 authentication rsa-sig
isakmp policy 5 encryption des
isakmp policy 5 hash md5
isakmp policy 5 group 1
isakmp policy 5 lifetime 86400
isakmp policy 10 authentication pre-share
isakmp policy 10 encryption des
isakmp policy 10 hash md5
isakmp policy 10 group 1
isakmp policy 10 lifetime 86400
```

continues

Example 12-9 *IKE Policy (Continued)*

```
isakmp policy 20 authentication rsa-sig
isakmp policy 20 encryption des
isakmp policy 20 hash sha
isakmp policy 20 group 1
isakmp policy 20 lifetime 43200
```

Some points to note about the configuration are as follows:

- The IKE policy with a sequence number of 20 implements the IKE policy for connecting PIX 2 and Router A.
- The IKE identity mode is set to hostname to permit RSA signatures authentication.
- The IKE policies with sequence numbers of 5 and 10 pertain to previously configured IKE policies.

Configure VPN Concentrator to PIX Firewall Site to Site

This section covers how to configure site-to-site VPNs using the Cisco VPN 3000 Concentrator to a PIX Firewall.

The network topology in Figure 12-3 shows that the VPN 3000 Concentrator C1 can set up IPSec tunnels to PIX 2 in a site-to-site (LAN-to-LAN) topology. The goal is for C1 to initiate IPSec to PIX 2, securing traffic of all Site 1 hosts to all Site 2 hosts. Static crypto maps are used in PIX 2.

Figure 12-3 *Network Topology*

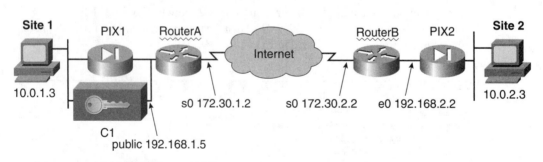

- Concentrator initiates IPSec to PIX2
- Secures all traffic between site 1 and site 2 hosts

IKE Policy

The IKE policy for connecting C1 and PIX 2 is shown in Table 12-4. Note that preshared keys are used for IKE authentication and that the other IKE parameters are the default values.

Table 12-4 *IKE Policy*

Parameter	Concentrator 1	PIX 2
Encryption algorithm	DES	DES
Hash algorithm	MD5	MD5
Authentication method	Preshare	Preshare
Key exchange	768-bit Diffie-Hellman	768-bit Diffie-Hellman
IKE SA lifetime	86,400 seconds	86,400 seconds
Peer IP address	192.168.2.2	192.168.1.5

IPSec Policy

The IPSec policy uses **esp-des** and **esp-md5-hmac**, so a new transform set needs to be created on PIX 2. All hosts in the 10.0.1.0 network connect through IPSec to all hosts in the 10.0.2.0 network at Site 2 (behind PIX 2). PIX 2 statically maps the 10.0.2.0 hosts to a global IP address network of 192.168.2.0 (although only one host is statically mapped in the example). The IPSec policy can be seen in Table 12-5.

Table 12-5 *IPSec Policy*

Policy	Concentrator 1	PIX 2
Transform set	ESP-DES	ESP-DES
	ESP-MD5-HMAC	ESP-MD5-HMAC
Peer host name	PIX2	N/A
Peer IP address	192.168.2.2	192.168.1.5
Hosts to be encrypted	10.0.1.0	192.168.2.0
Traffic to be encrypted	IP	IP
SA establishment	IKE	IKE

Configuration Procedure

The overall configuration procedure for the Concentrator and the PIX Firewall is as follows:

Step 1 Configure IKE proposals on the Concentrator.

Step 2 Add a new IPSec LAN-to-LAN connection on the Concentrator.

Step 3   Configure the PIX Firewall to implement the IKE and IPSec policy.

Step 4   Verify that IPSec works on the Concentrator and the PIX Firewall.

Step 1: Configure IKE Proposals

The first step involves configuring IKE proposals on the VPN Concentrator under Configuration | System | Tunneling Protocols | IPSec | IKE Proposals.

By default, the Concentrator has several IKE policy suites set up. You may be able to use one of the policies. Verify that an existing policy will work by selecting the policy and then clicking the **Modify** button. You can also copy and modify an existing policy or add a new policy.

You can activate a policy or move a policy to a higher (or lower) priority (similar to assigning an IKE policy with a lower sequence number on a Cisco router or PIX Firewall). The IKE Proposals screen can be seen in Figure 12-4.

Figure 12-4   *VPN Concentrator IKE Proposals Screen*

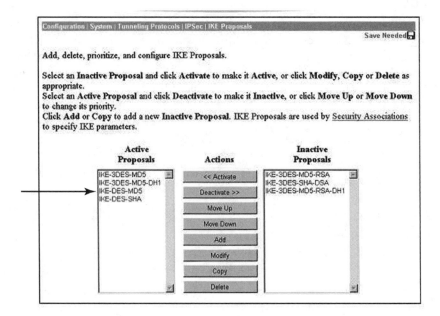

Selecting a policy and modifying it leads you to the Configuration | System | Tunneling Protocols | IPSec | IKE Proposals | Modify window, as shown in Figure 12-5.

Verify that the IKE proposal matches the IKE policy for the IPSec peer.

Figure 12-5 *VPN Concentrator IKE Proposal Modify Screen*

Configuration | System | Tunneling Protocols | IPSec | IKE Proposals | Modify

Modify a configured IKE Proposal.

Proposal Name	IKE-DES-MD5	Specify the name of this IKE Proposal.
Authentication Mode	Preshared Keys	Select the authentication mode to use.
Authentication Algorithm	MD5/HMAC-128	Select the packet authentication algorithm to use.
Encryption Algorithm	DES-56	Select the encryption algorithm to use.
Diffie-Hellman Group	Group 1 (768-bits)	Select the Diffie Hellman Group to use.
Lifetime Measurement	Time	Select the lifetime measurement of the IKE keys.
Data Lifetime	10000	Specify the data lifetime in kilobytes (KB).
Time Lifetime	86400	Specify the time lifetime in seconds.

Apply   Cancel

Step 2: Add an IPSec LAN-to-LAN Connection

The second step in configuring the Concentrator for a LAN-to-LAN connection to the PIX Firewall is to add a new LAN-to-LAN connection at the Configuration | System | Tunneling Protocols | IPSec LAN-to-LAN window, as shown in Figure 12-6.

Figure 12-6 *Add IPSec LAN-to-LAN*

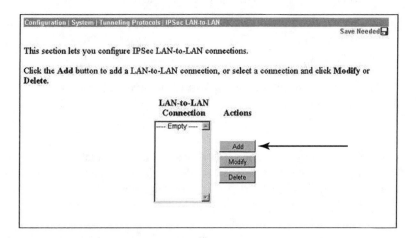

Click **Add** to add a new connection, which leads you to the Configuration | System | Tunneling Protocols | IPSec LAN-to-LAN | Add window.

Configuration of IPSec LAN-to-LAN cannot be done in Quick Configuration. The Concentrator provides a wizard for LAN-to-LAN connections.

A continuation of Step 2 includes going to the Configuration | System | Tunneling Protocols | IPSec LAN-to-LAN window, as shown in Figure 12-7, and clicking **Add** to configure the IPSec parameters as follows:

Step 1 Enter the name for the LAN-to-LAN connection.

Step 2 Set the peer value to be the IP address assigned to the outside interface of the remote PIX Firewall.

Step 3 Enter an alphanumeric string value for the preshared key to match that of the peer or select a digital certificate.

Step 4 Select the authentication and encryption values to match the IPSec policy. Select the IKE proposal configured in Step 1.

Step 5 Set the local network to be the network address that the private interface is on (that is, 10.0.1.0).

Set the wildcard mask to be the local network's subnet mask (that is, 0.0.0.255), similar to a wildcard mask on a Cisco router access list.

Step 6 Set the destination network to be a network on the peer's private network (that is, 192.168.2.0 for the PIX 2's statics).

Set the wildcard mask to be the local network's subnet mask (that is, 0.0.0.255).

Step 7 Click **Add**.

You can optionally select the **Network Auto Discovery** check box, which does a type of tunnel endpoint discovery.

NOTE You could optionally configure network lists in the Configuration | Policy Management | Traffic Management | Network Lists window, then apply them here. Network lists are similar to access lists, simplifying IPSec configuration.

The Configuration | System | Tunneling Protocols | IPSec LAN-to-LAN | Add | Done window appears after clicking **Add** in the Configuration | System | Tunneling Protocols | IPSec LAN-to-LAN window.

Figure 12-7 *Add IPSec LAN-to-LAN Window*

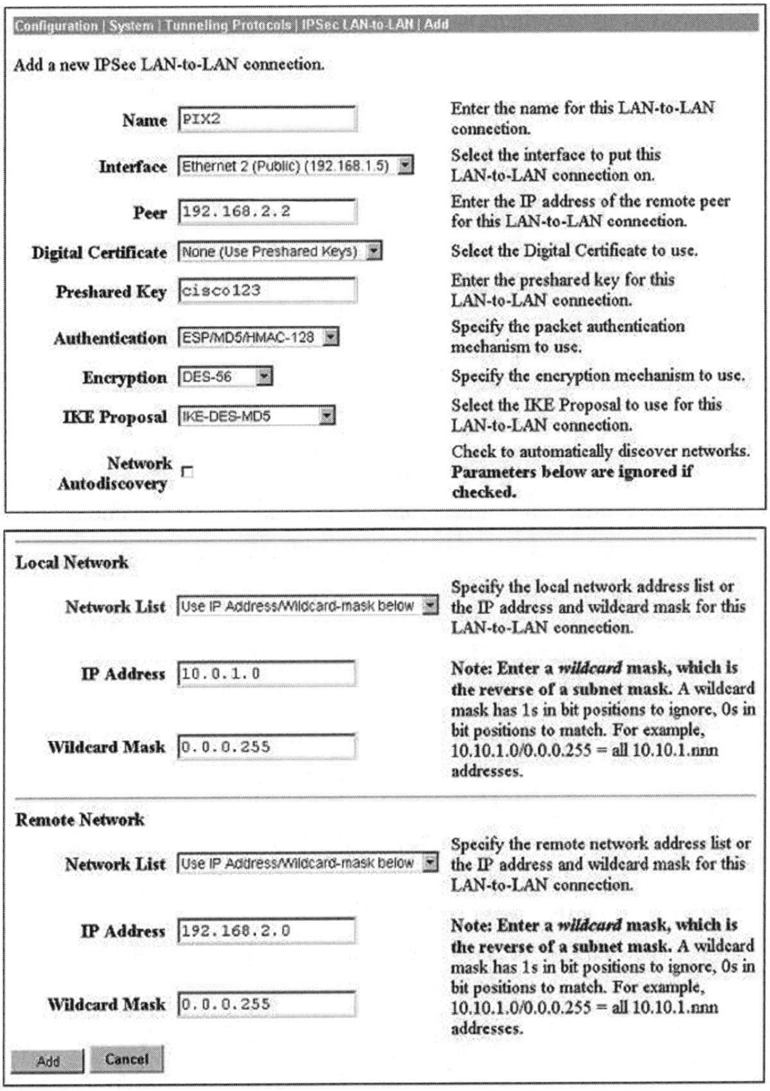

The window, as shown in Figure 12-8, provides a synopsis of the IPSec tunnel just created. Clicking **OK** brings you to the Configuration | System | Tunneling Protocols | IPSec LAN-to-LAN window.

Figure 12-8 *IPSec LAN-to-LAN Done*

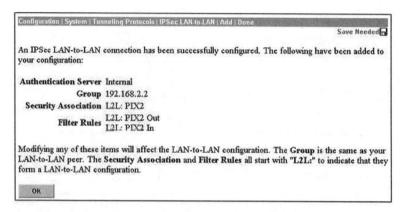

The Configuration I System I Tunneling Protocols I IPSec LAN-to-LAN window now shows the new LAN-to-LAN tunnel. Click **Modify** to modify the IPSec parameters. Note that the LAN-to-LAN connection is now applied to the public interface and is active.

Creating a LAN-to-LAN connection also creates a group in Configuration I User Management I Groups. Configuration I User Management I Groups I Modify allows you to see the Identity, General, and IPSec parameters. Under the **Identity** tab in Configuration I User Management I Groups I Modify, you can see the group name (the peer IP address). The Password field is set to the preshared key value and should not be changed.

The LAN-to-LAN connection can be seen in Figure 12-9.

Figure 12-9 *IPSec LAN-to-LAN*

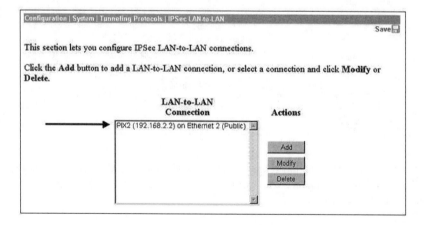

Step 3: PIX Configuration

The third step in configuring the Concentrator to PIX topology is to configure the PIX Firewall to implement the IKE and IPSec security policy to match that of the Concentrator. Example 12-10 lists a partial configuration of PIX 2.

Example 12-10 *IKE and IPSec Configuration of PIX 2*

```
pix2# write terminal
access-list 106 permit ip 192.168.2.0 255.255.255.0 10.0.1.0 255.255.255.0
crypto ipsec transform-set mine2 esp-des esp-md5-hmac
crypto map peerc 10 ipsec-isakmp
crypto map peerc 10 match address 106
crypto map peerc 10 set peer 192.168.1.5
crypto map peerc 10 set transform-set mine2
crypto map peerc interface outside
isakmp enable outside
isakmp key cisco123 address 192.168.1.5 netmask 255.255.255.255
isakmp identity address
isakmp policy 30 authentication pre-share
isakmp policy 30 encryption des
isakmp policy 30 hash md5
isakmp policy 30 group 1
isakmp policy 30 lifetime 86400
```

Some points to note about the configuration are as follows:

- Access list 106 is a mirror image of the IPSec network configuration on C1.

- Access list 106 points to the hosts behind C1 and the statics on PIX 2.

- PIX 2 is configured with a static crypto map named peerc.

- The IKE preshared key matches that on C1.

- The IKE policy has a sequence number of 30, which is different from any existing IKE policy.

Step 4: Verify IPSec Operation

The fourth step in configuring the Concentrator to PIX topology is to test and verify that everything is working properly. You can use the **show crypto map** command on PIX 2. The command provides a useful summary of IPSec configuration details. Output for PIX 2 is shown in Example 12-11.

Example 12-11 **show crypto map** *on PIX 2*

```
pix2(config)# show crypto map

Crypto Map: "peerc" interfaces: { outside }

Crypto Map "peerc" 10 ipsec-isakmp
  Peer = 192.168.1.5
```

continues

Example 12-11 show crypto map *on PIX 2 (Continued)*

```
access-list 106 permit ip 192.168.2.0 255.255.255.0
  10.0.1.0 255.255.255.0 (hitcnt=18)
Current peer: 192.168.1.5
Security association lifetime: 4608000 kilobytes/28800 seconds
PFS (Y/N): N
Transform sets={ mine2, }
```

Some additional verification steps that you can take include the following:

- Use the **write terminal**, **show isakmp**, **show isakmp policy**, **show access-list**, **debug crypto ipsec**, and **debug crypto isakmp** commands on the PIX.
- Configure Concentrator system events for IKE and IPSec, and then view the event log.
- Test and verify that an IPSec tunnel is created between the protected hosts.

Extended Authentication

The PIX Firewall supports the Extended Authentication (Xauth) feature within the IKE protocol. Xauth lets you deploy IPSec VPNs using Terminal Access Controller Access Control System Plus (TACACS+) or Remote Authentication Dial-In User Service (RADIUS) as your user authentication method. This feature, which is designed for VPN Clients, provides a user authentication by prompting the user for username and password and then verifies them with the information stored in your TACACS+ or RADIUS database. Xauth is negotiated between IKE phase one (IKE device authentication phase) and IKE phase two (IPSec SA negotiation phase). If Xauth fails, the IPSec SA is not established, and the IKE SA is deleted.

NOTE   A complete discussion of configuring Xauth on the PIX Firewall is beyond the scope of this book. Only the necessary commands and information for configuring Xauth with VPN Clients is covered.

The IKE mode configuration feature (covered in the section "IKE Mode Configuration—PIX Firewall") is also negotiated between IKE phase one and two. If both features are configured, Xauth is performed first.

NOTE   The VPN Client remote user must be running the Cisco VPN 3000 Client version 2.5 or the Cisco Secure VPN Client version 1.1.

The **aaa-server** command lets you specify an authentication, authorization, and accounting (AAA) server group. The PIX Firewall lets you define separate groups of TACACS+ or RADIUS servers for specifying different types of traffic, such as, a TACACS+ server for inbound traffic and another for outbound traffic. Another use is for all outbound HTTP traffic to be authenticated by a TACACS+ server, and all inbound traffic to use RADIUS.

AAA server groups are defined by a tag name that directs different types of traffic to each authentication server. If the first authentication server in the list fails, the AAA subsystem fails over to the next server in the tag group.

```
aaa-server group_tag (if_name) host server_ip key timeout seconds
```

group_tag	An alphanumeric string that is the name of the server group. Use the *group_tag* in the **aaa** command to associate **aaa authentication** and **aaa accounting** command statements to an AAA server.
if_name	The interface name on which the server resides.
host *server_ip*	The IP address of the TACACS+ or RADIUS server.
key	A case-sensitive, alphanumeric keyword of up to 127 characters that is the same value as the key on the TACACS+ server. Any characters entered past 127 are ignored. The key is used between the Client and server for encrypting data between them. The key must be the same on both the Client and server systems. Spaces are not permitted in the key, but other special characters are.
seconds	Specifies the duration that the PIX Firewall retries access four times to the AAA server before choosing the next AAA server.

The Xauth feature is optional and is enabled on the PIX Firewall using the following command:

```
crypto map map-name client authentication aaa-group-tag
```

map-name	The name of the crypto map set.
aaa-group-tag	The name of the AAA server that will authenticate the user during IKE authentication. The two AAA server options available are TACACS+ and RADIUS.

Use the same AAA server name within the **aaa-server** and **crypto map client authentication** command statements.

Making an Exception for Security Gateways

If you have both security gateway and VPN Client peers terminating on the same interface and have the Xauth feature configured, configure the PIX Firewall to make an exception to this feature for the security gateway peer. With this exception, the PIX Firewall does not challenge the security gateway peer for a username and password. The command that you employ to make an exception to the Xauth feature depends on the authentication method you are using within your IKE policies.

Xauth Example—PIX Firewall

To configure Xauth on your PIX Firewall, perform the following steps:

Step 1 Set up your basic AAA server.

```
pixfirewall(config)#aaa-server NT1 outside host 10.0.1.10 secret123
```

This example specifies that the authentication server with the IP address 10.0.1.10 resides on the inside interface and is in the default TACACS+ server group. The key secret123 is used between the PIX Firewall and the TACACS+ server for encrypting data between them.

Step 2 Enable Xauth.

Be sure to specify the same AAA server *group-tag* within the **crypto map client authentication** command statement as was specified in the **aaa-server** command statement.

```
pixfirewall(config)#crypto map mymap client authentication NT1
```

In this example, Xauth is enabled at the crypto map *mymap* and the server specified in the group *NT1* is used for user authentication.

Wildcard Preshared Keys

A wildcard can be thought of as a value that allows a match to be made against any other value. For example, you use wildcard masks in Cisco IOS access control lists (ACLs) to match against various Layer 3 addresses.

Wildcard preshared keys allow the enterprise gateway to have a key entry that matches any unknown peer, as opposed to specifying keys for each possible remote host.

NOTE Using wildcard preshared keys can lead to a potential security risk if the key used is compromised. Cisco recommends the use of additional authentication, such as Xauth, if wildcard preshared keys are used.

To specify that the PIX Firewall should allow VPN connections from any peer that has a matching key, use the wildcard preshared keys command.

```
isakmp key keystring address peer-address [netmask]
```

keystring	Specify the authentication preshared key. Use any combination of alphanumeric characters up to 128 bytes. This preshared key must be identical at both peers.
peer-address	Specify the peer IP address for the preshared key.
netmask	(Optional) The IP address of 0.0.0.0. can be entered as a wildcard, indicating the key could be used for any peer that does not have a key associated with its specific IP address.

Note that the peer address is not specified when using wildcard preshared keys. You just enter 0.0.0.0 as the netmask.

An example wildcard preshared key follows:

```
Pixfirewall(config)#isakmp key this-is-a-test-key address 0.0.0.0
```

The full isakmp configuration for a Cisco PIX Firewall that is using wildcard preshared keys can be seen in Example 12-12.

Example 12-12 *ISAKMP Wildcard Preshared Keys*

```
Pixfirewall(config)#show isakmp

isakmp key cisco1234 address 0.0.0.0 netmask 0.0.0.0
isakmp identity address
isakmp policy 30 authentication pre-share
isakmp policy 30 encryption des
isakmp policy 30 hash md5
isakmp policy 30 group 1
isakmp policy 30 lifetime 86400
```

IKE Mode Configuration

This section covers IKE mode configuration. IKE mode configuration is designed to address the issues that arise when VPN Clients are assigned dynamic IP addresses.

In Client-initiated access VPNs, the remote users' VPN Client starts Point-to-Point Protocol (PPP) links with the local Internet service provider (ISP) network access servers (NASs). After the VPN Client has been assigned a dynamic IP address by the ISP, it is difficult for the corporate gateway to administer scalable IPSec policy for all of these VPN Clients. Figure 12-10 shows that a new IPSec policy is required for each VPN Client, because each has a dynamic IP address that is assigned by different ISPs and is outside of the corporate subnet's IP address range.

Figure 12-10 *VPN Client IKE Requirements*

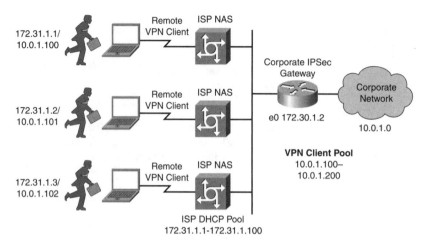

- **ISP assigns dynamic outside IP address via DHCP and PPP**
- **Mode configuration assigns dynamic inside addresses**
- **Addresses assigned from VPN client pool**

IKE mode configuration is an IKE negotiation that occurs between IKE phase one and IKE phase two. The gateway assigns a dynamic IP address to the VPN Clients, replacing any current IP address configuration on the VPN Clients. IKE mode configuration secures the connection between the VPN Clients and ISPs with an IPSec tunnel and allows for dynamic IP addressing of VPN Clients from the gateway. With IKE mode configuration, you can download IP addresses (and other network-level configuration, such as your IPSec policy) to VPN Clients as part of an IKE negotiation.

The gateway administrator can add VPN Clients to the network without having to reconfigure the gateway or the VPN Clients.

To implement IPSec VPNs between remote access Clients with dynamic IP addresses and a corporate gateway, you have to dynamically administer scalable IPSec policy on the gateway once each Client is authenticated. With IKE mode configuration, the gateway can set up scalable policy for a very large set of Clients, regardless of the IP addresses of those Clients.

There are two types of IKE mode configuration:

- Gateway initiation—Gateway initiates the configuration mode with the Client. When Client responds, the IKE modifies the sender's identity, the message is processed, and the Client receives a response.

- Client initiation—Client initiates the configuration mode with the gateway. The gateway responds with an IP address that is allocated for the Client.

IKE Mode Configuration—PIX Firewall

This section looks at the IKE mode configuration for a PIX Firewall when Client VPNs are introduced.

The following is a summary of the major steps to perform when configuring IKE mode configuration on your PIX Firewall:

Step 1 Define the pool of IP addresses. Existing local address pools are used to define a set of addresses. Use the **ip local pool** command to define a local address pool.

Step 2 Reference the pool of IP addresses in the IKE configuration. Use the **isakmp client configuration address-pool local** command to configure the IP address local pool you defined to reference IKE.

Step 3 Define which crypto maps should attempt to configure Clients, and whether the PIX Firewall or the Client initiates the IKE mode configuration. Use the **crypto map client-configuration address** command to configure IKE mode configuration.

Step 1: Define the Pool of IP Addresses

In this example of the **ip local pool** command, the pool name is vpn-pool. This IP address pool has a range from 172.31.1.1 to 172.31.1.100.

```
ip local pool pool_name pool_start-address[-pool_end-address]
```

pool-name	Name of a specific local address pool
pool_start-address	Lowest IP address in the pool
pool_end-address	Highest IP address in the pool

Step 2: Reference the Pool of IP Addresses

The **isakmp client configuration address-pool local** command is used to configure the IP address local pool to reference IKE.

Before using this command, use the **ip local pool** command to define a pool of local addresses to be assigned to a remote IPSec peer.

```
isakmp client configuration address-pool local pool-name [interface-name]
```

pool-name	Specifies the name of a local address pool to allocate the dynamic Client IP
interface-name	The name of the interface on which to enable ISAKMP negotiation

Step 3: Define Crypto Maps

Use the **crypto map client configuration address** command to configure IKE mode configuration on your PIX Firewall. With the **crypto map client configuration address** command, you define the crypto map that should attempt to configure the peer.

```
crypto map map-name client configuration address initiate | respond
```

map-name	The name of the crypto map set
initiate	Indicates that the PIX Firewall will attempt to set IP addresses for each peer
respond	Indicates that the PIX Firewall will accept requests for IP addresses from any requesting peer

Making an Exception for Security Gateways

If you have both a security gateway and VPN Client peers terminating on the same interface and have the IKE mode configuration feature configured, configure the PIX Firewall to make an exception to this feature for the security gateway peer. With this exception, the PIX Firewall does not attempt to download an IP address to the peer for dynamic IP address assignment. The command that you employ to bypass the IKE mode configuration feature depends on the authentication method you are using within your IKE policies.

The following shows an IKE authentication method using **no-config-mode** with a preshared key:

```
isakmp key keystring address ip-address [netmask] [no-xauth] [no-config-mode]
```

The following shows an IKE authentication method using **no-config-mode** with RSA signatures:

```
isakmp peer fqdn fqdn [no-xauth] [no-config-mode]
```

IKE Mode Configuration—Cisco IOS

Having covered the IKE mode configuration for the Cisco PIX Firewall, you will now look at the same configuration, but for Cisco IOS.

The configuration for Cisco IOS follows the same three steps as the PIX Firewall did. These are:

Step 1   Define the pool of IP addresses. Existing local address pools are used to define a set of addresses. Use the **ip local pool** command to define a local address pool.

Step 2   Reference the pool of IP addresses in the IKE configuration.

Step 3   Define which crypto maps should attempt to configure Clients and whether the IOS router or the Client initiates the IKE mode configuration.

Step 1: Define the Pool of IP Addresses

On a Cisco router running IOS, use the **ip local pool** command to create one or more local address pools from which IP addresses are assigned when a peer connects, and to add another range of addresses to an existing pool. The default address pool is then used on all point-to-point interfaces after the **ip address-pool local** global configuration command is issued. To use a specific, named address pool on an interface, use the **peer default ip address pool** interface configuration command. You can use existing local address pools to define a set of addresses. The IP address pool must be within the IP range of the corporate subnet. In this example, the pool name is vpn-pool. This IP address pool has a range from 172.31.1.1 to 172.31.1.100.

```
ip local pool {default | pool-name low-ip-address [high-ip-address]}
```

default	Default local address pool that is used if no other pool is named.
pool-name	Name of a specific local address pool.
low-ip-address	Lowest IP address in the pool.
high-ip-address	(Optional) Highest IP address in the pool. If this value is omitted, only the *low-IP-address* IP address is included in the local pool.

Step 2: Reference the Pool of IP Addresses

To configure the IP address local pool to reference IKE on your router, use the **crypto isakmp client configuration address-pool local** command in global configuration mode.

```
crypto isakmp client configuration address-pool local pool-name
```

pool-name	Specifies the name of a local address pool

Step 3: Define Crypto Maps

To configure IKE mode configuration on your router, use the **crypto map client-configuration address** command in global configuration mode.

```
crypto map tag client configuration address [initiate | respond ]
```

tag	The name that identifies the crypto map
initiate	A keyword that indicates that the router will attempt to set IP addresses for each peer
respond	A keyword that indicates that the router will accept requests for IP addresses from any requesting peer

Tunnel Endpoint Discovery

Tunnel Endpoint Discovery is an enhancement to the IPSec feature. Defining a dynamic crypto map allows you to be able to dynamically determine an IPSec peer; however, only the receiving router has this ability. With Tunnel Endpoint Discovery, the initiating router can dynamically determine an IPSec peer for secure IPSec communications.

Dynamic Tunnel Endpoint Discovery allows IPSec to scale to large networks by reducing multiple encryptions, reducing the setup time, and allowing for simple configurations on participating peer routers. Each node has a simple configuration that defines the local network that the router is protecting and the IPSec transforms that are required.

Tunnel Endpoint Discovery has the following restrictions:

- The IKE exchange cannot occur until the peer is identified. You can identify the peer using the **crypto dynamic-map** command. Using the **discover** keyword with this command, the receiving router sends a probe out to receive a response from the peer router.

- This feature is only available on dynamic crypto maps. The dynamic crypto map template is based on the dynamic crypto map performing peer discovery. Although there are no access list restrictions on the dynamic crypto map template, the dynamic crypto map template should cover data originating from the protected traffic and the receiving router using the **any** keyword. When using the **any** keyword, include explicit **deny** statements to exempt routing protocol traffic before entering the **permit any** command.

To create a dynamic crypto map entry with Tunnel Endpoint Discovery configured, use the following command:

```
crypto map map-name map-number ipsec-isakmp dynamic dynamic-map-name [discover]
```

discover	Enter the **discover** keyword on the dynamic crypto map to enable peer discovery. After the dynamic crypto map template permits an outbound packet, peer discovery occurs when the packet reaches an interface configured with the dynamic crypto map.

An example of this would be:

```
(config)#crypto map mymap 10 ipsec-isakmp dynamic mydynamicmap discover
```

Perfect Forward Secrecy

Perfect forward secrecy (PFS) is a cryptographic characteristic associated with a derived shared secret value. With PFS, if one key is compromised, previous and subsequent keys are not compromised, because subsequent keys are not derived from previous keys.

When a key is refreshed, the old key is combined with some new value. This means that new keys are, in part, dependent on previous values. Periodically generate a fresh key so that it is very difficult for an attacker, who may have found one key, to try to discover any subsequent value.

PFS can be requested as part of the IPSec SA. With PFS, the session key is completely regenerated by a Diffie-Hellman exchange every time the IPSec SAs are renegotiated.

The reasoning behind PFS is that it is a good idea to change the secret key being used for encryption after some period of time (or after a specified number of bytes have been encrypted). Changing keys makes it more difficult for an attacker to derive the key.

Configuring PFS—PIX Firewall

The configuration of PFS on the PIX Firewall is relatively simple. Adding the following command to the crypto map configuration enables PFS:

```
Pixfirewall(config)#crypto map mymap 10 set pfs group 2
```

This command specifies that PFS should be used whenever a new SA is negotiated for the crypto map "mymap 10." The 1024-bit Diffie-Hellman prime modulus group is used when a new SA is negotiated using the Diffie-Hellman exchange. This is ascertained from the group 2 setting.

```
crypto map map-name seq-num set pfs [group1 | group2]
```

set pfs	Specifies that IPSec should ask for PFS.
group1	Specifies that IPSec should use the 768-bit Diffie-Hellman prime modulus group when performing the new Diffie-Hellman exchange.
group2	Specifies that IPSec should use the 1024-bit Diffie-Hellman prime modulus group when performing the new Diffie-Hellman exchange.

Configuring PFS—Cisco IOS

As with the PIX Firewall, PFS configuration on a Cisco IOS router is also very straightforward.

To configure PFS on a Cisco IOS router, from crypto-map configuration mode, enter the following command:

```
Router(config-crypto-map)#set pfs group2
```

This enables PFS using the Diffie-Hellman group 2 algorithm.

set pfs [group1 | group2]

set pfs	Specifies that IPSec should ask for PFS.
group1	Specifies that IPSec should use the 768-bit Diffie-Hellman prime modulus group when performing the new Diffie-Hellman exchange.
group2	Specifies that IPSec should use the 1024-bit Diffie-Hellman prime modulus group when performing the new Diffie-Hellman exchange.

IPSec with Network Address Translation

Network Address Translation (NAT) is designed for IP address simplification and conservation, as it enables private IP internetworks that use nonregistered IP addresses to connect to the Internet. NAT operates on a router connecting two networks together and translates the private (not globally unique) addresses in the internal network into legal addresses before packets are forwarded on to another network. As part of this functionality, NAT can be configured to advertise only one address for the entire network to the outside world. This provides additional security, effectively hiding the entire internal network from the world behind that address. NAT has the dual functionality of security and address conservation and is typically sold in remote access environments.

Also called Port Address Translation (PAT) or port-level multiplexed NAT, *NAT overload* is used to translate all internal (local) private addresses to a single outside (global—usually registered) IP address. Unique port numbers on each translation are used to distinguish between the conversations.

With NAT overload, a translation entry containing full address and port information is created. A port translation might be created if another translation is using that port number with that outside or global address. This is necessary to eliminate any ambiguity about which translation needs to be applied to each packet traversing the router.

Figure 12-11 shows an example of NAT.

Figure 12-11 *NAT Example*

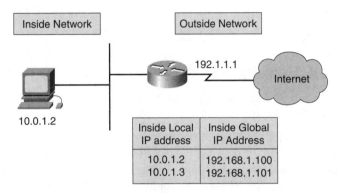

Note: 10.0.1.2 is translated to 192.168.1.100

ip nat inside source static 10.0.1.2 192.168.1.100

In the example, the address 10.1.1.2 is being translated into 192.1.1.100 before it is sent to the Internet.

The important thing to remember is that NAT happens before IPSec in the outbound path, and IPSec happens before NAT in the inbound path. So IPSec works with the translated addresses in terms of identifying the flows that it needs to protect. This also means that the IPSec packet cannot be subsequently translated anywhere between the source and destination, because modifying the IPSec-protected packet in any form will fail IPSec authentication, thus invalidating the packet.

When using IPSec with NAT, remember that the ISAKMP key uses the translated address. This principle should be applied to all configurations.

A sample of this can be seen Example 12-13.

Example 12-13 *NAT—IPSec Example*

```
ip subnet-zero
ip nat inside source static 10.0.1.2 192.168.1.100
no ip domain-lookup
ip domain-name redclay
crypto isakmp policy 1
authentication pre-share
crypto isakmp key thiskeyisbad address 192.168.2.2
```

NOTE   The ISAKMP key uses the translated address. This principle should be applied to all configurations.

NOTE	Authentication Header (AH) transforms will not work with NAT or PAT. Use the esp-sha-hmac and esp-md5-hmac transforms if authentication is required.

Configure PIX Firewall for Cisco VPN 3000 Client

This section covers how to configure the PIX Firewall version 5.2 and later and the Cisco VPN 3000 Client version 2.5 and later for interoperability.

The network topology in Figure 12-12 shows that the remote user with a VPN 3000 Client installed sets up an IPSec tunnel to the PIX Firewall by remote access. The PIX Firewall is configured for wildcard preshared keys, dynamic crypto maps, Xauth, and IKE mode configuration. It also has VPN groups configured with the **vpngroup** command to enable the PIX Firewall to push IPSec policy to the VPN 3000 Client. Preshared keys are used for authentication, although the PIX Firewall and VPN 3000 Client also support digital certificates. Cisco Secure ACS TACACS+ is used for user authentication by Xauth.

Figure 12-12 *Topology Overview*

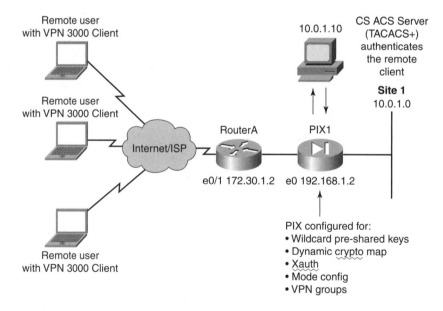

PIX Firewall Configuration

This section covers the configuration required on the PIX Firewall, before moving on to cover the configuration of the VPN Client. You will see how to address the PIX configuration in two sections, looking at the general and IPSec configuration first and then the IKE configuration. The following is a sample configuration for the PIX Firewall to support the VPN 3000 Client. The configuration includes commentary.

Configure an access list for the PIX Firewall and VPN 3000 Clients. The source is the PIX1's outside interface IP address, and the destination is a subnet pointing to the inside address assigned to the VPN 3000 Client as specified in the **ip local pool** command.

```
access-list 80 permit ip host 192.168.1.2 10.0.1.0 255.255.255.0
ip address outside 192.168.1.2 255.255.255.0
ip address inside 10.0.1.1 255.255.255.0
```

Set up a pool of IP addresses that will be assigned to the VPN Clients by IKE mode configuration.

```
ip local pool dealer 10.0.1.20-10.0.1.29
```

Use **nat 0** to point to the access list so that you do not have to define static translations.

```
nat (inside) 0 access-list 80
route outside 0.0.0.0 0.0.0.0 192.168.1.1 1
```

Set up the CS ACS server for Xauth user authentication. CS ACS (or a remote database it uses such as Microsoft Windows NT) must be configured with usernames and passwords and must point to the PIX Firewall as a network-attached storage (NAS). The TACACS+ key ("tacacskey" in this example) must match in CS ACS and in the PIX Firewall.

```
aaa-server t+ protocol tacacs+
aaa-server t+ (inside) host 10.0.1.10 tacacskey timeout 5
sysopt connection permit-ipsec
```

Set up a transform set that will be used for the VPN 3000 Clients. Note that AH is not supported in the VPN 3000 Client. You must set both an ESP encryption algorithm and an ESP authentication hashed message authentication code (HMAC) for the VPN 3000 Client.

```
crypto ipsec transform-set aaades esp-des esp-md5-hmac
```

Set up a dynamic crypto map to enable the VPN 3000 Clients to connect to the PIX Firewall. You must set a transform set in the dynamic map as a minimum. You might also want to set up an access list for additional security.

```
crypto dynamic-map dynomap 10 set transform-set aaades
```

Configure IKE mode configuration.

```
crypto map vpnpeer client configuration address initiate
```

Create a crypto map and assign the dynamic crypto map to it.

```
crypto map vpnpeer 20 ipsec-isakmp dynamic dynomap
```

Configure Xauth to point to the TACACS+ server.

```
crypto map vpnpeer client authentication t+
```

Apply the crypto map to the PIX Firewall interface.

```
crypto map vpnpeer interface outside
```

Configure the ISAKMP policy just as you would with any IPSec peer.

```
isakmp enable outside
```

Configure IKE mode configuration-related parameters.

```
isakmp client configuration address-pool local dealer outside
```

Configure the ISAKMP policy.

```
isakmp policy 10 authentication pre-share
isakmp policy 10 encryption des
isakmp policy 10 hash md5
isakmp policy 10 group 1
isakmp policy 10 lifetime 86400
```

Configure the VPN group to support pushing mode configuration parameters to the Client. The VPN group name of vpnpeer1 must match the group name in the VPN 3000 Client. The VPN group password must match the password in the VPN 3000 Client. You can also configure the VPN group to push Domain Name System (DNS), Windows Internet Naming Service (WINS), domain name, and split tunneling information to the VPN 3000 Client.

```
vpngroup student1 address-pool dealer
vpngroup student1 idle-time 1800
vpngroup student1 password ********
```

VPN 3000 Client Configuration

Having covered the required configuration of the PIX Firewall, you will now cover the configuration for the Cisco VPN 3000 Client that is required to establish an IPSec VPN to the PIX Firewall.

You must configure the VPN 3000 Client to interoperate with the PIX Firewall. You need to create a new connection entry (*vpnpeer1*, as shown in Figure 12-13). The host name or IP address of the peer should be the PIX Firewall outside interface.

After creating the new entry called *vpnpeer1*, you then have to set the properties for the new connection. If you are using preshared keys for authentication, you must make sure the group name (*student1* in this case) matches the VPN group name on the PIX Firewall, and that the password (the preshared key) matches the VPN group password. You could use digital certificates for authentication instead of preshared keys. The related screen can be seen in Figure 12-14.

Figure 12-13 *VPN 3000 Client to PIX Firewall Example*

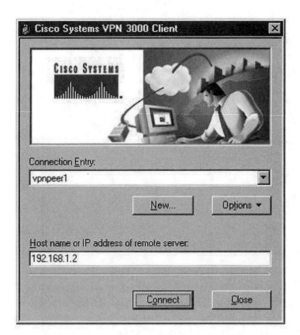

Once this is configured, the PIX Firewall uses IKE mode configuration to push the IPSec policy, defined with the **vpngroup** command, to the VPN 3000 Client. The Client IP address (shown in Figure 12-15) is set by the PIX Firewall **ip local pool** and **vpngroup** commands.

After these configuration steps, the VPN 3000 Client forms an IPSec VPN with the Cisco PIX Firewall.

Figure 12-14 *VPN 3000 Client to PIX Firewall Properties*

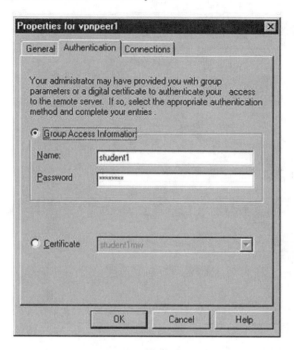

Figure 12-15 *VPN 3000 Client to PIX Firewall Connection Status*

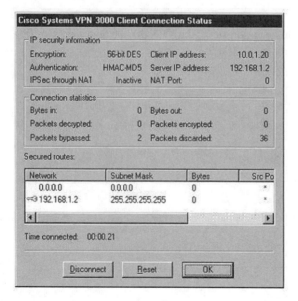

Configure PIX Firewall for Cisco Secure VPN 1.1 Client

After looking at the PIX Firewall to VPN 3000 VPN Client, now look at the steps to configure the PIX Firewall to establish an IPSec VPN with the Cisco VPN 1.1 Client.

Looking at the network topology displayed in Figure 12-16, you have multiple Clients who need access to the corporate network. The Clients' IP addresses are unknown. The PIX Firewall needs to be configured accordingly. In this case, you will use wildcard preshared keys, dynamic crypto maps, Xauth, and mode configuration.

Figure 12-16 *VPN 1.1 Client to PIX Firewall Topology*

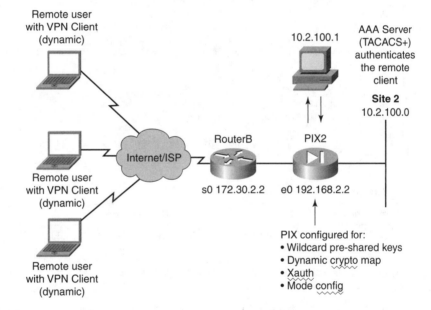

PIX Firewall Configuration

Example 12-14 shows a snippet of the required configuration with the IPSec-related commands displayed in shading. After the displayed configuration, you will find an explanation of these commands in Table 12-6.

Example 12-14 *IPSec Configuration*

```
ip address outside 192.168.2.2 255.255.255.0
ip address inside 10.2.100.1 255.255.255.0
global (outside) 1 192.168.2.4
nat (inside) 1 0.0.0.0 0.0.0.0 0 0
static (inside,outside) 192.168.2.6 10.2.100.6 netmask 255.255.255.255 0 0
    static (inside,outside) 192.168.2.7 10.2.100.7 netmask 255.255.255.255 0 0
conduit permit tcp host 192.168.2.6 eq www any
```

continues

Example 12-14 *IPSec Configuration (Continued)*

```
conduit permit tcp host 192.168.2.7 eq smtp any
conduit permit icmp any any
route outside 0.0.0.0 0.0.0.0 192.168.2.1 1
ip local pool mypool 10.2.100.1-10.2.100.250
sysopt connection permit-ipsec
sysopt ipsec pl-compatible
crypto ipsec transform-set strong esp-des esp-sha-hmac

crypto dynamic-map dynmap 10 set transform-set strong
crypto map mymap 10 ipsec-isakmp dynamic dynmap
crypto map mymap client configuration address respond
crypto map mymap client configuration address initiate
crypto map mymap interface outside
isakmp enable outside
isakmp key cisco1234 address 0.0.0.0 netmask 0.0.0.0
isakmp client configuration address-pool local mypool outside
isakmp policy 10 authentication pre-share
isakmp policy 10 encryption des
isakmp policy 10 hash sha
isakmp policy 10 group 1
isakmp policy 10 lifetime 300

aaa-server TACACS+ (inside) host 10.2.100.1 thekey timeout 20
crypto map mymap client authentication TACACS+
```

Table 12-6 *Explanation of PIX Commands*

Command	Description
ip local pool mypool 10.2.100.1-10.2.100.250	Define the pool of IP addresses for mode configuration.
crypto ipsec transform-set strong esp-des esp-sha-hmac	Set the encryption to DES and SHA.
crypto dynamic-map dynmap 10 set transform-set strong	Configure a dynamic map and assign the transform set.
crypto map mymap 10 ipsec-isakmp dynamic dynmap	Add the dynamic map into a regular crypto map set.
crypto map mymap client configuration address respond **crypto map mymap client configuration address initiate**	Crypto map is configured for gateway- or Client-initiated mode configuration.
crypto map mymap interface outside	Assign the crypto map to the outside interface.
isakmp enable outside	Enable ISAKMP on the outside interface.
isakmp key cisco1234 address 0.0.0.0 netmask 0.0.0.0	A wildcard preshared key is set up.

Table 12-6   *Explanation of PIX Commands (Continued)*

Command	Description
isakmp client configuration address-pool local mypool outside	Mode configuration is set up to reference mypool and to enable the ISAKMP negotiation on the outside interface.
isakmp policy 10 authentication pre-share **isakmp policy 10 encryption des** **isakmp policy 10 hash sha** **isakmp policy 10 group 1** **isakmp policy 10 lifetime 300**	Configure the ISAKMP policy for preshared keys, encryption algorithm DES, hash algorithm sha, Diffie-Hellman group 1, and a lifetime of 300 seconds.
aaa-server TACACS+ (inside) host 10.2.100.1 thekey timeout 20	An AAA server group is specified.
crypto map mymap client authentication TACACS+	Xauth is enabled, and the AAA server that will authenticate the user is specified, along with the crypto map that should evaluate the traffic.

VPN 1.1 Client Configuration

Figure 12-17 shows the completed information in the VPN 1.1 Client Config Security Policy Editor.

Note the following information:

- The remote party identity is set to the IP address of the subnet behind the PIX. This is the subnet to which you want to encrypt traffic.

- The secure gateway tunnel is set to the outside interface IP address of the PIX.

Once the Client Config information has been entered, the identity information has to be entered. Figure 12-18 shows the completed My Identity screen in the VPN 1.1 Security Policy Editor.

Note the following information:

- All the values under My Identity remain as the defaults.

- You must configure the preshared key.

To configure a preshared key, click the **Pre-Shared Key** button that is displayed at the bottom of Figure 12-18. This takes you to the Pre-Shared Key dialog box, as shown in Figure 12-19. You enter the preshared key of cisco1234 to match the PIX preshared key configuration explained previously.

Figure 12-17   *VPN 1.1 Client Security Policy Editor*

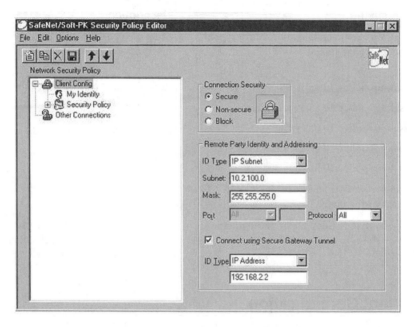

Figure 12-18   *VPN 1.1 Security Policy Editor, My Identity*

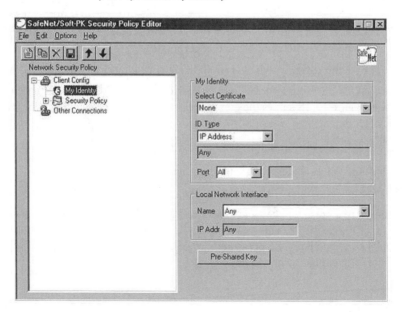

Figure 12-19   *VPN 1.1 Pre-Shared Key Dialog Box*

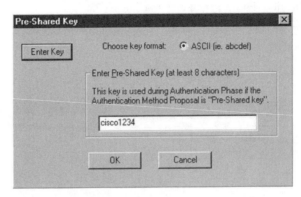

The next step in the configuration is to enter information on the **Security Policy** tab of the Security Policy editor. The **Security Policy** tab and the required information are displayed in Figure 12-20.

Figure 12-20   *VPN 1.1 Security Policy*

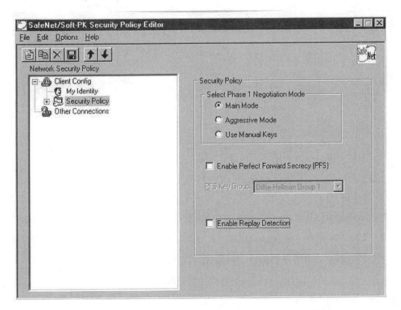

<table>
<tr><td>**NOTE**</td><td>Notice that replay detection is not being used, so this option is unchecked. (The default is checked.)</td></tr>
</table>

At this point, the **Security Policy** tab is expanded to provide two more options. These are Authentication (Phase 1) and Key Exchange (Phase 2).

Figure 12-21 shows the completed Authentication (Phase 1) screen for the IPSec connection to the PIX Firewall.

Figure 12-21 *VPN 1.1 Authentication*

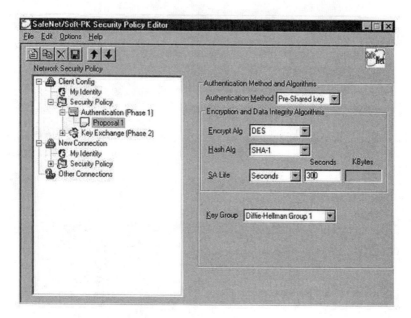

Note the following information:

- The authentication method is preshared.
- The encryption algorithm is DES. Set it to match the encryption algorithm on the PIX Firewall.
- The hash algorithm is SHA-1. Set it to match the hash algorithm on the PIX Firewall.
- The SA life is 300 seconds. Set it to match the lifetime on the PIX Firewall.
- The key group is Diffie-Hellman Group 1. Set it to match the key group on the PIX.

Figure 12-22 shows the completed Key Exchange (Phase 2) screen for the IPSec connection to the PIX Firewall.

Figure 12-22   *VPN 1.1 Key Exchange*

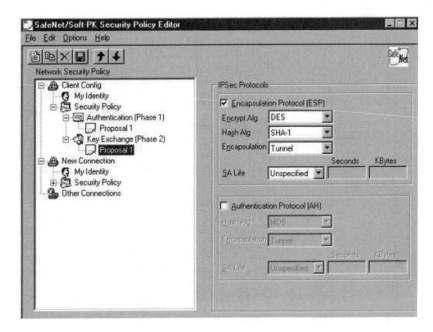

Note the following information:

- The ESP box is checked.

- The encryption algorithm is set to DES. This corresponds to choosing esp-des on the PIX Firewall.

- The hash algorithm is set to SHA-1. This corresponds to choosing esp-sha-hmac on the PIX Firewall.

- The SA life is unspecified. This means the Client will use the SA life specified on the PIX Firewall.

The final step in the configuration is to ensure that all other connections are left unsecured. This can be seen in Figure 12-23.

This completes the steps required to configure the VPN 1.1 Client to the Cisco PIX Firewall.

Figure 12-23 *VPN 1.1 Other Connections*

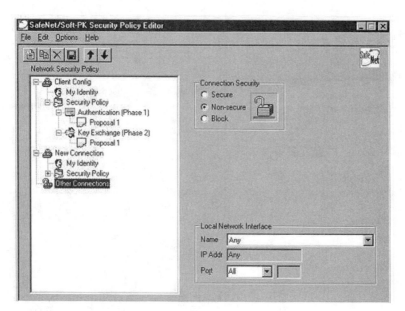

Configure Cisco IOS for Cisco Secure VPN 1.1 Client

Now that you have looked at configuring the Cisco PIX Firewall to the Cisco VPN 1.1 Client, this section covers Cisco IOS router to VPN 1.1 configuration. This example uses the same network topology as for the PIX to VPN 1.1 Client that was shown in Figure 12-16 and the exact same VPN 1.1 Client configuration. Example 12-15 provides a sample IOS configuration. A full explanation of the commands is presented in Table 12-7.

Example 12-15 *IOS Configuration*

```
routerB(config)# ip local pool mypool 10.2.100.1 10.2.100.250
routerB(config)# crypto ipsec transform-set strong esp-des esp-sha-hmac
routerB(cfg-crypto-trans)# exit
routerB(config)# crypto dynamic-map dynmap 10
routerB(config-crypto-map)# set transform-set  strong
routerB(config-crypto-map)# exit
routerB(config)# crypto map mymap 10 ipsec-isakmp dynamic dynmap
routerB(config)# crypto map mymap client configuration address respond
routerB(config)# crypto map mymap client configuration address initiate
router(config)# interface serial 0
router(config-if)# crypto map mymap
router(config)# crypto isakmp key cisco1234 address 0.0.0.0

router(config)# crypto isakmp client configuration address-pool local mypool
router(config)# crypto isakmp policy 10
```

Example 12-15 *IOS Configuration (Continued)*

```
router(config-isakmp)# authentication pre-share

router(config-isakmp)# encryption des

router(config-isakmp)# hash sha
router(config-isakmp)# group 1
router(config-isakmp)# lifetime 300
router(config-isakmp)# exit
router(config)# tacacs-server host 10.2.100.1 key thekey
```

Table 12-7 *Explanation of IOS Commands*

Command	Explanation
ip local pool mypool 10.2.100.1 10.2.100.250	Define the pool of IP addresses for mode configuration.
crypto ipsec transform-set strong esp-des esp-sha-hmac	Set the encryption to DES and Secure Hash Algorithm (SHA).
crypto dynamic-map dynmap 10	Configure a dynamic map.
set transform-set strong	Assign the transform set to the crypto map.
crypto map mymap 10 ipsec-isakmp dynamic dynmap	Add the dynamic map into a regular crypto map set.
crypto map mymap client configuration address respond crypto map mymap client configuration address initiate	Crypto map is configured for gateway- or Client-initiated mode configuration.
interface serial 0	Enter interface configuration mode.
crypto map mymap	Assign the crypto map to the interface.
crypto isakmp key cisco1234 address 0.0.0.0	A wildcard preshared key is set up.
crypto isakmp client configuration address-pool local mypool	Mode configuration is set up to reference mypool.
crypto isakmp policy 10 authentication pre-share encryption des hash sha lifetime 300	Configures the isakmp policy for preshared keys, encryption algorithm DES, hash algorithm sha, Diffie-Hellman group 1, and a lifetime of 300 seconds.

Summary

This final chapter looked at the scalability and advanced configuration features that are supported in the Cisco IPSec implementation. It started by looking at features such as dynamic crypto maps, Tunnel Endpoint Discovery, and PFS. The chapter finished by looking at the Cisco VPN 3000 Client and the Cisco VPN 1.1 Client with configuration for both the Cisco PIX and the Cisco IOS.

Review Questions

1 When configuring dynamic crypto maps, what is the suggested method for setting the priority of the referenced crypto map?

2 What command on Cisco IOS displays a summary of how the IPSec policy is configured?

3 Traffic is being sent from 192.168.1.1 to 10.0.1.1, and it is failing. Explain this by looking at the following output.

```
pix2(config)# show crypto map

Crypto Map: "peerc" interfaces: { outside }

Crypto Map "peerc" 10 ipsec-isakmp
  Peer = 192.168.1.5
  access-list 106 permit ip 192.168.2.0 255.255.255.0
    10.0.1.0 255.255.255.0 (hitcnt=18)
  Current peer: 192.168.1.5
  Security association lifetime: 4608000 kilobytes/28800 seconds
  PFS (Y/N): N
  Transform sets={ mine2, }
```

4 To configure an IPSec VPN between two Cisco IOS routers, it is common to use a generic routing encapsulation (GRE) tunnel and then apply the crypto map to the tunnel interface. Can this be done on a IOS router to PIX VPN?

5 When using wildcard preshared keys, what does Cisco also recommend you use to increase security?

6 What command on the PIX Firewall would enable PFS group 2 for crypto map mymap 10?

7 What must be configured on the PIX Firewall to allow the Firewall to push IPSec policies down to the Cisco VPN 3000 Clients?

8 True or False: On the Cisco VPN 1.1 Client, replay detection is enabled by default.

9 What command on the PIX Firewall creates a pool of IP addresses from 10.2.100.1 to 10.2.100.250 for use by remote VPN Clients?

10 When enabling the use of a wildcard preshared key, what address do you use for the peer address and peer netmask?

Answers to Review Questions

Chapter 1

1 What are the three types of VPNs?

Answer: The three types of VPNs are access, intranet, and extranet.

2 What type of VPNs link outside customers, suppliers, partners, or communities of interest to an enterprise customer's network over a shared infrastructure using dedicated connections?

Answer: Extranet VPNs.

3 IPSec consists of which two components?

Answer: Authentication Header (AH) and Encapsulating Security Payload (ESP).

4 You configure an IPSec transform set to use AH. Is the data payload encrypted?

Answer: No, you require ESP for encryption. AH just provides authentication and antireplay services.

5 You want to establish an extranet VPN over the Internet. Which type of IPSec mode (transport or tunnel) would be the best solution in this scenario?

Answer: Because of the public nature and the unpredictable delivery of the Internet, it would be best to use IPSec tunnel mode. Then a pseudo-one-hop VPN would be established.

6 Which is the most secure encryption algorithm: DES, 3DES, or Diffie-Hellman?

Answer: DES is 56-bit, 3DES is 168-bit, and Diffie-Hellman is either 768-bit or 1024-bit. This makes Diffie-Hellman the strongest algorithm of the three.

7 Step one of configuring IPSec is defining interesting traffic. What Cisco IOS feature do you use to define this?

Answer: You use an extended IP access list to define interesting traffic.

8 With preshared keys, can each of the keys be different or must each be the same (have the same value as the other's public key)?

Answer: With preshared key encryption, both of the keys have to be *exactly the same at both ends of the VPN*.

9 What is used to relay the shared key to the VPN peer?

Answer: Diffie-Hellman is used to relay the shared key to the VPN peer.

10 IKE peers authenticate themselves using one of four methods. What are these four methods?

Answer: The four IKE authentication methods are preshared keys, RSA signatures, RSA encryption, and CA digital certificates.

Chapter 2

1 VPN Accelerator Cards (VACs) are available for which models of the Cisco Secure PIX Firewall?

Answer: The Cisco PIX VAC is available for the PIX 515, 520, 525, and 535 Firewalls.

2 Which PIX model is predominantly designed for the SOHO or ROBO user?

Answer: The Cisco Secure PIX 506 Firewall is designed for the small office, home office (SOHO) and remote office, branch office (ROBO) market.

3 What is the clear text throughput of a Cisco Secure PIX 525 Firewall?

Answer: The clear text throughput of a Cisco Secure PIX 525 Firewall is 370 Mbps.

4 What is the lowest specification model in the VPN 3000 Concentrator series?

Answer: The lowest specification VPN Concentrator 3000 is the 3005.

5 If you had a small branch office that wanted an upgradable VPN solution for up to 100 users at any one time, which model of the VPN Concentrator 3000 series would you choose?

Answer: In this instance, either the 3005 or the 3015 would handle the job, but the requirement specifies that the unit must be upgradable. The 3005 is not hardware-upgradable, therefore the 3015 would be the best solution.

6 Which is the lowest specification router that can perform IPSec VPN termination?

Answer: The lowest specification router that can perform IPSec VPN termination is the Cisco 800 series.

7 If you required a VPN Concentrator that could terminate 7500 IPSec tunnels, which model or models could you use?

Answer: The only model that you could use would be the VPN 3080, as this supports up to 10,000 IPSec tunnels. The VPN 3060 supports only 5000 IPSec tunnels, so this would not meet the requirement of 7500 IPSec tunnels.

8 How many IPSec tunnels can the PIX 535 terminate?

Answer: The PIX 535 can terminate 2000 IPSec tunnels.

9 What is the highest specification model in the VPN 3000 Concentrator Series?

Answer: The highest specification VPN 3000 Concentrator is the 3080.

10 Which PIX Firewall boasts 1 Gbps clear text throughput?

Answer: The PIX 535 is the latest addition to the Cisco Secure PIX Firewall family, and it offers 1 Gbps clear text throughput.

Chapter 3

1 How many tasks are involved in configuring IPSec?

Answer: There are four tasks involved in configuring IPSec.

2 Do you configure IKE phase one or IKE phase two first?

Answer: You configure IKE phase one first, then IKE phase two.

3 What command is used to display information about the crypto map?

Answer: The command show crypto map is used to display information about the crypto map.

4 How do you apply a crypto map to an interface?

Answer: To apply a crypto map to an interface, you use the crypto map *mymap* command, where mymap is the name of the crypto map you wish to apply to the interface.

5 With Diffie-Hellman, there are two options, which are group 1 and group 2. Group 1 uses 768-bit encryption; what does group 2 use?

Answer: Diffie-Hellman group 2 uses 1024-bit encryption.

6 What port does ISAKMP use?

Answer: ISAKMP uses UDP port 500.

7 To allow ISAKMP, ESP, and AH through an access list, what would you have to allow?

Answer: To allow ISAKMP, ESP, and AH through an access list, you have to allow UDP port 500 (ISAKMP), IP protocol number 50 (ESP), and IP protocol number 51 (AH).

8 What command would create a transform set that uses ESP authentication with MD5, ESP encryption with 56-bit DES, and tunnel mode?

Answer: The command to create a transform set that uses ESP authentication with MD5, ESP encryption with 56-bit DES, and tunnel mode would be crypto ipsec transform-set noAH esp-md5-hmac esp-des.

9 What command globally enables ISAKMP?

Answer: To enable ISAKMP globally, you enter the command crypto isakmp enable from global configuration mode.

10 IPSec peers authenticate each other during ISAKMP negotiations using the preshared key and the ISAKMP identity. The identity can be either the router's IP address or what other method?

Answer: Host name. IPSec can use either the peer IP address or the peer host name. Name resolution must exist if host name is used. This can be by DNS or a static name mapping.

Chapter 4

1 What command displays the configured access lists on a router that is part of an IPSec VPN?

Answer: The generic command that displays access lists on any router, whether participating in an IPSec VPN or not, is show access-lists.

2 Currently, which CA servers can be used by Cisco IOS devices?

Answer: Cisco IOS devices can use the following CA services:

- **Entrust Technologies, Inc.—Entrust/PKI 4.0**

- **VeriSign—OnSite 4.5**

- **Baltimore Technologies—UniCERT v3.05**

- **Microsoft Corporation—Windows 2000 Certificate Services 5.0**

3 To use the Entrust PKI CA Server, what version of Cisco IOS is required?

Answer: To use the Entrust PKI CA Server, you must be using Cisco IOS release 11.(3)5T or later.

4 When you generate an RSA key pair on an IOS router, what are you prompted for?

Answer: When you generate RSA keys, you are prompted to enter a modulus length.

5 What command displays your configured IKE policies?

Answer: The command to display your configured IKE policies is show crypto isakmp policy.

6 Before you can generate an RSA key pair, what two items must be set on the IOS router?

Answer: Before generating the RSA key pair, you must set the host name and IP domain name of the router. If you do not do this the command will not run.

7 How do you globally enable IKE?

Answer: You globally enable IKE by entering the command crypto isakmp enable at global configuration mode.

8 What command generates the RSA key pair?

Answer: The RSA key pair is generated with the crypto key generate rsa global configuration command.

9 To use the Microsoft 2000 CA, what version of IOS is required?

Answer: The Microsoft 2000 CA server requires the router to be using at least IOS 12.05(T) to work.

10 How do you view the certificates that are stored on your router?

Answer: To view the certificates stored on your router, enter the show crypto ca certificates command.

Chapter 5

1 What command will display the configured ISAKMP preshared keys on the Cisco IOS router?

Answer: The command show crypto isakmp key will display the configured ISAKMP preshared keys on the Cisco IOS router.

2 Which values are compared during the main mode exchange?

Answer: The values compared during main mode exchange are

- **Encryption algorithm**
- **Hash algorithm**
- **Authentication method**
- **Diffie-Hellman group**
- **SA lifetime**

3 You are using IPSec over a GRE Tunnel. The GRE Tunnel has the Serial 0 interface set as the tunnel source. Where do you have to apply the relevant crypto map?

Answer: When using a logical interface such as a GRE Tunnel interface, you have to apply the crypto map to both the logical interface and the physical interface. Therefore, the relevant crypto map would need to be applied to the tunnel 0 interface and the Serial 0 interface.

4 You apply a crypto map to an interface. What happens to traffic that does not match the IPSec access list associated with the crypto map?

Answer: Traffic passing through the interface that does not match the IPSec access list will simply be routed as normal.

5 What is the priority value of the default ISAKMP policy?

Answer: The default ISAKMP policy has a priority of 65535.

6 You have a problem with the VPN establishment on a Cisco router where the error message mentions that the sanity check has failed. What is the probable cause of this?

Answer: If you receive a sanity check error message, it probably indicates that the preshared keys do not match.

7 Within the ISAKMP policy, what is the default hash algorithm?

Answer: Within the ISAKMP policy, the default hash algorithm is SHA. This cannot be seen in the configuration and can only be seen with the show crypto isakmp policy command.

8 How do you display real-time information on your router about the state of the ISAKMP negotiation?

Answer: The command to display real-time information on your router about the state of the ISAKMP negotiation is debug crypto isakmp. You have to ensure that logging is enabled to the console or terminal line that you are connecting to the router.

9 What command would apply the crypto map called MyMap to the Serial 0 interface? Assume you are in interface configuration mode.

Answer: The command to apply the crypto map called MyMap to the Serial 0 interface is

```
Router(config-if)#crypto map MyMap
```

10 Which command produces the following output?

```
ID Interface        IP-Address      State  Algorithm            Encrypt  Decrypt
 1 <none>           <none>          set    DES_56_CBC                 0        0
 8 Serial1          30.0.0.1        set    HMAC_MD5+DES_56_CB         0      749
 9 Serial1          30.0.0.1        set    HMAC_MD5+DES_56_CB       749        0

Crypto adjacency count : Lock: 0, Unlock: 0
```

Answer: The output shown is from the show crypto engine connections active command.

Chapter 6

1 What command enables you to view the default IPSec policy parameters?

Answer: The command show isakmp policy displays the default policy, as well as any defined policies.

2 With PIX v5.0, can you terminate an IPSec VPN on the inside interface?

Answer: PIX Firewall version 5.0 software supports IPSec termination on the outside interface only. PIX Firewall version 5.1 software supports IPSec termination on any interface.

3 When typing in the **isakmp policy** commands, what keyword enables preshared authentication?

Answer: The keyword required is .preshare.

4 What global command configures the PIX firewall so that IPSec VPN traffic will flow through the firewall, bypassing any conduits and access lists?

Answer: Use the sysopt connection permit-ipsec command in IPSec configurations to permit IPSec traffic to pass through the PIX Firewall without a check of conduit or access-list command statements. An access-list or conduit command statement must be available for inbound sessions.

5 When creating a crypto access list, what do you do to ensure that specific traffic is encrypted?

Answer: You have to permit the traffic to ensure that it gets encrypted. Denied traffic is sent in clear text.

6 What command enables ISAKMP on the outside interface?

Answer: Entering the command isakmp enable outside enables ISAKMP on the outside interface.

7 What is the default value for the **isakmp identity** command?

Answer: The default for isakmp identity is to use the IP address of the remote peer.

8 What is the default Diffie-Hellman key size?

Answer: The default Diffie-Hellman group is 1. This specifies a 768-bit key size.

9 What commands displays the transform sets that are configured on the PIX Firewall?

Answer: The command show crypto ipsec transform-set displays the transform sets configured on the firewall.

10 What two modes of identity for ISAKMP are supported by the PIX firewall?

Answer: The two modes for the isakmp identity command are IP address or host name.

Chapter 7

1 SCEP stands for what?

Answer: SCEP stands for Simple Certificate Enrollment Protocol.

2 What is the maximum RSA key modulus size?

Answer: The maximum RSA key modulus size is 2048 bits.

3 In its default state, which PIX-compatible CA does not support SCEP?

Answer: The Microsoft Certificate Services 5.0 does not natively support SCEP.

4 Why must you set the time and date on a PIX Firewall before enabling CA support?

Answer: The clock must be accurately set before generating RSA key pairs and enrolling with the CA server because the keys and certificates are time-sensitive.

5 What is the minimum RSA key modulus size?

Answer: The minimum RSA key modulus size is 512 bits.

6   What are the RSA key pairs used for?

Answer: RSA key pairs are used to sign and encrypt IKE key management messages and are required before you can obtain a certificate for your PIX Firewall.

7   What command allows you to save the PIX Firewall's RSA key pairs; the CA, the RA, and PIX Firewall's certificates; and the CA's CRLs in the persistent data file in Flash memory between reloads?

Answer: The ca save all command allows you to save the PIX Firewall's RSA key pairs; the CA, the RA, and PIX Firewall's certificates; and the CA's CRLs in the persistent data file in Flash memory between reloads.

8   Which peer authentication method is considered to be the stronger, preshared or RSA encryption?

Answer: RSA encryption is considered to be stronger than preshared as a peer authentication method.

9   What command removes the PIX Firewall's RSA key pairs; the CA, the RA, and PIX Firewall's certificates; and the CA's CRLs from the persistent data file in Flash memory?

Answer: The no ca save command removes the PIX Firewall's RSA key pairs; the CA, the RA, and PIX Firewall's certificates; and the CA's CRLs from the persistent data file in Flash memory.

10 What command deletes all RSA keys that were previously generated by your PIX Firewall?

Answer: The command ca zeroize rsa deletes all RSA keys that were previously generated by your PIX Firewall.

Chapter 8

1   On a Cisco IOS router, the command **show crypto isakmp key** will display the configured preshared keys. What command will do this on the Cisco Secure PIX Firewall?

Answer: There is no way on a Cisco Secure PIX Firewall to display the preshared key once it has been entered into the configuration.

2   What command on the PIX Firewall would place crypto map newmap to the outside interface?

Answer: The command crypto map newmap interface outside would place the crypto map newmap on the outside interface.

3 What is the purpose of the **sysopt connection permit-ipsec** command?

Answer: The sysopt connection permit-ipsec command allows the PIX Firewall to bypass the adaptive security algorithm.

4 On the Cisco PIX Firewall, what command shows you the number of free, used, and active crypto connection maps?

Answer: The command show crypto engine will display the number of free, used, and active crypto connection maps.

5 What is the default SA lifetime?

Answer: The default SA lifetime is 86,400 seconds. This equates to 24 hours.

6 What configuration mode on the Cisco PIX Firewall do you enter the ISAKMP information from?

Answer: On the PIX Firewall, you enter all configurations from global configuration mode. Unlike the Cisco IOS, there is no specific configuration mode for ISAKMP.

7 What would be the access list on a PIX Firewall to encrypt all traffic from the network 10.1.0.0/16 to 192.168.2.0/25?

Answer: The PIX access list to encrypt all traffic from the network 10.1.0.0/16 to 192.168.2.0/25 would be

```
PIX(config)#access-list 101 permit ip 10.1.0.0 255.255.0.0
    192.168.2.0 255.255.255.128
```

8 By default, is all IPSec traffic allowed or disallowed through the firewall?

Answer: By default, all IPSec traffic is disallowed through the firewall. A NAT translation and conduit/access list must exist for IPSec traffic to flow through the firewall, as in any other traffic flow. However, if a crypto map is assigned to an interface, IPSec traffic for that crypto map is allowed to bypass the ASA with the default sysopt connection permit-ipsec command.

9 When you view the IPSec configuration of a PIX Firewall, what character is used to mask the preshared key?

Answer: The PIX Firewall uses eight asterisks (*) to mask the preshared key.

10 Does the Cisco PIX use a wildcard or subnet mask for IPSec access lists?

Answer: The Cisco PIX uses subnet masks in all access lists.

Chapter 9

1 What is the minimum configuration on the CLI to use the browser-based VPN Manager?

Answer: In order to use the browser-based VPN Manager, you must configure at least one interface IP address from the CLI. This should ideally be the private (inside) interface, although the configuration will work with the public (outside) interface.

2 When connecting a console to use the CLI, what cable should you use?

Answer: You must use a straight Ethernet cable to connect to the console port. A standard Cisco console cable will not work.

3 When using the browser-based VPN Manager for the first time, what is the default username and password pair?

Answer: When using the browser-based VPN Manager for the first time, the default username and password pair is admin/admin.

4 Looking at the left pane of the VPN Manager, what are the three selectable options?

Answer: Looking at the left pane of the VPN Manager, the three selectable options are Configuration, Administration, and Monitoring.

5 You configure the private IP address with the CLI and then reboot the Concentrator and try to access the VPN Manager using Internet Explorer. You cannot access the VPN Manager. What is the probable cause of this?

Answer: When you make a configuration change with the CLI, it is not automatically applied to the nonvolatile memory of the Concentrator. There is a manual Save option from the main CLI menu to save the configuration in its current state.

6 From a networking point of view, along with the IP addresses for the private and public interfaces, what else is required in order for the Concentrator to work in an internetwork?

Answer: The VPN Concentrator, as all IP devices, must know the egress point of its local network to reach other networks. This is normally configured using a static default route, although the Concentrator will also operate within an OSPF area.

7 What are the four options for IP address assignment on the VPN Concentrator?

Answer: The four options are Use Client Address, Per User, Use DHCP, and Configured Pool.

8 Which program menu item launches the VPN Client and initiates the VPN communication?

Answer: The VPN Dialer program item launches the VPN Client and initiates the VPN communication.

9 What is the recommended MTU size for IPSec over UDP?

Answer: Recommended MTU size for IPSec over UDP is 1400 bytes. This is set at the Client by using the MTU Size program menu item.

10 The VPN Concentrator can act in a way similar to a DHCP server or a DHCP relay agent. If it is acting similar to a DHCP server, what else must you configure on the VPN Concentrator?

Answer: If the VPN Concentrator is acting like a DHCP server, you must also create the pools of IP addresses and assign these to the specific IPSec groups.

Chapter 10

1 What is the certificate request also known as?

Answer: The certificate request is also known as a Public Key Cryptography Standards (PKCS) #10 certificate request.

2 The RSA signing is an algorithm designed by RSA Laboratories and defined by what?

Answer: The RSA signing is an algorithm designed by RSA Laboratories and defined by PKCS#1.

3 What is an identity certificate?

Answer: An identity certificate is a certificate issued by a CA to an entity that binds the device's public key to a set of information that identifies the device.

4 What is a certificate validity period?

Answer: A certificate is valid for a specific period of time. The validity period (range) is set by the CA and consists of "Valid from" and "Valid to" fields. In the Concentrator, when you try to add a certificate, the validity range is compared against the system clock. If the system clock is not within the validity range—either too early or too late—you get an error message.

5 What is a certificate revocation list?

Answer: A certificate revocation list (CRL) is a list issued by the CA that contains certificates that are no longer valid. CRLs are signed by the CA and are released periodically or on demand. CRLs are valid for a specific amount of time, depending on the CA vendor used.

6 To use a digital certificate on the VPN 3000 Client, where must the certificate reside?

Answer: In order for a client using the VPN 3000 Client to use a digital certificate, the certificate must reside and be installed on the local PC.

7 You receive an expiration error when loading your identity certificate; what is the first item to check?

Answer: In the event that you receive an expiration error when loading your identity certificate, ensure that the Concentrator's date and time is correctly set.

8 In a hierarchical CA environment, what is the top of the hierarchy also known as?

Answer: In a hierarchical environment, the ability to sign is delegated through a hierarchy. The top is the root CA, which signs certificates for subordinate authorities. Subordinate CAs, in turn, sign certificates for lower-level CAs.

9 How many certificates are based in the VPN Concentrator?

Answer: Two certificates are based in the Concentrator. These are the Root certificate and the identity certificate.

10 When using Microsoft certificate services, where are the certificates stored when downloaded?

Answer: Microsoft certificate services load both an identity certificate and a root certificate in the Internet Explorer certificate store.

Chapter 11

1 How can you get access to the event log on the VPN Concentrator, besides through the VPN Manager?

Answer: In addition to the VPN Manager (HTTP) method, you can also use Telnet or FTP to retrieve the event log.

2 When manipulating images over TFTP, what happens if you name a file with the same name as an existing file?

Answer: If either filename is the same as an existing file, TFTP overwrites the existing file without asking for confirmation.

3 How many events does the event log hold by default?

Answer: By default, the event log holds 2048 events. After that, the event log will wrap new events.

4 What rights are required to view event logs?

Answer: Administrative rights are required to view event logs.

5 Looking at the System LED status, what does an amber LED signify?

Answer: An amber System LED indicates that the system has crashed and halted.

6 From the Administration index screen, which option do you choose to delete a system file?

Answer: From the Administration index screen, you choose the File Management option to delete a system file.

7 On average, how long does a full reboot take?

Answer: A full reboot takes between 60 and 75 seconds.

8 You want to limit the workstations that are allowed to access the VPN Manager of the Concentrator to only the ones where specific users will be working. What option is available to do this?

Answer: You can achieve this by creating an administrator access control list. You can specify the individual workstations that are allowed to access the VPN Manager by IP address.

9 When performing a software update of the VPN Concentrator software, where must you locate the system software image in order for the VPN Manager to upload it to the Concentrator?

Answer: The new Concentrator software image must be locally accessible to the machine where the VPN Manager is running. In other words, it is required to be on a physical or network connected drive that is accessible to the system on which the VPN Manager is running.

10 What are the default and maximum session timeout values?

Answer: The default session timeout is 600 seconds. There is no maximum session timeout value.

Chapter 12

1 When configuring dynamic crypto maps, what is the suggested method for setting the priority of the referenced crypto map?

Answer: Any crypto map entries that reference dynamic crypto map sets should be the lowest priority crypto map entries in the crypto map set (that is, have the highest sequence numbers) so that the other crypto map entries are evaluated first. That way, the dynamic crypto map set is examined only when the other (static) map entries are not successfully matched.

2 What command on Cisco IOS displays a summary of how the IPSec policy is configured?

Answer: The show crypto map command displays a summary of how the IPSec policy is configured.

3 Traffic is being sent from 192.168.1.1 to 10.0.1.1, and it is failing. Explain this by looking at the following output.

```
pix2(config)# show crypto map

Crypto Map: "peerc" interfaces: { outside }

Crypto Map "peerc" 10 ipsec-isakmp
  Peer = 192.168.1.5
  access-list 106 permit ip 192.168.2.0 255.255.255.0
    10.0.1.0 255.255.255.0 (hitcnt=18)
  Current peer: 192.168.1.5
  Security association lifetime: 4608000 kilobytes/28800 seconds
  PFS (Y/N): N
  Transform sets={ mine2, }
```

Answer: The configured access list is:

```
access-list 106 permit ip 192.168.2.0 255.255.255.0
  10.0.1.0 255.255.255.0
```

The source address of 192.168.1.1 would not be permitted by the access list, so it would not be encrypted and sent across the IPSec tunnel.

4 To configure an IPSec VPN between two Cisco IOS routers, it is common to use a generic routing encapsulation (GRE) tunnel and then apply the crypto map to the tunnel interface. Can this be done on an IOS router to PIX VPN?

Answer: No, the Cisco PIX will pass GRE traffic, but you cannot terminate a GRE tunnel on a PIX interface.

5 When using wildcard preshared keys, what does Cisco also recommend you use to increase security?

Answer: Using wildcard preshared keys can lead to a potential security risk if the key used is compromised. Cisco recommends the use of additional authentication, such as Xauth, if wildcard preshared keys are used.

6 What command on the PIX Firewall would enable PFS group 2 for crypto map mymap 10?

Answer: The following command on the PIX Firewall would enable PFS group 2 for crypto map mymap 10:

```
Pixfirewall(config)#crypto map mymap 10 set pfs group 2
```

7 What must be configured on the PIX Firewall to allow the Firewall to push IPSec policies down to the Cisco VPN 3000 Clients?

Answer: VPN groups have to be configured with the vpngroup command to allow the PIX Firewall to push IPSec policies to the VPN 3000 Client.

8 True or False: On the Cisco VPN 1.1 Client, replay detection is enabled by default.

Answer: This is true. On the Cisco VPN 1.1 Client, replay detection is enabled by default.

9 What command on the PIX Firewall creates a pool of IP addresses from 10.2.100.1 to 10.2.100.250 for use by remote VPN Clients?

Answer: The following command on the PIX Firewall creates a pool of IP addresses from 10.2.100.1 to 10.2.100.250 for use by remote VPN Clients:

```
ip local pool mypool 10.2.100.1-10.2.100.250
```

10 When enabling the use of a wildcard preshared key, what address do you use for the peer address and peer netmask?

Answer: When enabling a wildcard preshared key, you use 0.0.0.0 for the peer address and 0.0.0.0 for the peer netmask.

INDEX

Numerics

0 access-list acl_name, 165
0 access-list acl_name command, 165
3DES (triple Data Encryption Standard), 11, 47, 166

A

aaa-server command, 329
access rights, 299–300
access contol list. *See* ACLs
Access VPNs, 5
access-list command, 83, 130
access-list global configuration command, 163
ACLs (access control lists), 142, 300
    crypto, 86–88
    IPSec, 75–76
        configuring, 67
        PIX Firewalls, 224–225
        troubleshooting, 149
    PIX Firewall, 163–165
    wildcard preshared keys, 330
activity, monitoring, 285–294
adaptive security algorithm (ASA), 215
adding
    ACLs, 300
    IPSec LAN-to-LAN connections, 323
    permit statements, 75
    users, 250–251
addresses (IP)
    assigning, 243
    pools, 335
administration
    certificates, 304
    Cisco VPN 3000 Concentrator, 295–304
    files, 302–303
    sessions, 296
Administrators, 299
aggressive mode, IKE, 27
agreements, D-H key agreements, 18–20
AH (Authentication Header), 8, 72, 141
algorithms
    ASA, 215
    HMAC, 20
    HMAC-MD5-96, 21

    HMAC-SHA-1-96, 21
    IPSec, 71
    SHA, 166
Altiga Networks VPN command (Start menu), 254
applications
    IOS, 47–48
    VPN Concentrator, 52
        3000 series, 52–61
        5000 series, 61
applying
    crypto maps, 92–94
    interfaces (PIX Firewall), 174–175
ASA (adaptive security algorithm), 215
assignment, IP addresses, 243
authentication, 123
    CAs, 123, 197–198
    certificate-based, 37–39, 270
    HMAC, 166
    IPSec
        ACLs, 75–76
        checking current configuration, 74–75
        configuring, 67
        defining policies, 71–74
        preparing IKE, 68
        selecting IKE policies, 68–70
        testing peers, 75
    preshare method, 160
    SCEP, 190
    SHA, 166
    VPN 3000 Concentrator, 251
    Xauth, 328–329
Authentication Header (AH), 8, 72, 141

B

Baltimore Technologies, 114
Baltimore Technologies CA servers, 191
booting Cisco VPN 3000 Concentrator, 298
browsers. *See also* interfaces
    Browser Manager, 236
    VPN 3000 Concentrator, 239–251

C

CA (Certificate Authority)
    authentication, 197–198

J–K

L

M

Q

R

S

W

X–Z

Hey, you've got enough worries.

Don't let IT training be one of them.

Get on the fast track to IT training at InformIT,
your total Information Technology training network.

 | **www.informit.com** |

■ Hundreds of timely articles on dozens of topics ■ Discounts on IT books from all our publishing partners, including Cisco Press ■ Free, unabridged books from the InformIT Free Library ■ "Expert Q&A"—our live, online chat with IT experts ■ Faster, easier certification and training from our Web- or classroom-based training programs ■ Current IT news ■ Software downloads ■ Career-enhancing resources

Train with authorized Cisco Learning Partners.

Discover all that's possible on the Internet.

One of the biggest challenges facing networking professionals is how to stay current with today's ever-changing technologies in the global Internet economy. Nobody understands this better than Cisco Learning Partners, the only companies that deliver training developed by Cisco Systems.

Just go to **www.cisco.com/go/training_ad**. You'll find more than 120 Cisco Learning Partners in over 90 countries worldwide.* Only Cisco Learning Partners have instructors that are certified by Cisco to provide recommended training on Cisco networks and to prepare you for certifications.

To get ahead in this world, you first have to be able to keep up. Insist on training that is developed and authorized by Cisco, as indicated by the Cisco Learning Partner or Cisco Learning Solutions Partner logo.

Visit **www.cisco.com/go/training_ad** today.

CISCO SYSTEMS

EMPOWERING THE
INTERNET GENERATION™

CCIE Professional Development

Cisco BGP-4 Command and Configuration Handbook

William R. Parkhurst, Ph. D., CCIE

1-58705-017-X • AVAILABLE NOW

Cisco BGP-4 Command and Configuration Handbook is a clear, concise, and complete source of documentation for all Cisco IOS Software BGP-4 commands. If you are preparing for the CCIE exam, this book can be used as a laboratory guide to learn the purpose and proper use of every BGP command. If you are a network designer, this book can be used as a ready reference for any BGP command.

Cisco LAN Switching

Kennedy Clark, CCIE; Kevin Hamilton, CCIE

1-57870-094-9 • AVAILABLE NOW

This volume provides an in-depth analysis of Cisco LAN switching technologies, architectures, and deployments, including unique coverage of Catalyst network design essentials. Network designs and configuration examples are incorporated throughout to demonstrate the principles and enable easy translation of the material into practice in production networks.

Routing TCP/IP, Volume I

Jeff Doyle, CCIE

1-57870-041-8 • AVAILABLE NOW

This book takes the reader from a basic understanding of routers and routing protocols through a detailed examination of each of the IP interior routing protocols. Learn techniques for designing networks that maximize the efficiency of the protocol being used. Exercises and review questions provide core study for the CCIE Routing and Switching exam.

Routing TCP/IP, Volume II

Jeff Doyle, CCIE, Jennifer DeHaven Carroll, CCIE

1-57870-089-2 • AVAILABLE NOW

Routing TCP/IP, Volume II, provides you with the expertise necessary to understand and implement BGP-4, multicast routing, NAT, IPv6, and effective router management techniques. Designed not only to help you walk away from the CCIE lab exam with the coveted certification, this book also helps you to develop the knowledge and skills essential to a CCIE.

Cisco Press   **www.ciscopress.com**

Cisco Press Solutions

Enhanced IP Services for Cisco Networks
Donald C. Lee, CCIE

1-57870-106-6 • AVAILABLE NOW

This is a guide to improving your network's capabilities by understanding the new enabling and advanced Cisco IOS services that build more scalable, intelligent, and secure networks. Learn the technical details necessary to deploy Quality of Service, VPN technologies, IPsec, the IOS firewall and IOS Intrusion Detection. These services will allow you to extend the network to new frontiers securely, protect your network from attacks, and increase the sophistication of network services.

Developing IP Multicast Networks, Volume I
Beau Williamson, CCIE

1-57870-077-9 • AVAILABLE NOW

This book provides a solid foundation of IP multicast concepts and explains how to design and deploy the networks that will support appplications such as audio and video conferencing, distance-learning, and data replication. Includes an in-depth discussion of the PIM protocol used in Cisco routers and detailed coverage of the rules that control the creation and maintenance of Cisco mroute state entries.

Designing Network Security
Merike Kaeo

1-57870-043-4 • AVAILABLE NOW

Designing Network Security is a practical guide designed to help you understand the fundamentals of securing your corporate infrastructure. This book takes a comprehensive look at underlying security technologies, the process of creating a security policy, and the practical requirements necessary to implement a corporate security policy.

Cisco Press

www.ciscopress.com

Cisco Press Solutions

EIGRP Network Design Solutions

Ivan Pepelnjak, CCIE

1-57870-165-1 • AVAILABLE NOW

EIGRP Network Design Solutions uses case studies and real-world configuration examples to help you gain an in-depth understanding of the issues involved in designing, deploying, and managing EIGRP-based networks. This book details proper designs that can be used to build large and scalable EIGRP-based networks and documents possible ways each EIGRP feature can be used in network design, implmentation, troubleshooting, and monitoring.

Top-Down Network Design

Priscilla Oppenheimer

1-57870-069-8 • AVAILABLE NOW

Building reliable, secure, and manageable networks is every network professional's goal. This practical guide teaches you a systematic method for network design that can be applied to campus LANs, remote-access networks, WAN links, and large-scale internetworks. Learn how to analyze business and technical requirements, examine traffic flow and Quality of Service requirements, and select protocols and technologies based on performance goals.

Cisco IOS Releases: The Complete Reference

Mack M. Coulibaly

1-57870-179-1 • AVAILABLE NOW

*Cisco IOS Releases: The Complete Referenc*e is the first comprehensive guide to the more than three dozen types of Cisco IOS releases being used today on enterprise and service provider networks. It details the release process and its numbering and naming conventions, as well as when, where, and how to use the various releases. A complete map of Cisco IOS software releases and their relationships to one another, in addition to insights into decoding information contained within the software, make this book an indispensable resource for any network professional.

Cisco Press   **www.ciscopress.com**

Cisco Press Solutions

Residential Broadband, Second Edition

George Abe

1-57870-177-5 • AVAILABLE NOW

This book will answer basic questions of residential broadband networks such as: Why do we need high speed networks at home? How will high speed residential services be delivered to the home? How do regulatory or commercial factors affect this technology? Explore such networking topics as xDSL, cable, and wireless.

Internetworking Technologies Handbook, Third Edition

Cisco Systems, et al.

1-58705-001-3 • AVAILABLE NOW

This comprehensive reference provides a foundation for understanding and implementing contemporary internetworking technologies, providing you with the necessary information needed to make rational networking decisions. Master terms, concepts, technologies, and devices that are used in the internetworking industry today. You also learn how to incorporate networking technologies into a LAN/WAN environment, as well as how to apply the OSI reference model to categorize protocols, technologies, and devices.

OpenCable Architecture

Michael Adams

1-57870-135-X • AVAILABLE NOW

Whether you're a television, data communications, or telecommunications professional, or simply an interested business person, this book will help you understand the technical and business issues surrounding interactive television services. It will also provide you with an inside look at the combined efforts of the cable, data, and consumer electronics industries' efforts to develop those new services.

Performance and Fault Management

Paul Della Maggiora, Christopher Elliott, Robert Pavone, Kent Phelps, James Thompson

1-57870-180-5 • AVAILABLE NOW

This book is a comprehensive guide to designing and implementing effective strategies for monitoring performance levels and correctng problems in Cisco networks. It provides an overview of router and LAN switch operations to help you understand how to manage such devices, as well as guidance on the essential MIBs, traps, syslog messages, and show commands for managing Cisco routers and switches.

Cisco Press   **www.ciscopress.com**

Cisco Press Fundamentals

Internet Routing Architectures, Second Edition
Sam Halabi with Danny McPherson
1-57870-233-x • AVAILABLE NOW

This book explores the ins and outs of interdomain routing network design with emphasis on BGP-4 (Border Gateway Protocol Version 4)--the de facto interdomain routing protocol. You will have all the information you need to make knowledgeable routing decisions for Internet connectivity in your environment.

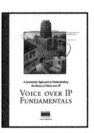

Voice over IP Fundamentals
Jonathan Davidson and James Peters
1-57870-168-6 • AVAILABLE NOW

Voice over IP (VoIP), which integrates voice and data transmission, is quickly becoming an important factor in network communications. It promises lower operational costs, greater flexibility, and a variety of enhanced applications. This book provides a thorough introduction to this new technology to help experts in both the data and telephone industries plan for the new networks.

For the latest on Cisco Press resources and Certification and

Training guides, or for information on publishing opportunities, visit

www.ciscopress.com

Cisco Press

Cisco Press books are available at your local bookstore, computer store, and online booksellers.